D0204717

CONSUMER CULTURE

A Reference Handbook

Other Titles in ABC-CLIO's
CONTEMPORARY WORLD ISSUES
Series

CONSUMER CULTURE

A Reference Handbook

Douglas J. Goodman and Mirelle Cohen

CONTEMPORARY WORLD ISSUES

ABC-CLIO

Santa Barbara, California
Denver, Colorado
Oxford, England

Library of Congress Cataloging-in-Publication Data

Goodman, Douglas J.
    Consumer culture : a reference handbook / Douglas J. Goodman, Mirelle Cohen.
            p. cm. — (Contemporary world issues)
Includes index.
    ISBN 1-57607-975-9 (hardcover : alk. paper)   1-57607-976-7 (e-book)
    1. Consumption (Economics)—Social aspects. 2. Consumers. I. Cohen, Mirelle. II. Title. III. Series.
    HC79. C6G665 2003
    306.3—dc22

                                                                2003020916
08   07   06   05   04   10 9 8 7 6 5 4 3 2 1

Note: Parts of chapters 2 and 3 are to be published as "Consumption as a Social Problem" in G. Ritzer, ed., The Handbook of Social Problems, *Thousand Oaks, CA: Sage, 2003.*

This book is also available on the World Wide Web as an e-book. Visit abc-clio.com for details.

ABC-CLIO, Inc.
130 Cremona Drive, P.O. Box 1911
Santa Barbara, California 93116-1911

This book is printed on acid-free paper ∞.
Manufactured in the United States of America

Contents

List of Tables

Preface

The analyst is always involved in the culture that he or she is studying. This is accepted as necessary in the social sciences. It is why anthropologists generally engage in participant observation by living with the culture that they study, and it is why sociologists generally study their own culture. Despite its necessity, it is also seen as a danger, because we cannot help but bring prejudices, stereotypes, habits of thought, and assumptions to the culture that we are studying.

That there are dangers associated with our necessary engagement with a culture is true of the study of any culture, but it is especially true of consumer culture for three reasons. First, the study of consumer culture does not have the rich history of scholarship that we see in the study of cultures shaped by production. To study the effects of the division of labor, industrialization, vocations, or changes in the mode of production, the sociologists can turn to a formidable body of theory and research: Émile Durkheim, Max Weber, and Karl Marx, to name just a few. These great analysts of society wrote at the time when our modern culture was forming, and they provide us with a standpoint from which to understand our present concerns.

There are a number of reasons for this lack of study, but there are two main ones. In the early modern period, the changes in consumption (discussed in chapter 1) were not as obvious as the changes in production (the building of factories, separation of home and workplace, growth of cities, etc.). The other main reason is that men were primarily concerned with work and production whereas women where mainly concerned with consumption (discussed in chapter 4). People then, and some even today, do not feel that what women do is as important as what men do.

The second reason that the study of consumer culture is especially difficult is that we tend to think of consumption as a natural thing that is independent of historical and social context. Since people always and everywhere must consume, we assume that a consumer culture must have always existed and everywhere been the same. Although few people are totally ignorant of the history of production (for example, the steam engine, the production line, computers), most will find the history of consumption related in chapter 1 as well as the discussion of the changing relation between consumer culture and inequality in chapters 4 and 5 almost completely new.

The third reason for the difficulty of studying consumer culture relates more directly to this book. Scholars today, especially those who wish to write books that will be read, must think in terms of the consumption of their work. This means that the very thing that we are studying has shaped every aspect of this book: the main ideas that we have chosen to present, the examples that we have used to illustrate these ideas, the structure of the sentences, the word choices, and so forth. This book is inextricably intertwined with consumer culture, and the reader could pay the authors no higher compliment than to use some of the insights and tools presented in these chapters to critique this very book.

This book is both a scholarly analysis and a consumer product. In line with our attempt to present a scholarly analysis, this book is meant to be informative, challenging, and critical. As a consumer product, we have tried to make this book accessible, useful, and entertaining. This book supposes that the reader is intimately knowledgeable about consumer culture—indeed an expert on how to use consumer culture for the reader's economic advantage and amusement. Nevertheless, we do not assume that the reader will be familiar with the history of consumer culture or what makes consumer culture unique. It is our intent to use historical and sociological analysis to reveal what is extraordinary in our everyday, taken-for-granted practices of consumption.

Chapter 1 is a necessarily short and simplified history of consumer culture. This chapter uses history not to throw names and dates at the reader, but to reveal that what we often believe to be natural, such as a concern with fashion, is in fact, historically unique. Consumption has changed, not only in how we do it, but in how we think about it.

Chapter 2 looks at the contradictions of consumer culture. For example, our culture contains messages that, on one hand, consumers are sovereign and, on the other hand, consumers are manipulated dupes. The chapter examines both the economic background of these contradictions and their political effects.

Chapter 3 examines one particularly important contradiction in detail: We use consumption to express our disgust with consumption. Our very criticisms of consumption are often part of making consumer culture stronger. The chapter examines a number of forms of this contradiction, including its international expression.

Both chapters 4 and 5 examine the way that inequality works in consumer culture. Chapter 4 argues that inequality that works by stigmatizing groups or individuals is being subverted by consumer culture. Chapter 5 argues that inequality that works through anonymous global connections is made stronger by consumer culture. Together the two chapters contend that the way that inequality works in consumer culture is different than it has worked in other cultures and different than most of us think that it works. Chapter 5 concludes by discussing the political ramifications of this change.

The rest of the chapters are intended to provide the reader with resources for further research, whether for their own curiosity or for papers and assignments. Chapter 6 presents a short description of those people, events, trends, and organizations that are important to the story that we wanted to tell in this book. Chapter 7 provides a description of organizations, associations, and agencies concerned with consumer culture, as well as information for contacting them. Chapter 8 consists of an annotated list of books, chapters, articles, and videos that further discuss consumer culture.

1

From Consumption to Consumer Culture

We live in a consumer culture. Consumption pervades our everyday lives and structures our everyday practices. The values, meanings, and costs of what we consume have become an increasingly important part of our social and personal experiences. Occasionally, we may wonder at the amount of time we spend consuming, thinking about consuming, and preparing to consume. It may even occur to us that not all cultures have been so focused on consumption. Nevertheless, we know relatively little about how our culture came to be this way, nor are we aware of the full extent to which consumption has shaped our social life.

The news media is filled with information about consumption—not only in the form of advertising, but also as news about businesses, lifestyles, and economic indicators. But the news does not provide the basis for understanding a consumer culture because these news items were written as reports on current problems and interests—on the financial problems of a company or the latest fashion trends. Such stories do not tell us how we came to be a culture that identifies freedom with consumer choice or that sees consumption as a means of self-fulfillment and shopping as a form of entertainment. They do not tell us how consumption became one of the central organizing motifs of our society.

For the most part, we only become aware of consumption when it is a problem: when a slowing economy keeps people from buying houses, when cars are built with a concern for salability rather than safety, when there are shortages of the latest version of what we have come to view as necessary, when we realize the environmental degradation caused by producing what is in fashion and discarding what is out of fashion, or when we read about the adverse effects that a globalized consumer culture has on other parts of the world. Understanding a social phenomena often begins with recognizing a problem, but it cannot end there. We need to understand the social and historical context of a consumer society.

In order to understand our consumer society, we should look at more than the obvious economic processes and practices of exchange. We should look at the way in which these economic processes and practices of exchange give people *meaningful* objects to incorporate into their social interactions and their personal biographies.

All cultures have found meanings in material goods. Anthropologists and sociologists have long told us that every object possesses a meaning. Objects may represent our social status or they may be concrete symbols of our most intimate experiences. They may represent a memory of our past, a sign of our current identity, or a symbol of what we hope to be. Except perhaps as a philosophical exercise, it is useless to try to separate out the real object from its meaning.

Consumption, then, is about meaning. Consumption can be defined as the set of practices through which commodities become a part of a particular individual. The archetypal model here would be eating, in which a commodity becomes a physical part of the individual, but more important are those practices where commodities become part of the individual symbolically. Goods are consumed not only for their material characteristics, but even more for what they symbolize—their meanings, associations, and their involvement in our self-image.

These symbolic meanings are certainly social, but that does not mean that society determines the meaning of the object in any absolute way. Different people can find different meanings in the same object. We certainly find this when we move from culture to culture. Objects made for the most mundane functions, such as grinding food or clasping a robe, may show up in another culture as an objet d'art. But even within the same culture, the meaning of the object can vary. Many yard sales have been the stage for the magical transformation of an object from useless trash to valuable collectible.

Consumption is not simply the acquiring of a product's predetermined meanings. Instead, it should be seen as a form of social interaction—perhaps as participation in a social language. Consumption is not a one-way process going from social definition to individual use but a process of negotiation and contestation. Martial metaphors are often used, seeing the consumer as a guerrilla attempting to outflank the big guns of the advertiser. But it is perhaps better to see consumption as a playground where war is sometimes played, along with hide-and-seek, dress-up, and many other barely organized games.

The social production of meaning and the individual's appropriation of meaning are inevitably linked aspects of a single cultural process. This is why the consumption of a socially meaningful object always involves the production of individual meaning. No matter how strong the social meanings that are promoted through advertising, as soon as a consumer acquires an object, he or she immediately produces an interpretation of that object, a story that gives it special significance. No matter how many other people may own that same pair of pants or how many billboard models may advertise them, they become my pants that I bought in San Francisco and wore hiking the Cascades with my best friend and stained with a coffee spill when I heard the surprising news and which I still keep despite the fact that my waist has now expanded beyond all hope of ever fitting into them again. As the French sociologist Pierre Bourdieu puts it, "the consumer helps to produce the product he consumes, by a labor of identification and decoding" (1984, 100).

Consumption as a Culture

It is tempting to regard consumption as a practice that can be discussed independent of its social and historical context, since it is assumed to be a ubiquitous aspect of all social life. Such a view of consumption misses the different roles that consumption can play in various cultures, and it misses the historical development of these diverse relations between culture and consumption. In this book, consumption will be examined as socially and historically variable. These practices and their meanings differ from culture to culture and—the focus of this chapter—they differ historically.

Consumption is an important topic for those who wish to understand our society precisely because it is unquestioned. It is this unquestioned quotidian aspect that suggests that we are in a consumer culture. While consumption is an act, consumer culture is a way of life.

In general, we can speak of a culture whenever we can talk about a community as an agent or as having an intention. For example, at a number of points we will write that consumer culture "does" something or "presents" itself as something. When such statements are not patently absurd, we are speaking of something like a culture. We must remember that when we use the term *culture,* we are not saying that everyone in that community shares those values or practices, nevertheless, a culture is more than a convenient generalization. The term *culture* indicates values and practices that individuals can reject but usually at a price—at least of feeling different and more likely the price of becoming the focus of some form of social control.

It is quite likely that never before in history has consumption become one of the central values of a culture. Consumption has always occurred, but in previous societies, consumption was primarily a reflection of other values such as kinship systems or forms of hierarchy. In these other societies, one would have been socialized into patterns of consumption that were tasteful or appropriate to one's social position; but in modern society, one learns simply to consume, and tasteful or appropriate consumption is only one of the myriad choices. It is this focus on consumption as a central value that makes ours a consumer culture.

It appears that consumer culture had its beginnings in Western capitalism. The norms, objects, practices, and power structures of our society have cohered increasingly around consumption. Those cultural practices that represent alternatives to consumer culture, such as bourgeois high culture, are becoming increasingly commodified, and—as we will discuss in chapter 3—even those practices that are explicitly anticonsumption, such as environmental concerns, have become a way to sell more commodities.

Consumption no longer seems to simply reflect our cultural values; it has itself become a cultural value. It has entered into the warp and woof of the fabric of modern life. All forms of social life—from education to sexual relations to political campaigns—are now seen as consumer relations. Every public space, every occasion for public gathering, every creative expression is seen as an opportunity to encourage more consumption. Our lives apparently amount to little more than a diversity of opportunities to consume.

Consumer culture has been incredibly successful. Not only has it been successful in satisfying our needs and desires, but it has also been successful in redefining what our needs are and in expanding our desires. If we accept these desires as natural or inevitable, then consumer society seems natural and inevitable as well. If, however, we have some misgivings about this culture, want to change it, or aim to reject it altogether, then we must begin to understand it as a sociohistorical phenomenon that could have been different.

Traditional Consumption

Before the Industrial Revolution of the eighteenth century, what people consumed was, for the most part, either made by the family or made locally by people with whom the consumer had a personal relation. Towns had shops where people could buy things, but these shops tended to be an extension of the craftsman's workshop. In fact, the word *shop* meant porch of a residence in Old Saxon. You could not go "shopping" in the modern sense of browsing, because there were no shops with a mixture of goods, and there was rarely anything on display, since most items were made to order. Furthermore, entering a shop entailed an obligation to buy. The main practice that occurred in these shops was not browsing, but bargaining. There were no fixed prices and no marked prices even to act as a guide.

The closest thing in early Europe to what we would call shopping occurred in the weekly markets and seasonal fairs. Markets were only open one day a week, but there you could browse through the products of the nearby countryside and the goods made by local craftsmen. "Since people went there on set days, it was a natural focus for social life," states historian Fernand Braudel (1982, 29). "It was at the market that townspeople met, made deals, quarreled, perhaps came to blows." One can still attend such weekly markets in small towns and daily markets in large cities throughout Europe, Africa, and South America and find them operating very much as they did in the preindustrial era.

Fairs usually had more of a selection and drew sellers from outside the community and even from other countries. The biggest fairs were virtually international markets. However, fairs were generally held only once a year. A few of the larger dealers had booths, but most just used a temporary table, and many craftsmen and peddlers simply spread their goods on the ground or walked among the crowds.

The historical pattern in America was somewhat different. Unlike in Europe, where markets and fairs preceded the development of shops, in America shops emerged as the prevailing way of buying and selling in its early colonial period. This was because the colonial period was dominated by such corporations as the British East India Company, which controlled the provisions. Some of the posts set up by the large trading companies even resembled chain stores. It was not until the eighteenth century that markets and fairs became popular in the United States.

However, nowhere in Europe or America was there anything that could be called a consumer culture before the nineteenth century. Certainly, there was consumption earlier than the nineteenth century, and it was related to the culture, but it would have to be said that consumption was in the service of other culturally defined status systems rather than the central value of that system. Consumption might have represented royal power or family relations, but consumption was not itself a value system.

Fashion

Before there could be a consumer culture, there first had to be an interest in fashion. Fashion includes clothing, but also any object where there is a concern for what is different, new, and improved, and which allows us to express our individuality. One sociologist declared that, "one cannot understand the modern consumer society and the meaning of consumption in a modern society if the social mechanism of fashion, a self-dynamic social process, is not properly understood and analysed" (Gronow 1997, xi).

Fashion is so central to modern-day consumption and so much a part of expressing our individuality that it is difficult to imagine a culture in which it is not a major force. It is equally difficult to grasp how great a change it introduced into people's everyday lives and expectations. To understand the uniqueness of consumer culture, we must realize that fashion has not always been of concern to people. Not all cultures have been interested in the novelty produced by fashionable change, and even where there has been interest, there has rarely been the means to pursue fashion. People seem to have always been interested in the beautiful or in signs of status, but the pursuit of the new for its own sake, of novelty as an individual expression, is itself something new and novel.

Historians (McCracken 1988; Braudel 1973) have convincingly traced the beginning of Western culture's concern with fashion to the sixteenth-century court of Elizabeth I (1533–1603; see profile of Queen Elizabeth I in chapter 6). It was there that we saw the beginnings of a conception of fashion that would spread to the middle class, making possible a consumer culture. It was at that time, in the last quarter of the sixteenth century in England, that consumption first took off amongst the European nobility. This has been attributed to two important developments. First, Queen Elizabeth I used the dramatic spectacle of fashion as a display of governmental power. Second, she forced social competition among the nobility by removing them from their locality where they were clearly superior and forcing them to attend the London court where they had to compete with equals.

Before this time, consumption had always been a family matter that involved an organization that spanned the generations. Commodities were chosen because of their ability to grow more valuable as they grew older, with the idea that they would be passed down to succeeding generations. Newness and novelty were seen as the marks of commonness. However, the Elizabethan nobleman now began to spend less for his family and more to secure his place in this new social competition. Goods selected as markers in a social competition required very different characteristics than those purchased to be handed down. There was no longer a concern for increasing value over time; instead, the consumer focused on the ability of the commodity to express the individuality of the consumer, his or her difference from others of the same social rank.

Of course, this was not the first time that consumption was used for social competition, but what occurred next in European history is almost unprecedented. During the seventeenth and eighteenth centuries, this competitive consumption spread beyond the court to create new institutions and lay the foundation for a consumer culture—that is, a culture that does not simply use consumption as one tool in its status system, but for which consumption becomes a central value. Historians tell us of a gradual increase in consumption during the time of the Elizabethan court, but they describe a dramatic takeoff in the early eighteenth century as the fashion system took hold outside the court (Breen 1993, 251–252).

One of the opening events of this consumer revolution was the wild enthusiasm with which the English greeted the cheap calico and muslin imported from India around the turn of the century. The sudden demand for this cloth was one of the first indications that fashion was assuming an unprecedented importance that extended beyond the elite. At about the same time, there was a huge increase in the import of certain food items, specifically sugar, tea, and coffee (Mintz 1985; see tables 1.1 and

Table 1.1 A History of Sugar Consumption in Great Britain

8000 B.C.	Sugarcane is first domesticated in New Guinea.
6000 B.C.	Sugar is diffused from New Guinea to the Philippines and India, and possibly Indonesia.
1000 A.D.	Sugar is introduced into Western Europe.
1096 A.D.	Sugar reaches Venice, and Venice subsequently becomes a major reexporting center for Europe.
1100 A.D.	Sugar is introduced to England.
1319 A.D.	The first documented shipload of sugar is sent directly to England.
1627 A.D.	Settlement of Barbados is established. It becomes England's major sugar-producing colony.
1650 A.D.	Sugar moves from being a luxury and a rarity to a commonplace necessity.
1655– 1660 A.D.	Jamaica is colonized by the British. During the next 100 years, it will receive 662,400 slaves, primarily employed on British sugar plantations. By 1660, England consumes 1,000 hogsheads of sugar, and British colonies export 2,000 hogsheads (96,666 gallons) of sugar.
1700 A.D.	England consumes 50,000 hogsheads (3.25 million gallons) of sugar (4 pounds per capita), and British colonies export 18,000 hogsheads (1.2 million gallons).
1753 A.D.	110,000 hogsheads (7.1 million gallons) of sugar are imported to England (12 pounds per capita), and another 6,000 (290,000 gallons) hogsheads are exported elsewhere by British colonies.
1830 A.D.	Total British colonial production rises to 572,000 tons, an increase of more than 233 percent in 30 years.
1890 A.D.	World production exceeds 6 million tons, a 500 percent increase in 30 years.
1900 A.D.	Sugar has firmly entered the diet of every working family and supplies nearly one-fifth of the calories in the English diet.

Source: Adapted from Sidney W. Minz. 1985. *Sweetness and Power: The Place of Sugar in Modern History.* New York: Viking Press.

Table 1.2   Tea Imports for Home Consumption: 1700–1799 (Annual Average)

	England and Wales		Thirteen Colonies	
Year	Legal Pounds per Capita	Estimated Legal and Illegal Pounds per Capita	Legal Pounds per Capita	Estimated Legal and Illegal Pounds per Capita
1700–1709	0.01	—	—	—
1710–1719	0.05	—	—	—
1720–1729	0.10	—	—	—
1730–1739	0.17	0.50	—	—
1740–1749	0.29	1.00	—	—
1750–1759	0.49	1.10	0.11	0.43
1760–1769	0.81	1.60	0.19	0.80
1770–1779	0.70	1.40	0.13	—
1780–1789	1.26	2.00	—	—
1790–1799	2.00	2.10	—	—

Source: Adapted from Carole Shammas. 1993. "Changes in English and Anglo-American Consumption from 1550–1800." In *Consumption and the World of Goods*, John Brewer and Roy Porter, eds., 184. London: Routledge.

1.2). This was significant because of the speed with which these items changed from the luxuries of elites into everyday necessities for the masses. Also significant was that the cloths, sugar, tea, and coffee (we will have more to say about coffee in chapter 5) were produced in areas remote from Europe, then introduced into mass trade. It was the first evidence of the globalizing effect of consumer culture.

The historian Sydney Mintz describes the importance of this change:

> The consumption of these items by proletarian consumers marked a turning-point in western history. Masses of European working people, none of whom had ever before had access to products coming from more than a few miles away, now became the everyday consumers of what had quite recently been remote and precious luxuries. As they did so, their relationship to their own labour changed. Without recognizing it, they became dependent upon markets that far exceeded their own visions of the world. . . . The meaning of work, the definition of self, the very nature of material things must have seemed to change, as commodities, in the new capitalist sense, became commonplace. What it meant to be a person would now become a different thing, too.

Mintz further describes,

> A newly emerging world in which working people
> produced less and less of what they themselves con-
> sumed; in which they filled most of their needs by sell-
> ing their labour for wages and buying what they con-
> sumed in an impersonal market; and in which their
> purchases became a measure of some kind of their own
> identities.... To say that these substances became a
> measure of people's identities is to claim that the
> people who consumed them somehow changed in
> their own eyes or the eyes others, by buying and con-
> suming them. Part of this assertion is the idea that the
> newly emerging capitalist world carried within it dif-
> fering conceptions both of what an individual was, and
> of what an individual might become. (1993, 266–267)

Throughout this period, prosperous merchants and aristocrats began to fill their homes with such imported goods as foreign paintings, oriental rugs, china tea services, and furniture
made from tropical woods. Even among the less than prosperous,
there was an increased interest in decorating the dining room and
the bedroom. Much of this decorating involved the newly industrialized manufactured goods such as textile products, pottery,
glass, and paper. These increasingly affordable items spread
quickly, becoming so common that they appeared in the homes of
peasants and laborers. This rapid spread of consumer goods was
aided by both demographic changes and, perhaps most importantly, the Industrial Revolution. It would be a mistake, however,
to think that the Industrial Revolution happened independently
of what could be called a consumer revolution—or even worse, as
has been often assumed, that the Industrial Revolution caused the
change in consumption. One clue is that the industries that blos-
somed in the Industrial Revolution were primarily those in the
consumer sector rather than those in the heavy industrial section
(Wyrwa 1998, 444).

The change in consumption guaranteed that those who industrialized would have a market. Consumers who are interested in fashion will buy what is new and novel. This makes
them more interested in the latest industrial product than in the
traditional craft of their neighbors. Furthermore, they will buy
the next style when it comes out instead of waiting for the old to
need replacing after years of patching. Neil McKendrick, a his-

torian of this period, tells us that "the consumer revolution was the necessary analogue to the Industrial Revolution, the necessary convulsion on the demand side of the equation to match the convulsion on the supply side" (1983, 9). The increasing mechanization and rationality on the production side went hand in hand with fashionable triviality, impulse buying, product obsolescence, and a fascination with all that was ephemeral. In Braudel's words, "the future belonged to societies which were trifling enough, but also rich and inventive enough, to bother about changing colours, materials and styles of costume" (1982, 235–236).

The new attitude toward consumption meant that those with the means would try new things simply for the change. Even those who currently could not afford them had a reason to work harder to get the surplus. What made this period different from the past was that those who had much seemed eager to add to the excess with every passing fashion, and those who had little struggled to the best of their ability to buy what they could.

As commodities became more diverse and included more imported and manufactured goods, the medieval pattern of shopping at markets and fairs was replaced by a new urban pattern of shopping in permanent shops that tended to be clustered together in certain areas. The shops were usually a family affair. Clients were mostly from the neighborhood, and they would have known both the shopkeeper and each other. Clients shopped daily and mainly bought necessities. They were indifferent to packaging and took no notice of anything like a brand name. The shopkeeper took a client's order, fetched the articles from behind the counter, measured them out, haggled over the prices, wrapped them, and either took cash or debited the sum to the account book. The idea that the seller could encourage increased consumption never occurred to these merchants. This was the next major development in the history of consumer culture.

Fashioning Demand

We have long known that the Industrial Revolution was driven in large part by the scientific understanding and mastery of the forces of nature. We are just now beginning to see that the parallel consumer revolution was also driven by a new kind of understanding and mastery, in this case, of fashion and the marketplace.

A few people began to see that fashion was a phenomena that could be understood and controlled.

Although fashions may change rapidly and continually, there is always some social uniformity in the changes. Fashion is characterized by trends, and it cannot exist without people—those who set these trends and identifiable groups that follow. An understanding of the malleability of fashion trends could be used by those producing and selling consumer goods. Consumer demand could be controlled to suit the needs of the producers. Larger and more predictable markets could be created without impeding, indeed even encouraging, fashionable change.

According to Grant McCracken (1988), Josiah Wedgwood was one of the pioneers in this new understanding of fashion and the marketplace (see profile of Josiah Wedgwood in chapter 6). Wedgwood was a manufacturer and retailer of pottery in eighteenth-century England. He was able to channel the elite's pursuit of the latest and most novel styles of ceramic into a profitable fashion for the many. Wedgwood's genius was to recognize that if the rich and elite could be induced to adopt fashions, then the other classes would soon follow.

There are only certain societies where it is possible for a fashion to spread from a higher class to a lower class. First, the spread of fashion has to be allowed by the norms and laws of the society. Second, the fashion has to be affordable for those in the lower class. Finally, the classes must be close enough with some fluidity between them that those in the lower class could imagine themselves owning what those in the upper class have. Only in such societies will a lower class be able to, or even wish to, emulate the consumption of the higher class.

Eighteenth-century England—with its fluid social structure, rising wages, growing bourgeoisie, and relative egalitarianism—presented the right mix of ingredients for social emulation to become a strong cultural force. In England during this period, there was a widespread ambition to climb from one rank up to the next. In this pursuit, possessions were both tools and symbols of social promotion. Therefore, those in the lower class were eager to possess whatever the upper class deemed fashionable. Wedgwood realized the immense financial potential of such social emulation—if it could be properly controlled. The fashionable commodity he focused on was pottery.

The emergence of one fashion often leads to the introduction of other fashions. The spread of imported hot beverages such as tea, coffee, and chocolate created a demand for pots and cups for drinking them (and, as we will see in chapter 5, a demand for coffeehouses). At first, this was not a demand for British pottery, since only Asian porcelains, that is, "china," could stand up to the hot liquid without cracking. As a result, the new fashion did not immediately affect the production side. It was not long before English manufacturers developed firing processes that rivaled those used on imported pottery. However, more important than the changes in production were the changes in marketing these products.

To examine these changes in marketing, we focus here on Wedgwood, but there were others at this same time whose marketing campaigns encouraged an unprecedented surge of spending that spread across Europe. Few, however, understood what they were doing as well as Wedgwood.

The leaders in fashion at that time were the upper classes. Wedgwood learned to closely observe what they were buying in order to predict what the lower classes would buy next. He used innovative techniques to keep his products in step with subtle changes in fashion among the upper class. More importantly, until Wedgwood, the upper class's choice of a new fashion was made according to their own whims or, at most, the monarchy's direction. Wedgwood learned to use marketing in order to direct upper-class taste. He went to endless trouble and expense in order to curry their favor. He gave them free samples of his latest products, pandered to their whims, asked their advice, and accepted their custom orders. In this way, he was able to identify his own products with the elite, thereby making his commodities attractive objects to those who wanted to emulate the elite.

It was this commercialization of fashion that was the chief way in which consumer demand was changed by eighteenth-century innovations. These innovations included the manipulation of fashion leaders, a more rapid obsolescence of style, the speedier diffusion of fashion knowledge, the use of marketing techniques, and the targeting of previously excluded social groups, especially the newly emerging middle class.

Department Stores

Throughout the seventeenth and eighteenth centuries, novelty and diversity were appearing everywhere. Nevertheless, most of the change affected the wealthy city dwellers. The poor and those living in the country and small towns still shopped much as their grandparents had done. A large gap developed between the specialized luxury shops of London and Paris that catered to the fashionable and the town and village merchants that provided traditional staples to familiar customers.

However, by the end of the eighteenth century, retail shops selling a wide variety of ready-made goods were well established throughout even the smaller towns of England and France and had become a familiar part of most European capitals. This trend continued in the nineteenth century, as a true middle class became increasingly important. For the most part, the newfound wealth of the growing middle class was spent on consumption, and precisely what was consumed was increasingly dictated by fashion.

The verb "to shop" began to be used in the eighteenth century as more and more shops were filled with more and more goods. Nevertheless, the idea of "shopping" had yet to change significantly. Purchasing anything was still a complex, personal transaction. The time spent in a shop was taken up with evaluating the knowledge, skill, and honesty of the shopkeeper and with arguing over the price. Shopping had not yet become a form of leisure and entertainment.

However, along with the expansion of retail, there was also a transformation by the end of this period that amounted to a "revolution" in retailing. The shop was transformed by new techniques of selling. Clearly marked prices replaced prices based on haggling. Reputation based on hearsay gave way to the creation of reputation by means of advertisement. Shops began to use displays to entice customers in. Shops were transformed from establishments that existed solely to fulfill customers' known wants into places designed to attract customers and to create new wants. Retail stores in the larger urban areas had reached such a size, handled such a wide variety of goods, and began to use such new retailing techniques that it was probably incorrect to think of them simply as "large general stores." They were becoming something very different—department stores.

The simultaneous occurrence of a retail revolution in France, the United States, and England in the late nineteenth century has led to a rivalry over which country should be acclaimed the birthplace of the department store. Most accounts name France's Bon Marché, opened in 1869, as the first department store (Miller 1981; see table 1.3). Other accounts name the later but more di-

Table 1.3   Early Department Stores

1670	Hudson's Bay Company is established and given control over the fur trade in much of the Canadian territory. It is now a department store.
1838	"David Jones" opens in Sydney, Australia; "Bainbridge and Company" opens in Newcastle, England, featuring fixed prices.
1846	A. T. Stewart's "Marble Palace" opens in New York.
1857	"Macy's" opens in New York.
1863	"Whitely's of London" opens. By 1872, it had incorporated ten neighboring stores and taken on the name of "Universal Provider."
1869	"Bon Marché of France" opens.
1877	John Wanamaker's "New Kind of Store" opens in Philadelphia.
1881	"Marshall Fields" opens in Chicago.
1885	Henry Charles Harrod opens "Harrods of London."
1904	Billed as the oldest department store in Japan, "Mitsukoshi" opened in 1673 as a kimono shop and becomes a department store in 1904.
1907	"Globus" is the first department store in Switzerland.
1909	Gordon Selfridge opens "Selfridge's of London."

verse Macy's, John Wanamaker's "New Kind of Store," or perhaps Stewart's "Marble Palace." But the debate over which was truly the first may be left aside. What is important is the fact that there was a widespread urban phenomena of the period, and thus our attention might be better focused on what these stores had in common.

In both North America and Europe, the transition from small shop to department store took shape at roughly the same time as more fundamental transformations were occurring in the countries' economic structures—most notably, a strong and sustained economic expansion. Wherever the transition started, it was not long before every major city had its centerpiece downtown department store that came to represent that city's indigenous essence.

Perhaps more important than the emergence of the department store itself was that the department store's style of presentation inevitably forced all retailers to change. The department store pioneered and perfected many of the new techniques in retailing, such as window displays, the display of goods in interiors, fixed prices, and cash sales. All of these marked a distinct break with the past and constituted the "birth of modern retail." Indeed, it is difficult to overestimate the role of these new department stores in the cultivation of a consumer culture.

Three of the changes in retailing are particularly important. First, it was primarily through the department store that shopping became a leisure activity, in contrast to the purposeful acquisition of goods. Where leisure once meant freedom from work and economic responsibility, now the economic sphere and leisure became increasingly intertwined. As many of us have discovered to our chagrin, the leisure of shopping usually ends up costing us something. Second, the main aim of the retail establishment was changed by the department store. Instead of the preplanned acquisition of particular items, the department store is devoted to the arousal of previously unimagined desires. We often enter the department store knowing only that we want—the department store itself provides the substance of our desire. The third change was the deliberate targeting of the middle class. The number of people who had the right to these desires was expanded beyond the elite and, as we will describe more fully later, the department store became the royal court of the middle class.

Most significant for this examination, though, is the department stores' social functions as "cathedrals of consumption" (Zola 1980) and their effect on the imagination by providing "visions of excess" (Bataille 1985) or "dream worlds" (Williams 1982). The abundant use of marble, carpets, ornaments, balconies, and displays induced in shoppers the same sort of awe that they felt in cathedrals, while it captured and stimulated their imagination with visions of what they could own or, at least, what they could want to own.

A legend of retailing is that the future founder of Bon Marché, Aristide Boucicaut, lost his way in the Paris Exposition of 1855 (see profile of Aristide Boucicaut in chapter 6). He was dazzled by the spectacle of the goods on display and delighted in the surprises that met his every turn. The exposition presented a dream world of sumptuous display where the browser could imagine possessing all of the commodities offered. Boucicaut realized that spectacle and browsing were integral to the success of the exposition and that these elements had tremendous potential for retailing.

Experts have distinguished department stores from traditional retail stores by their level of capitalization, diversity of merchandise, methods of selling, and structure and styles of management. But the most conspicuous characteristic distinguishing the department store is its use of displays. As goods were increasingly standardized and the act of consumption became more impersonal, the display of items became correspondingly more important. With the standardization of goods and prices, the activity of purchasing became one of comparing the relative worth of different items. One of the most important aspects of this new shopping experience was browsing the items that were on display. The importance of display is now taken for granted, but it was a novel idea in the mid-nineteenth century. Goods that were displayed for comparison became their own sort of art form, especially in window displays.

The spectacle of the department store involved more than just the commodities, however. These displays of commodities merged into other spectacles such as concerts, fashion shows, pageants, and other extravaganzas. There were also a range of leisure and rest facilities such as rest rooms, reading rooms, writing rooms, silence rooms, restaurants, exhibitions, and concert halls, so that a visit to a department store was presented less as acquiring and purchasing and more as luxury and leisure. For example, Chicago's Marshall Fields had thirty-nine marble-floored lavatories with three maids in each. When it opened in 1902, six orchestras played on the various floors, roses adorned every counter, but nothing was permitted to be sold on that first day. It was only for display and fantasy. As Kim Humphrey explains, "Shopping, even for everyday items, had now almost entirely lost its status as an activity and become simply an experience. It had lost a materiality and become a cultural event" (1998, 114). Transforming shopping into a leisure activity depended on many of these innovations that were developed by the department store—the displays, the spectacle, the leisure areas. But one of the most important changes was the transformation of the personal relation between shopkeeper and customer into an impersonal relation between strangers. This allowed the focus to be on the object rather than the person. You only knew the person you were trading with through the object. Before purchasing the object, you may have never met; after the transaction, you may never see each other again. This impersonal relationship proved beneficial to the consumer. If you wanted to try something new, out of character, or above your station, who was to know?

The actual act of purchasing became insignificant compared to the activity of shopping. The department store was a permanent fair, a dream world, a spectacle of excessive proportions. Going to the store became an event and an adventure. One came less to purchase a particular article than simply to visit, to browse, to see what was new, to try on new fashions and even new identities.

Buying became secondary. It was often just an added excitement, a way to spice up the primary experience of shopping.

Some shops in France put a sign in their windows saying *entrée libre,* which meant that one could enter without needing to make a purchase. Because buying was no longer obligatory, even the poor could enter the stores—although there was little they could actually buy. Since all classes could enter, each class in its own way could achieve a form of consumerhood through what has been called "the democratization of luxury." Luxury was available as an experience—even if only a viewing experience— to anybody who wanted it.

But it was especially middle-class women who were attracted to this new practice, a day's shopping. The department store offered them one of the few places for public activity. In fact, the department store presented itself as a new kind of community: not merely a huge sales hall, but a meeting place, a site for female sociability and arguably also emancipation, since it made part of "the public" safe for women. In this safe public arena, the department store taught middle-class women their new civic roles: to be consumers.

Middle-Class Culture Is Consumer Culture

The professionalization of public and private bureaucracies created a steadily rising number of white-collar jobs. In addition, there were an increasing number of small-business owners. The emergence of department stores coincided with the rise of this new middle class. Middle-class families had money to spare for a few luxuries and were gradually switching the emphasis of their housekeeping expenditure from food to fashion.

Department stores specifically targeted middle-class consumers, who were spending on a much wider variety of goods than ever before, as they struggled to rig themselves out with the paraphernalia of gentility. They had more money to spend, but it had to be spent on more things, and therefore they were cost conscious. The department stores sought to provide traditional upper-class services at lower prices. Roland Marchand explains how useful the department stores were to the upwardly mobile consumer:

> Suppose a newly promoted railway clerk and his wife
> wanted to celebrate their fresh prosperity by moving

> for the first time to a house with a drawing-room.
> They could go to a cabinetmaker and expose their ig-
> norance and their strictly limited means, and to an up-
> holsterer and do the same, and perhaps to a print-
> seller and a china-shop and an ironmonger and so
> forth, and wrestle with the unfamiliar problems of fur-
> nishing for themselves. Or they could walk around a
> department store and inspect the displays of many
> grades of chairs, carpets, curtains, find out what was
> the stylish thing, all clearly labeled and priced. At the
> same time the sight of all sorts of other items, orna-
> ments, pictures, mirrors, knick-knacks, would suggest
> ideas they had never imagined. (1995, 234)

In effect, the department store was the middle-class world—
a world where middle-class culture itself was on display, complete with middle-class costumes, middle-class occasions, and
middle-class ambitions. The very range of middle-class lifestyles
were to be found on the store's shelves and counters and floors.

Furthermore, the department store became the main vector
for social homogenization. It disseminated the values and lifestyle of the urban upper-middle class to middle-class society as a
whole. It did this by lowering prices to a level that allowed middle-class commodities to become mass-consumer items. But it
also disseminated middle-class culture by becoming a kind of
cultural primer. The department store showed people how they
should dress, how they should furnish their home, and how they
should spend their leisure time. It defined ideals and goals for
middle-class society. It illustrated how people should live if they
were successful or on their way to becoming successful or even
merely wished to appear successful.

It was not simply that department stores educated consumers about what was new, modern, and fashionable; they also
made this information seem necessary for the middle-class
woman who truly cared about her family. All of this involved advertising, which developed as an industry in its own right, notably with the emergence of increasingly popular mail-order catalogs that allowed the spectacular display of goods to be viewed
in the home.

Mail-order houses—such as Montgomery Ward and Sears
and Roebuck—slanted the appeal of their advertisements to a
rural consumer, and for many an isolated small-town inhabitant,
the large, lavishly illustrated catalog became an important cultural

Table 1.4   Comparison of Sears and Montgomery Ward Department Stores, 1945 and 1954

	Sears			Montgomery Ward		
	Sales (in millions)	Profit (in millions)	Number of Stores	Sales (in millions)	Profit (in millions)	Number of Stores
1945	$1,045.3	$35.8	—	$654.8	$22.9	—
Percent of total	61.5	61.0		38.5	39.0	
1954	$2,965.4	$147.3	699	$887.3	$35.2	568
Percent of total	76.7	80.7		23.3	19.3	

Source: Calculated from data in Boris Emmet and John E. Jeuck. 1950. Catalogues and Counters: A History of Sears, Roebuck and Company. Chicago: University of Chicago Press, 650 and 664.

document (see profile of Aaron Montgomery Ward in chapter 6 and table 1.4). Thus, beginning with the department store, the middle classes of the large cities and small towns became more alike. Through advertising, through catalogs, and through pilgrimages to downtown stores, the middle class shared in a common culture. For the first time, we see the emergence of a class that was almost totally defined by consumption.

During this same period, there was a transformation of advertising. Posters, handbills, and even sandwich boards had long been used, but these were usually associated with local products. The change in the role of advertising was especially evident in the United States where mass production began to make a national market possible. Beginning with "patent" medicines after the Civil War, advertising encouraged customers to ask local merchants for particular national brands rather than simply accepting merchandise from whatever source the merchant preferred. In less than twenty years, national advertising transformed local tastes into a mass market. Advertising used customer demand to force merchants into a national market whether the merchants wanted to or not. This set the stage for the entire country to become a homogenous consumer culture dominated by middle-class tastes.

The middle class that appeared in advertisements, in the pages of the catalogs, and in department store displays was no longer defined by a certain shared lifestyle but rather by the suggestion that its members bought certain goods. Being middle class meant a certain pattern of consumption. This allowed the department store—the principal medium of consumption—to become both the supplier and the creator of middle-class identity. "Middle class" could be identified with whatever the store had to sell.

The values and habits of the middle class were translated into marketable goods. In department store displays, advertisements, and mail-order catalogs, the concept of a proper middle-class household was transformed into particular furnishings, a set of outfits, and a collection of leisure items. At the same time, new needs were created almost systematically, so that the definition of the middle class could fluctuate with changes in the consumer goods available. Clothing fashions were the clearest example of this. It was not simply that clothing styles varied from year to year or that complete changes occurred. There were also entirely new kinds of clothing to fit entirely new kinds of wants—apparel for particular sports, for driving, and for cooking, and different outfits for different leisure pursuits.

As local consumer tastes were transformed into a national demand dominated by middle-class culture, advertising began to feature a new kind of differentiation based on the brand name. Because the market was swamped with uniform mass-produced commodities, brands were introduced to allow customers to distinguish between standardized products. Because of this, the role of advertising changed. Rather than focusing on the actual attributes of the product, advertisements began to build an image around a product's brand. In many cases, this image took the form of an invented personality (Aunt Jemima), which often evoked traditions (Old Granddad Whiskey). In other cases, the image was attached to certain class aspirations (Cadillac) or to the exotic (Gypsie Queen cigarettes) or the religious (Quaker Oats).

Through the department stores, the middle classes gradually became fashion conscious. The stores helped to create the demands to which they catered. Through their displays and advertisements, middle-class culture became consumer culture and its central theme was the visions of excess that constituted the unique attraction of the department store. With the brand, the product itself became less and less important, while the invented image took center stage. The idea of consumption was gradually changed from a function of need to a function of fantasy.

After the Department Store

The remarkable and prolonged prosperity after World War I brought the middle-class culture being sold by the department stores within reach of the working class. Even the depression in

Table 1.5   Facts about Malls

1819	London's Burlington Arcade opens—one of the world's earliest retail shopping arcades.
1851	The Crystal Palace Exhibition features a nineteen-acre building that is walled and roofed in glass and that has many characteristics of the modern mall.
1867	The world's first shopping "mall," the Galleria Vittorio Emanuele, is built in Milan, Italy.
1923	The first shopping mall in the United States and the world's first automobile-oriented shopping center, the Country Club Plaza, opens near Kansas City, Missouri.
1946	There are eight shopping malls in the United States by the end of World War II.
1956	Southdale, the first enclosed mall, opens near Minneapolis, Minnesota.
1970s	Studies show that the typical American spends more time at the mall than at any other place except home or work.[a]
1980s	Giant megamalls are developed. The West Edmonton Mall in Alberta, Canada, opens in 1981 with more than 800 stores and a hotel, an amusement park, a miniature-golf course, a church, a "water park" for surfing, a zoo, and a 438-foot-long lake. However, the number of centers under construction nationwide begins to decline in 1988.[a]
1990s	By 1992, there are 38,966 operating shopping centers in the United States, 1,835 of them large, regional malls.[a]
	In 1992, the largest enclosed shopping and entertainment facility in the United States—the Mall of America—opens in Bloomington, Minnesota.
	A 1994 Roper poll finds that only 10 percent of respondents say they shop at malls "very often" (down from 16 percent in 1987), while 24 percent say they do not go to malls at all (up from 12 percent in 1987).[b]
	Another survey finds the average shoppers' monthly time spent in malls declined from twelve hours in 1980 to only four hours in 1990.[c]

Source Notes:
[a] Kenneth Jackson. 1996. "All the World's a Mall: Reflections on the Social and Economic Consequences of the American Shopping Center." *The American Historical Review* 101, no. 4: 1111–1121.
[b] "Fifteen Ways to Fix the Suburbs." 1995. *Newsweek* 125, no. 20 (15 May): 46–53.
[c] Tim Cavanaugh. 1996. "Mall Crawl Palls." *American Demographics* 18, no.9: 14–16.

the 1930s seemed only to increase the hold of consumer culture on the Western world, since it eliminated many of the local stores that were still able to compete with the newer forms of retailing. By the end of World War II, consumer culture presented itself as the way in which a troubled society could be restored and reconstructed. Consumption and democratic citizenship became increasingly intertwined in official and popular rhetoric.

However, by the late 1950s, the department store no longer was seen as one of the great symbols of modern retailing and was even beginning to look like it was itself no longer in fashion. Its place of importance was taken by the shopping mall (a collection of independent retail stores, services, and a parking area), which is designed, constructed, and maintained as a unit by a separate management firm (see table 1.5).

The increasing dependence on automobiles and the growth of suburbs had an important effect on the location and form of shopping districts. Middle-class customers began to avoid downtown areas where parking was difficult and were instead attracted to suburban malls with plenty of parking. These malls often included department stores as anchors, but the department store was demoted to only one attraction among others.

Soon, shopping malls were not just being incorporated into already-existing suburbs to provide shopping for a nearby population. Instead, they began to shape the development of the new suburbs. New highways, services, and housing were built around the mall. The suburbs followed the shopping mall, as consumption increasingly became one of the main driving forces for social change.

These changes also promoted cultural changes. The cultural forms associated with groups of like-minded people attending unique performances—such as symphonies, plays, and operas—began to fade. In their place grew the easily reproducible, mass-market cultural forms such as movies, chain restaurants, and theme parks. The change in culture tracked the change from downtown department store to suburban mall.

In the time between the emergence of the department store and the dominance of the mall, there have been other important changes in consumption: Chain stores spread in the late nineteenth century; supermarkets became our main way of buying food in the 1930s; brands became even more important; experiences began to be viewed as consumable goods; credit cards made money irrelevant; self-service made consuming not only anonymous, but solitary. Most of the changes in consumption have occurred in two directions that seem at first sight to be contradictory; the act of consuming has grown simpler, while at the same time the organization of consumption has become increasingly complicated. Consumption is simpler in that buying something, making a thing our own, is an easy, efficient, impersonal, usually painless activity. But the choice of what commodity to buy, the way to purchase it, the meanings that it has, and the hidden network that has produced it have all become much more complex.

Nevertheless, this in no way changes the basic argument of this chapter. Fashion and its manipulation still dominate our culture. Consumption is still, and perhaps increasingly so, a form of leisure. Retailing is as much about creating new wants and needs as it is about fulfilling our present ones. Cultural forms are increasingly commodified. Subcultures are defined by what they buy. And our common culture is still a consumer culture.

References

Bataille, Georges. 1985. *Visions of Excess: Selected Writings.* Minneapolis, MN: University of Minnesota Press.

Bourdieu, Pierre. 1984. *Distinction: A Social Critique of the Judgement of Taste.* Cambridge, MA: Harvard University Press.

Braudel, Fernand. 1973. *Capitalism and Material Life, 1400–1800.* New York: Harper & Row.

———. 1982. *The Wheels of Commerce: Civilization and Capitalism, 15th–18th Century.* New York: Harper & Row.

———. 1992. *Civilization and Capitalism: Fifteenth–Eighteenth Century.* Berkeley, CA: University of California Press.

Breen, Tim. 1993. "The Meaning of Things: Interpreting the Consumer Economy in the Eighteenth Century." In J. Brewer and R. Porter, eds., *Consumption and the World of Goods,* 249–260. New York: Routledge.

Cavanaugh, Tim. 1996. "Mall Crawl Palls." *American Demographics* 18, no. 9: 14–16.

Emmet, Boris, and John E. Jeuck. 1950. *Catalogues and Counters: A History of Sears, Roebuck and Company.* Chicago: University of Chicago Press.

"Fifteen Ways to Fix the Suburbs." 1995. *Newsweek* 125, no. 20 (15 May): 46–53.

Gronow, Jukka. 1997. *The Sociology of Taste.* New York: Routledge.

Humphrey, Kim. 1998. *Shelf Life: Supermarkets and the Changing Cultures of Consumption.* Cambridge, UK: Cambridge University Press.

Jackson, Kenneth. 1996. "All the World's a Mall: Reflections on the Social and Economic Consequences of the American Shopping Center." *The American Historical Review* 101, no. 4: 1111–1121.

Marchand, Roland. 1995. *Advertising the American Dream: Making Way for Modernity, 1920–1940.* Berkeley, CA: University of California Press.

McCracken, Grant. 1988. *Culture and Consumption: New Approaches to the Symbolic Character of Consumer Goods and Activities.* Bloomington: Indiana University Press.

McKendrick, Neil. 1983. "The Consumer Revolution of Eighteenth-Century England." In N. McKendrick, J. Brewer, and J. Plumb, eds., *The Birth of a Consumer Society,* 7–33. London: Hutchinson.

Miller, Michael. 1981. *The Bon Marché: Bourgeois Culture and the Department Store, 1869–1920.* Princeton, NJ: Princeton University Press.

Mintz, Sydney W. 1985. *Sweetness and Power: The Place of Sugar in Modern History.* New York: Viking Press.

———. 1993. "The Changing Roles of Food in the Study of Consumption." In J. Brewer and R. Porter, eds., *Consumption and the World of Goods,* 261–273. New York: Routledge.

Shammas, Carole. 1993. "Changes in English and Anglo-American Consumption from 1550–1800." In J. Brewer and R. Porter, eds., *Consumption and the World of Goods,* 177–205. London: Routledge.

Williams, Rosalind. 1982. *Dream Worlds: Mass Consumption in Late-Nineteenth-Century France.* Berkeley: University of California Press.

Wyrwa, Ulrich. 1998. "Consumption and Consumer Society: A Contribution of the History of Ideas." In S. Strasser, C. McGovern, and M. Judt, eds., *Getting and Spending: European and American Consumer Societies in the Twentieth Century,* 431–447. Cambridge, UK: Cambridge University Press.

Zola, Émile. 1980. *Au bonheur des dames.* Paris: Gallimard.

2

The Contradictions of Consumer Culture

The following are a collection of bumper stickers about consumption: "When the Going Gets Tough, the Tough Go Shopping," "He Who Dies with the Most Toys Wins," "People Who Say Money Can't Buy Happiness Don't Know Where to Shop," "So Many Malls, and So Little Trunk Space," "I'm Spending My Grandkids' Inheritance," and "A Woman's Place Is in the Mall."

Only the most naive reader would think that these are celebrations of consumption. All of them have an ironic edge. All of them represent a truth about our society: We love consuming, but we are not quite comfortable with that feeling. This chapter argues that the contradictions in our feelings about consumption have their origin in the contradictions in our consumer culture.

Consumption is central to our society. It is an essential part of the values and concepts through which individuals understand their place in society. However, before we can understand the culture, we first must understand the economic system that is the basis of our consumer culture. Following an examination of that economic system, we will look at some of the contradictions of consumer culture—its contradictions with the demands of production with bourgeois culture and the contradictions in the view of the consumer. Finally, we will look at the effects that consumer culture has had on our political system.

Economics of Consumption

The capitalist economic system based on the ideal of a free market has become one of the main institutions of our society. Indeed, we seem to be currently engaged in a grand social experiment to see just how much of our society can be given over to the economic system. The market economy has assumed many of the functions—such as running schools and incarcerating lawbreakers—once thought to be the government's responsibility. We tend to see the economy as more responsive to the needs of the average person than is any government agency. Increasingly, the public sees the government as bureaucratic interference in the economy and not as protection from the excesses of the economic system.

An important part of this change has been the increasing emphasis on the role of the consumer in the economy. Consumption is now recognized by both experts and laypersons as the economy's driving force, and the ordinary consumer, rather than the producer, is seen as the central figure in the economic system. This, however, has not always been the case. It is useful to look briefly at the history of the change in economic thought from a focus on the producer to a focus on the consumer.

Economists, of course, have always had to recognize the existence of consumption, even if it had little place in their analysis. Adam Smith, the founder of modern economic theory, wrote that "consumption is the sole end and purpose of all production and the interest of the producer ought to be attended to, only so far as it may be necessary for promoting that of the consumer. The maxim is so perfectly self-evident, that it would be absurd to attempt to prove it" (Smith 1937, 625).

Despite economists' recognition of its importance, consumption never entered into early economic analysis because it was seen as either a response to a natural need or as the result of unnatural and morally reprehensible greed. Consumers either increased their consumption because increased income allowed them to provide for previously unmet natural needs or they were led into increased consumption because of what economist Alfred Marshall (1890) called an "unwholesome desire." Consequently, any policy to stimulate the economy by increasing consumption was either impossible or immoral. With this approach, there could be no recognition of an active consumer nor of a consumer culture.

However, the current economic view of consumption has moved from seeing it as an unwholesome desire to recognizing it as the central source of our economic strength. It is viewed as so important that after the terrorist attacks of 11 September 2001, President Bush promoted increased consumption as a patriotic duty. As the *New York Times* reported, "Indeed, in the twitchy post-September 11 economy, consumer confidence has become the *It* Statistic. With business investment shrinking and the markets on the fritz, free-spending shoppers are considered the last line of defense against a disastrous economic slide" (Walker 2003, C1).

We will trace this change in the economic view of consumption through four stages: (1) consumption as detrimental to the accumulation of wealth; (2) consumption as a propellant that keeps the economy rolling; (3) the consumer as a rational agent that determines the allocation of resources; and (4) the consumer as a social agent involved in complex ways with fashion trends, social competition, and emulation. We will briefly comment on each.

The idea of a capitalist economy began with the concept of accumulating wealth and rationally investing it, rather than spending it on pleasurable consumption. It has therefore always been part of the "spirit of capitalism" (Weber 2002) to discourage consumption because it was seen as inimical to the accumulation of wealth on which capitalism depends.

The economist who did the most to recognize the positive role of consumption was John Maynard Keynes (see profile of John Maynard Keynes in chapter 6). Writing during the Great Depression, Keynes argued that low consumption impeded recovery, and he therefore promoted increased consumption as the solution to the economic malaise (see description of the Great Depression in chapter 6). Keynes suggested state intervention to stimulate consumption, and this idea guided the economic policies of President Roosevelt's New Deal, President Kennedy's New Frontier, and President Johnson's Great Society, and continues to guide President George W. Bush's calls for patriotic consumption.

For Keynes, though, it made little difference what the consumer bought. Consumer buying did not enter the market as information so much as a propellant that stimulated the economy. The next step in understanding the economics of consumption saw the consumer not just as propellant, but also as the provider of information on which a rational economy could be based. This has come to be called the neoclassical approach.

The neoclassical approach sees the consumer as a rational, utilitarian purchaser. The economy might often go in the wrong direction—investing too much in one sector rather than another, producing too much or too little—but decisions by the rational consumer will sooner or later set the economy on the correct course. The best thing that a business can do is to pay attention to the choices of the consumer, and the best thing that the government can do is to leave consumers alone to make their choices. Governments could never adequately direct the economy because a rational economic order depends on the dispersed bits of information held by individual consumers.

This neoclassical view, which still dominates current economic thinking, depends heavily upon the rationality of the consumer (Stigler 1982, 52), despite the fact that study after study has shown that consumers are far from rational. The neoclassical view starts with the assumption that the economy is rational and reasons backwards that the consumer that steers it must therefore be rational as well. However, there is just as little evidence to support the rationality of the economy as there is to support the rationality of the individual consumer. Both seem to have at their core social processes—such as fashion trends, whims, and manipulated emotions—that the neoclassical model must see as extraneous and irrational.

Recently, there has been more acceptance of an approach to the economics of consumption that, like the neoclassical approach, recognizes the irreplaceable role of the consumer in steering the economy, but that also recognizes the social processes at the heart of the economy. In this more sociological approach, it is the very irrationality of the economy—its dependence on fashion trends, emulation, and competitive consumption—that makes the role of the consumer so necessary for steering the economy. It is not that the government does not have all of the information dispersed among rational individuals—if that were the case, then we could reinstate centralized planning once we had found a way to gather and organize all of the dispersed knowledge. Instead, it is precisely because the economy is not rational that consumers are irreplaceable. Only consumers are in touch with the never-entirely rational social processes that are at the center of our economic system.

In fact, Michael Porter (1990) has argued that consumers in touch with fashion trends are one of the most important resources determining the competitive advantage of a nation. The intensity of the Japanese interest in audio and photographic equipment, the Italian love of fashion, the German love of cars, the British love of gardening, the American love of fast food—all of these have resulted in industries that dominate the world market.

This is even truer in a globalizing world where the industry's domestic market of sophisticated, knowledgeable consumers provides a place to test new products. These consumers demand rapid improvements, are in touch with the latest fads, and are highly aware of the status effects of having the newest model. Sophisticated, knowledgeable consumers provide a continuing competitive advantage so long as the demands of the home market are not idiosyncratic and are predictive of trends in other countries. For example, the American consumer's interest in fast, inexpensive, and convenient food provides a competitive advantage so long as other countries are moving along the same path of putting more value on speed and predictability than on the quality of the food.

Today, nearly everyone recognizes the importance of consumption to our economy. We will next argue that this importance extends far beyond the economy. Consumption is more than just an economic transaction. Consumption has become central to our culture.

Consumer Culture and Its Contradictions

The shared concepts and values of a culture help people to relate their individual lives to larger themes. Historically, most cultures have been centered around a set of religious values and concepts. Alternatively, a few cultures have found their values and concepts in secular, intellectual, and aesthetic movements, usually called "high" culture. This is the type of culture that one refers to when speaking of the arts, manners, or education. We will be looking at something different from either of these: a consumer culture.

To say that we are a consumer culture means that our central shared values have to do with consumption. This is not to say that religion and high culture have disappeared from our society, but that they have become instances of consumer culture. People still have religion, but increasingly, they "shop around" for the right religion and choose one that fits their lifestyles. Religion is not a tradition that we are inextricably embedded in; instead, it is chosen, consumed, and sometimes discarded, returned, or exchanged like any other commodity.

Similarly, high culture has simply become a niche market in a consumer culture. From the perspective of marketers, people who go to classical concerts and art museums are a cluster group who also tend to buy Italian espresso machines, Volvo cars, and Pierre Cardin clothes. In other words, a preference for a certain type of "high" art has been reduced to a simple indication of the "type" of consumer items a person is most likely to buy. Even if we don't "prefer" high culture, it nonetheless occasionally finds its way into our experience of consumption. High culture is what we listen to while we are on hold waiting for customer service. It is what we pass on our way to the museum gift shop. It is what we buy to decorate our living rooms. Even where high culture is not simply a commodity, it functions more and more like a commodity, with an emphasis on the new, the latest, the attention-getting, the controversial, the shocking.

Despite its differences from previous cultures, consumer culture is still a set of meanings through which individuals can relate their individual lives to larger themes. In most societies, culture has been the way to transmit the established social meanings of objects, their appropriate use, or tasteful display. However, our culture has and continues to create a multitude of items that have no established social meanings. For example, what is the traditional meaning of a modem or a DVD player? Consequently, one of the main tasks of consumer culture has been the creation of new meanings, especially through advertising. In addition, consumer culture, like all cultures, must motivate us and give our individual lives meaning. The main point of this section is to argue that the meanings that make up consumer culture are contradictory with both the traditions out of which they have emerged and with the culture's own understanding of itself.

Contradictions between Consumer Culture and Capitalist Production

A capitalist economic system requires, by definition, the accumulation of capital, which is then consistently and rationally invested in production. Capitalism was able to emerge because it was originally linked to a culture that emphasized self-control, delayed gratification, and rational planning in the pursuit of clearly defined goals. However, a culture structured around production has, to a large extent, been transformed into a culture structured around consumption, and this is hardly a culture of self-control and delayed gratification. A culture that once saw work as a moral end in itself now sees work only as a means toward more consumption (Schor 2000).

Capitalism requires completely different attitudes from those who produce as compared to those who consume—even though they are usually the same person. The rational, calculating producer requires the irrational, impulsive consumer. If we were as rational in our consuming as we are in our producing, the economy would grind to a halt. Capitalist production still requires self-restraint, discipline, and frugality in our work, but our consumer culture promotes just the opposite. Whereas once we were encouraged to save and invest, we are now also encouraged to spend and go into debt. Daniel Bell in *The Cultural Contradictions of Capitalism* argued that the only solution to this contradiction is for us to become fragmented, to have one set of values at work and another when we consume. As Bell puts it, "One is to be straight by day, and a swinger at night" (1976, 72). But Bell did not believe that this fragmentation would be sustainable. He predicted that the industrialized world would soon enter a crisis because the capitalist economy is contradicted by a consumer culture that is focused on hedonism and novelty. According to Bell, consumer culture's pursuit of the new and improved and its rejection of all that is old-fashioned and passé have infected a culture that now rejects all traditions and that accepts new values with an ironic stance that degenerates into bitter attack once those values are no longer fashionable. We have lost all other overriding values motivating us to work—only the desire for more consumption remains. But, Bell believed that this value could not get us through an economic downturn in the way that a work ethic could.

More than twenty-five years later, Bell's analysis of the contradiction between a consumer culture and capitalist production appears to be absolutely correct. Capitalism seems even more driven by this contradiction than ever. However, his prediction appears to be absolutely wrong: The disjunction continues and even worsens, but it does not appear to be bringing us any closer to a cultural crisis. Indeed, it will be argued below that our very fragmentation now fuels our consumption as we purchase commodities that promise a lost wholeness.

Contradictions between Consumer Culture and Bourgeois Culture

Marxists, members of the aristocracy, and others who see themselves as outside of consumer culture have always had an animosity toward it. Marxists have argued that consumer culture rests on the exploitation of workers (Sklair 1995). Even where it seems to benefit the workers, that benefit is only a device to "buy off" their revolt and delay the triumph of the popular will (Marcuse 1992). Those who see themselves as part of an aristocratic tradition advance a more elitist condemnation (Gronow 1997). Consumer culture is, for them, a contradiction in terms. Nothing that can be popularly consumed could form the basis of a true culture. The aristocratic critique is based on the assumption that the triumph of consumerism is the triumph of the popular will, and this is precisely what they do not like.

The bourgeoisie were those shop owners and small businessmen who came to dominance as the feudal order faded. The bourgeoisie created a culture that was distinct from the landed aristocracy, and it was this culture that the middle class adopted as economic conditions changed. Because consumer culture became identified with bourgeois culture, the disdain of consumer culture by both Marxists and aristocrats is usually combined with a rejection of the bourgeoisie. Nevertheless, even though bourgeois culture is deeply intertwined with consumption, bourgeois culture has roots that preceded consumer culture (Schudson 1998), and despite the best efforts of modern advertising, bourgeois culture is still not entirely comfortable with the centrality of consumption. Consequently, we see a contradiction between consumer culture and the bourgeois culture out of which the former emerged. Bourgeois culture was related to the Christian, especially Protestant, religion (Weber 2002). Its early emphasis was on sacrifice and self-restraint. Identity and personal satisfaction were to be found in a career or vocation. In addition, it included a sense of family and community that encompassed but extended beyond the self-reliant individual (Ashcraft 1972).

All of these traits are inimical to consumer culture. Rather than sacrifice and self-restraint, hedonism and luxurious indulgence are emphasized. Consumer culture presents identity as being infinitely transformable with the purchase of new products (Halter 2000), and even on the production side, people are encouraged to be flexible, mobile, and transitory rather than devoting themselves to a lifelong vocation (Hage and Powers 1992). Finally, consumer culture emphasizes the individual over the community. It may take coordinated groups to produce objects, but these objects are usually consumed by individuals.

Consumer culture grew out of bourgeois culture, but parent and progeny are often at odds, and there is little hope that there will ever be a complete reconciliation between bourgeois culture and its "prodigal son." A bourgeois critique of consumer culture has persisted and helps to explain the long sociological neglect of consumption as a serious subject of study (Ritzer, Goodman, and Wiedenhoft 2001). And even ordinary shoppers are often subject to self-contempt because their consumption is so indulgent and unrestrained.

Michael Schudson (1998) lists three bourgeois objections to consumer culture. The first, which he calls the Puritan objection, criticizes the pursuit of material goods because it takes away from the spiritual. The second, which he calls Quaker, objects to the frivolity and indulgence that are not compatible with a life of simplicity and self-restraint. Finally, the third objection, which he calls republican, believes consumer culture has undermined the community, leading to political complacency and the lack of civic engagement.

There is a long history of bourgeois anticonsumption sentiments (Breen 1993; Horowitz 1985). Indeed, consumer culture has always developed in tandem with its own critique. We consume, but we often feel guilty about it. The belief that consumer culture is not compatible with spirituality, simplicity, and community is a strong part of our bourgeois heritage. The feeling that virtue lies in thrift and self-restraint, and sin in consumption, is still present, even when it has lost its religious roots. But just as our fragmentation fuels more consumption, so does our guilt and loss of spiritual meaning. Advertisers have found ways to use this guilt to get us to consume more. As we will describe below, people buy objects that promise spirituality, simplicity, and community.

The Consumer as Sovereign and as Dupe

The demands of capitalist production and its relation with bourgeois culture do not exhaust the contradictions of consumer culture. There is also a strong contradiction in regard to the rationality, autonomy, and power of the consumer. On the one hand, the consumer is sovereign. The consumer's rational choices determine the direction of the economy. Everything is designed with the intent (albeit often failing) to please the consumer. The rich and powerful of our society must listen to the consumers' voices and try to discern their fleeting whims. On the other hand, the consumer is often portrayed as nothing but a dupe, subject to uncontrolled impulses and manipulated by the most transparent tricks.

Probably the first thing that we think of in terms of manipulating the consumer is advertising. Billions of dollars are spent on advertising every year, and very little of that advertising is of the informational variety that the assumption of a rational consumer would lead one to expect. Advertising is increasingly pervasive. In 1880, only $30 million was spent on advertising in the United States; thirty years later, it had increased to $600 million (Durning 1992), and today, it is in excess of $200 billion in the United States and over $300 billion worldwide (Cardona 2002). Every day, North Americans are exposed to an estimated 12 billion display advertisements, 3 million radio commercials, and more than 200,000 television commercials. Not only are advertisements plastered on billboards, shown between breaks on television shows, popped up on our computer screens, and placed beside text in our newspapers, but they are also beamed into classrooms, played in elevators, featured as props in movies, displayed above the urinal in men's bathrooms, used as part of athletes' uniforms, and displayed in every place and in every manner that human ingenuity can devise. We seem to be currently engaged in a grand experiment to see just how much of our society can be given over to the economic system, and perhaps the riskiest part stems from the constant exposure of people—from cradle to grave, from waking to sleeping—to advertising.

Examining advertising makes it clear that the concept of a consumer culture includes much more than a direct relation between individuals and the objects they consume. To a large extent, that relation is mediated by the meanings attached to the objects. Of course, all cultures have attached traditional meanings to objects, but our culture is so flooded with a constant stream of new (and improved) products that they long ago exceeded all traditional meanings. Many objects depend, at least initially, on the meanings produced by advertising. Whatever its initial aim, advertising does more than sell products. It is an integral part of consumer culture. It not only attaches meanings to commodities, but also to the people who purchase and use them, as Daniel Bell explains:

The advertising in the women's magazines, the house-and-home periodicals, and sophisticated journals like the *New Yorker* was to teach people how to dress, furnish a home, buy the right wines—in short, the styles of life appropriate to the new statuses. Though at first the changes were primarily in manners, dress, taste, and food habits, sooner or later they began to affect more basic patterns: the structure of authority in the family, the role of children and young adults as independent consumers in the society, the patterns of morals, and the different meanings of achievement in the society. (1976, 69)

Indeed, the meanings produced by a consumer culture extend even to the personality of the consumer. It is not just a motorcycle or a white ball gown that one purchases, but the identity that goes with it. One becomes a biker or a debutante. Identities become commodities to buy, and like other commodities, there are competing identities on the market. As a 1991 cover of *Cosmopolitan* declared: "By changing the way you look . . . you can create a new you!"

One of the early leaders in advertising, Helen Woodward, identified the attraction of the purchasable identity in the following way: "To those who cannot change their whole lives or occupations, even a new line in a dress is often a relief. The woman who is tired of her husband or her home or a job feels some lifting of the weight of life from seeing a straight line change into a bouffant, or a gray pass into beige. Most people do not have the courage or the understanding to make deeper changes" (1926, 345; see profile of Helen Rosen Woodward in chapter 6).

It is in the ability to proffer new meanings and identities that consumer culture and advertising contain a strong dose of idealism. We are more attached to the ideal meaning of the object and to the ideal identity represented by the object than to the object itself. This is the phenomenon that Raymond Williams refers to when he writes that advertising is proof that people in modern capitalist societies are not materialist. Williams claims "if we were sensibly materialist, in that part of our living in which we use things, we should find most advertising to be of an insane irrelevance" (1980, 185). It is not that we are tricked by the meanings that advertisements deliver. To a large degree, it is the meaning—

the advertising, the brand, the logo, the Nike swoosh, the Polo pony—that is wanted, especially by the young. The actual commodity is just the convenient carrier of that meaning.

The idea that we wear the logo not the clothes, drink the advertising not the soda, and drive the image not the car has seemed to many to prove that we are being manipulated. Advertisers, it has been argued, create desires that consumers obediently express as if the desires were the consumers' own. This has been called the "hypodermic theory" of advertising—advertisements inject us with false needs (Key 1972). According to this theory, the desire to consume is largely the product of the manipulations of advertisers on an unsuspecting public. A passive public is duped into spending money on things it does not need.

Vance Packard's *The Hidden Persuaders* (1957) was an early and influential example of this viewpoint, arguing that our minds are controlled by the hidden, subliminal messages contained in advertising (see profile of Vance Packard in chapter 6). Packard's interviews with advertisers revealed their rather disturbing attitude toward the general public. He writes, "Typically they see us as bundles of daydreams, misty hidden yearnings, guilt complexes, irrational emotional blockages. We are image lovers given to impulsive and compulsive acts. We annoy them with our seemingly senseless quirks, but we please them with our growing docility in responding to their manipulation of symbols that stir us to action" (1957, 12).

Another influential book attacking consumer culture was Stuart Ewen's *Captains of Consciousness* (1976). Ewen argued that consumer society is a gigantic fraud, a conspiracy to manipulate the public and sell people items they do not need. Whereas those who controlled society were once captains of industry, society is now controlled through the manipulations of advertising by captains of consciousness.

These books have been followed by a steady succession of anticonsumption books, including most recently: *The Overspent American: Upscaling, Downshifting, and the New Consumer* (1998) by Juliet Schor, *No Logo: Taking Aim at the Brand Name Bullies* (2000) by Naomi Klein, *Culture Jam: How to Reverse America's Suicidal Consumer Binge—And Why We Must* (2000) by Kalle Lasn, and *Shoveling Fuel for a Runaway Train: Errant Economists, Shameful Spenders, and a Plan to Stop Them All* (2002) by Brian Czech, not to mention the magazines such as *Ad Cult* and *AdBusters*.

Of course, it is easy enough to dismiss this hypodermic theory by pointing to advertising's spectacular failures. New products with substantial advertising are introduced every day, and the vast majority of them fail. One of the most cited examples is the huge amount spent introducing and marketing the Edsel car, which became a laughable flop (Larrabee 1957).

Furthermore, it has been argued that the creation and control of meaning is not a one-way process. Advertisers may create saleable meanings for the new commodities, but consumers often create meanings of their own (Abercrombie 1994; de Certeau 1984; Fiske 1989). For example, hippies took the American flag and unpatriotically used it as clothing, punks took the safety pin and used it as bodily adornment, and rap DJs took the turntable and turned it into a creative instrument. None of these uses were intended or even imagined by those who created and marketed the products. Advertisers may often have the first word on meanings, and there is no disputing the power of that position, but consumers sometimes have the last word. Rather than simply a conduit for the producers' meanings, consumer objects are often a site of struggle over meaning.

Despite this struggle over meaning, few can doubt that advertising is aimed at controlling our behavior, and we must suspect that it is fairly successful. Otherwise, why would corporations continue to spend billions of dollars on it? Nevertheless, most people, although they often feel disdain for advertising, are not ready to revolt against the "captains of consciousness" and their "hidden persuaders." Perhaps this is because the sort of control that advertising exerts is not one that is experienced as disagreeable. It is not a rigid, constraining control, but exactly the opposite. Advertising manipulates us toward unrestraint in spending. It encourages us to enjoy forbidden pleasures, to break the old rules of thrift and self-discipline. One might say that it is controlling us to go out of control, at least where consuming is concerned. Controlling us to be, in a sense, out of control is a contradiction, but it is one that is easy to avoid examining too closely. Despite the contradiction, it is easy to think of this control as freedom and this manipulation as power.

What the vast amount of advertising really sells is consumer culture itself. Even if advertising fails to sell a particular product, the advertisements still sell the meanings and values of a consumer culture. As Christopher Lasch writes, "The importance of advertising is not that it invariably succeeds in its immediate purpose, much less that it lobotomizes the consumer into a state of passive acquiescence, but simply that it surrounds people with images of the good life in which happiness depends on consumption. The ubiquity of such images leaves little space for competing conceptions of the good life" (1994, 1387).

What advertising constantly sells is the idea that there is a product to solve each of life's problems—that the good life, the attractive personality, the appropriate taste can be purchased along with the object that we are told represents it. However, this promise is constantly broken. One of our first great disappointments is the discovery that buying that special toy does not bring us the infinite fun portrayed on television (Gunter and Furnham 1998). Nor, we soon discover, does buying those clothes gain us social acceptance. Our first car does not translate into freedom, and buying a beer does not surround us with beautiful members of the opposite sex. We buy the commodities, but the good life does not follow.

Donella Meadows explains why, despite our continued dissatisfaction, we continue to consume.

> People don't need enormous cars, they need respect. They don't need closets full of clothes; they need to feel attractive and they need excitement and variety and beauty. People don't need electronic equipment; they need something worthwhile to do with their lives. People need identity, community, challenge, acknowledgment, love, and joy. To try to fill these needs with material things is to set up an unquenchable appetite for false solutions to real and never-satisfied problems. The resulting psychological emptiness is one of the major forces behind the desire for material growth. (1992, 216)

The greatest contradiction that consumer culture has had to face is not with an economic system that values both the accumulation of capital and consumer extravagance, nor its contradiction with the bourgeois ethics out of which it emerged, nor the contradiction between the rational and irrational consumer. The greatest contradiction that consumer culture has had to deal with is that it does not deliver on its own promises, and this very mendacity fuels further consumption.

Consumer Contradictions in Politics

A consumer culture has effects far beyond actual consumption and its associated advertising. Such a culture tends to change all other institutions into something compatible with its consumerist values. We have already discussed how religions have changed from unquestioned traditions into belief systems that we "shop around" for in order to fit our lifestyles. The same sort of thing happens in higher education, where students are more and more frequently treated like consumers, and the mission of the school is increasingly shaped by its attempts to market itself to its target audience. Similarly, news becomes entertainment, artistic value is measured by price, and history is turned into theme parks. Indeed, it seems that every human expression, from art to sex to outrage, is either sold as a commodity or used to sell a commodity.

Of most concern to many is the effect that consumer culture has had on politics. The democratic model depends on citizens making rational decisions, but the same marketing techniques and advertising campaigns that have targeted the irrational consumer are now aimed at the irrational citizen. It is not just that people think they should be able to buy good government rather than creating and participating in it or that people place more trust in the efficiencies of a consumer-driven economy than a citizen-led government. It is rather that our very models of political freedom and civic participation come from consumption. Freedom now means the opportunity to indulge our impulses rather than the capacity to determine our destiny, and civic participation means choosing among prepackaged political candidates. In this way, the contradictions that are at the heart of consumer culture have infected our political system.

To some extent, consumer issues such as the cost of living, scarcity of goods, health and safety effects, and the conditions under which commodities are made or sold have always been of political concern. But it was in trying to end the Great Depression that the concerns of consumption and consumers became established as a central part of public discourse. The New Deal began a process that equated the consumer's freedom of choice with democracy and defined the American way of life through consumer goods. By the time of the Cold War, it was the difference between Soviet and American consumers that defined the conflict more than the difference between political citizens.

However, consumer culture has affected politics in more ways than just making the satisfaction of consumer demands a political priority. The consumer in the market has become the model for the political citizen. Indeed, some early enthusiasts proclaimed the consumer market to be more democratic than any government could be.

Edward Filene, founder of the Boston department store and early consumer expert, suggested that by buying commodities, consumers were voting with their dollars. In this way, "the masses of America have elected Henry Ford. They have elected General Motors. They have elected the General Electric Company, and Woolworth's and all the other great industrial and business leaders of the day" (1931, 98).

Charles McGovern describes the way that the fledgling advertising industry welcomed the analogy between consumer and citizen.

> In metaphors equating consumers with citizens and purchasing with voting, admen portrayed consumption as the true exercise of the individual's civic role and public identity; consumption was the ritual means of affirming one's nationality as an American. They identified their own work of persuasion as politics—the promulgation of ideas and programs for the common good to be affirmed or rejected through a public, communal, and voluntary process. The central political comparison in advertising was the electoral metaphor. (1998, 43)

There is, however, one glaring problem with this analogy. If consumers vote with their dollars, then some people have many more votes than others. Equality may be the goal in politics, but inequality is the rule in consumer markets. What the poor need but cannot afford simply does not appear in the market, while the wealthy's every whim is catered to by many.

As consumer markets became the model of democratic choice, political campaigns became more like advertising campaigns. This process has been described in detail in both Theodore H. White's *The Making of the President, 1960* (1961) and Joe McGinniss's *The Selling of the President, 1968* (1969). But it takes little analysis to convince us of the similarity of politics and advertising, because the parallel has become an accepted part of the political discussion. Pundits constantly refer to the success of political advertisements and the ability of the candidate to sell his or her image. Beyond the rhetoric, political campaigns regularly hire people who work in advertising, and techniques developed in the field of market research are widely used to analyze the preferences of voters. This has led individuals to view themselves as passive consumers rather than active citizens. People now expect politics to consist of selecting between prefabricated choices in which the political affiliation of the candidate works something like a brand name. In such an environment, issues are less important than style.

The wholesale adoption of advertising techniques for political campaigns began in earnest with Eisenhower's presidential campaign in 1952. In that year, only 5 percent of campaign expenditures went to broadcast media. By 1972, that figure had reached 15 percent for direct expenditures and undoubtedly much more when media consultants and production costs are included. Since then, political advertising has focused more on television (see table 2.1).

Some see a conspiracy behind this relation between politics and consumer culture. Consumer culture is believed to be part of

Table 2.1   Political Advertising on Television: Breakdown of Total Dollars Spent

Election Year	National Networks	Local Stations	Total
1970*	$260,900	$11,789,000	$12,049,900
1972	6,519,100	18,061,000	24,580,100
1974	1,486,200	21,781,600	23,267,800
1976	7,906,500	42,935,700	50,842,200
1978	1,065,800	56,545,000	57,610,800
1980	20,699,700	69,870,300	90,570,000
1982	861,900	122,760,300	123,622,200
1984	43,652,500	110,171,500	153,824,000
1986	459,300	161,184,000	161,643,300
1988	38,520,700	189,379,500	227,900,200
1990	—	203,313,300	203,313,300
1992	73,816,000	225,807,400	299,623,400
1994	—	354,961,400	354,961,400
1996	33,824,000	366,661,900	400,485,900
1998	—	498,890,600	498,890,600
2000	772,600	605,233,100	606,005,700

Sources: Adapted from Anthony Corrado. 2000. *Beyond the Basics: Campaign Finance Reform.* New York: Century Foundation Press, 31.
Television Bureau of Advertising, http://www.tvb.org/rcentral/mediatrendstrack/tvbasics/31_Political.asp.

* Political advertising was first measured as a category in 1970.

a larger scheme to tranquilize the public and to channel all discontent into a wish for more goods. Stuart Ewen argued that the captains of consciousness intend for us to consume ourselves "into social and political passivity" (1976, 204). Herbert Marcuse coined the term "repressive tolerance" to describe the way in which our leaders substitute consumer satisfaction for real freedom and weaken the capacity for protest through the propaganda of commodities (1965).

However, such a conspiracy theory is difficult to support, especially since those in charge seem to be as limited by the consumer model as those who are supposedly being controlled. Political leaders today need to watch the polls constantly, and their leadership is severely limited by the need to "sell" their programs to an electorate that is always looking for a better deal. This is not to say that the problems described by such critics as Ewen and Marcuse are not real, but that it seems more likely that they can be attributed to a pervasive culture than a conspiracy.

Political leaders at both ends of the spectrum have had difficulty adapting to this consumer culture. Liberals have been reluctant to adopt the marketing strategies of the big businesses that they have traditionally opposed, while conservatives have found it difficult to reconcile these strategies with their emphasis on family, community, and traditional values.

Edward Luttwak, a former Reagan administration official, describes the contradiction of conservative politics in terms that are analogous to the contradictions of consumer culture. "The contradiction between wanting rapid economic growth and dynamic economic change and at the same time wanting family values, community values, and stability is a contradiction so huge that it can only last because of an aggressive refusal to think about it" (de Graaf 1997, 50). Or perhaps we are so used to living this contradiction in consumer culture that we can no longer see it in other spheres.

Conclusion

It seems that our consumer culture is infected with contradictions. We are to be self-disciplined and self-indulgent, spiritual and materialist, calculating and impulsive. We are authentically cynical, traditionally radical. Consumption is experienced as a mix of pleasure and guilt, anticipation and fear, desire and trepidation. We both love and hate our consumer culture and our guilt, fear, trepidation, and hate involve us in this culture just as deeply as does our love.

Ambivalence about consumption is part of our consumer culture. Some believe that the consumers' desires need to be suppressed, while others are working to incite them. At different times, we see the consumer as sovereign and as victim; we see shopping as a process through which we create and express our identity and as the acting out of the advertisers' hypnotic suggestions; we see the shopping center as our community and as the destroyer of our community. We are unsure whether we are on the verge of unprecedented abundance and empowerment or social and environmental devastation.

References

Abercrombie, Nicholas. 1994. "Authority and Consumer Society." In R. Keat, N. Whiteley, and N. Abercrombie, eds., *The Authority of the Consumer*, 4357. New York: Routledge.

Ashcraft, Richard. 1972. "Marx and Weber on Liberalism as Bourgeois Ideology." *Comparative Studies in Society and History* 14, no. 2: 130–168.

Bell, Daniel. 1976. *The Cultural Contradictions of Capitalism*. New York: Basic Books.

Breen, Tim. 1993. "The Meaning of Things: Interpreting the Consumer Economy in the Eighteenth Century." In J. Brewer and R. Porter, eds., *Consumption and the World of Goods*, 249–260. New York: Routledge.

Cardona, Mercedes. 2002. "U.S. Will See Modest Boost in Ad Spending." *Advertising Age* 73: 22–23.

Corrado, Anthony. 2000. *Beyond the Basics: Campaign Finance Reform.* New York: Century Foundation Press.

Czech, Brian. 2002. *Shoveling Fuel for a Runaway Train: Errant Economists, Shameful Spenders, and a Plan to Stop Them All*. Berkeley: University of California Press.

de Certeau, Michel. 1984. *The Practice of Everyday Life*. Berkeley: University of California Press.

de Graaf, John. 1997. *Affluenza: The All-Consuming Epidemic*. San Francisco: Berrett-Koehler.

Durning, Alan. 1992. *How Much Is Enough?: The Consumer Society and the Future of the Earth*. New York: Norton.

Ewen, Stuart. 1976. *Captains of Consciousness: Advertising and the Social Roots of the Consumer Culture.* New York: McGraw-Hill.

Filene, Edward. 1931. *Speaking of Change: Selection of Speeches and Articles by Edward A. Filene.* New York: Private Press.

Fiske, John. 1989. *Reading the Popular.* Boston: Unwin Hyman.

Gronow, Jukka. 1997. *The Sociology of Taste.* New York: Routledge.

Gunter, Barrie, and Adrian Furnham. 1998. *Children as Consumers: A Psychological Analysis of the Young People's Market.* New York: Routledge.

Hage, Gerald, and Charles Powers. 1992. *Post-Industrial Lives: Roles and Relationships in the Twenty-First Century.* Thousand Oaks, CA: Sage.

Halter, Marilyn. 2000. *Shopping for Identity: The Marketing of Ethnicity.* New York: Schocken.

Horowitz, Daniel. 1985. *The Morality of Spending: Attitudes toward the Consumer Society in America, 1875–1940.* Chicago: Elephant Press.

Key, Wilson B. 1972. *Subliminal Seduction.* New York: Signet.

Klein, Naomi. 2000. *No Logo: Taking Aim at the Brand Name Bullies.* Toronto: Knopf Canada.

Larrabee, Eric. 1957. "The Edsel and How It Got That Way." *Harper's* 1231, no. 1: 123–146.

Lasch, Christopher. 1994. "The Culture of Consumption." In P. Stearns, ed., *Encyclopedia of Social History,* 1387–1388. New York: Garland.

Lasn, Kalle. 2000. *Culture Jam: How to Reverse America's Suicidal Consumer Binge—And Why We Must.* New York: Quill.

Marcuse, Herbert. 1965. "Repressive Tolerance." In R. Wolff, B. Moore, and H. Marcuse, eds., *A Critique of Pure Tolerance,* 81–123. Boston: Beacon Press.

———. 1992. *One-Dimensional Man: Studies in the Ideology of Advanced Industrial Society.* 2d ed. Boston: Beacon Press.

Marshall, Alfred. 1890. *Principles of Economics.* New York: Macmillan.

McGinniss, Joe. 1969. *The Selling of the President, 1968.* New York: Trident.

McGovern, Charles. 1998. "Consumption and Citizenship in the United States, 1900–1940." In S. Strasser, C. McGovern, and M. Judt, eds., *Getting and Spending: European and American Consumer Societies in the Twentieth Century,* 37–58. Cambridge, UK: Cambridge University Press.

Meadows, Donella H. 1992. *Beyond the Limits.* Post Mills, VT: Chelsea Green.

Packard, Vance. 1957. *The Hidden Persuaders.* New York: D. McKay.

Porter, Michael. 1990. *The Competitive Advantage of Nations.* New York: Free Press.

Ritzer, George, Douglas Goodman, and Wendy Wiedenhoft. 2001. "Theories of Consumption." In G. Ritzer and B. Smart, eds., *Handbook of Social Theory*, 410–427. Thousand Oaks, CA: Sage.

Schor, Juliet. 1998. *The Overspent American: Upscaling, Downshifting, and the New Consumer.* New York: Basic Books.

———. 2000. "The New Politics of Consumption." In J. Schor, ed., *Do Americans Shop Too Much?*, 3–36. Boston: Beacon Press.

Schudson, Michael. 1998. "Delectable Materialism: Second Thoughts on Consumer Culture." In D. Crocker and T. Linden, eds., *Ethics of Consumption: The Good Life, Justice, and Global Stewardship*, 249–268. Lanham, MD: Rowman and Littlefield.

Sklair, Leslie. 1995. *Sociology of the Global System.* 2d ed. Baltimore: Johns Hopkins University Press.

Smith, Adam. 1937. *An Inquiry into the Nature and Causes of the Wealth of Nations.* New York: Modern Library.

Stigler, George. 1982. *Economists and Public Policy.* Washington, DC: American Enterprise Institute for Public Policy Research.

Walker, Rob. 2003. "Anti-War Protests Give McDonald's a Taste of Brand-Power Backlash." *New York Times,* 30 March, C1.

Weber, Max. 2002. *The Protestant Ethic and the Spirit of Capitalism.* 3d ed. Los Angeles: Roxbury.

White, Theodore H. 1961. *The Making of the President, 1960.* New York: Atheneum.

Woodward, Helen. 1926. *Through Many Windows.* New York: Harper.

3

The Consumption of Anticonsumption

Consumption is a problem. One of the most interesting aspects of our consumer culture is that this statement really requires no argument. Consumer culture itself proclaims consumption to be a problem. For example, we are inundated with advertising that attacks the absurdity of advertising, people buy books that condemn consumption, and, indeed, as we will argue later in this chapter, products are often consumed to express disdain for consumption.

Whatever the problem, advertising has tried to position a product as its solution—not simply for the personal problems of halitosis, shyness, or unattractiveness, but also for social problems such as oppression or inequality. For example, advertising has always portrayed itself as on the side of liberation, especially from everything old and traditional. This usually takes the form of liberation from old commodities in favor of new and improved commodities, but there has sometimes been an actual political component. For example, advertisements for cigarettes were early public proclamations for women's equality. A leading advertiser of the 1920s described an advertising-inspired parade where, with the support of a prominent feminist, some young women lit "torches of freedom" (i.e., cigarettes) "as a protest against woman's inequality" (Ewen 1976, 161). Gender inequality could be solved by buying the right brand of cigarettes, the right toys for little girls, the right suit for the businesswoman.

By the middle of the 1950s, consumer culture and advertising were increasingly seen as parts of the problem rather than as solutions. People were beginning to realize that if there is any connection between increased consumption and happiness, it is a negative one (see table 3.1). A common theme of popular magazine articles, movies, and sermons, as well as of academic writing was the problem of conformity, of consumerism, and the loss of the work ethic. The appearance of this theme shows the

Table 3.1   Consumption and Happiness

Changes in Consumption	Changes in Quality of Life
Rise in per capita consumption in the United States between 1973 and 1993.	Despite the astounding economic growth between 1958 and 1980, Americans reported feeling significantly less well-off in 1980 than they had twenty-two years earlier.
In 1992, people were, on average, 4.5 times richer than their great-grandparents at the turn of the century.	Percent of Americans reporting that they were "very happy" were no more numerous in 1991 than in 1957.

Median size of a new house built in the United States:
    1949: 1,100 square feet
    1970: 1,385 square feet
    1993: 2,060 square feet
	51 percent decrease in quality of life in the United States since 1970, as measured by the index of Social Health.

Americans can choose from:
    Over 25,000 supermarket items
    200 kinds of cereal
    11,092 magazines
	75 percent of American workers ages twenty-five to forty-nine report that they would like to see a return to a simpler society with less emphasis on material wealth.

In 1987, the number of shopping centers in the United States (32,563) surpassed the number of high schools.	93 percent of American teenage girls report store-hopping as favorite activity.
By the time they graduate from high school, American teenagers are typically exposed to 360,000 advertisements.	Employed Americans spent 163 hours more per year on the job in 1991 than they did in 1969.
Since 1960, the daily average number of hours spent viewing television has risen by 39 percent.	
Doctors comprise the highest income group in theUnited States.	Doctors and lawyers comprise the professions with the highest proportion of unhappy people.
American parents spent 40 percent less time with their children in 1991 than they did in 1965.	69 percent of Americans would like to "slow down and live a more relaxed life."

Sources: EcoFuture. 2003. *All-Consuming Passion: Waking Up from the American Dream.* http://www.ecofuture.org/ pk/pkar9506.html; Joe Dominguez and Vicki Robin. 1993. *Your Money or Your Life: Transforming Your Relationship with Money and Achieving Financial Independence.* 2d ed. New York: Penguin; New Road Map Foundation. http://www.cn.org/zpg/acpmain.htm.

protean ingenuity of consumer culture in that advertising was able to present even this problem as solvable by more consumption. Because this innovation was so important to the spread of consumer culture, we will examine it in detail.

Hip Consumerism

Thomas Frank, in *The Conquest of Cool* (1997), has described changes in advertising as one of the most important processes behind the counterculture of the 1960s. Frank's main thesis is that the counterculture received its impetus from the momentous transformation that advertising underwent in the early 1960s. Advertising made the hatred of consumer culture one of its own themes and presented the consumer as a rebel against the "establishment" and conformity.

The counterculture of the 1960s was deeply critical of consumer culture. One of the founding documents of the counterculture, the Port Huron Statement, condemned marketing techniques intended to "create pseudo-needs in consumers" and to make "wasteful 'planned obsolescence' . . . a permanent feature of business strategy" (Miller 1987, 339). However, both critics and admirers have commented on the deep connections between consumer culture and the counterculture of the 1960s. Both promulgated a doctrine of hedonism, liberation, and continual transgression. Frank makes sense of this contradiction by demonstrating that consumer culture was itself critical of consumer culture, and the counterculture was, to a large extent, a reflection of that.

> The central theme that gives coherence to American advertising of both the early and late sixties is this: Consumer culture is a gigantic fraud. It demands that you act like everyone else, that you restrain yourself, that you fit in with the crowd, when you are in fact an individual. Consumer culture lies and seeks to sell you shoddy products that will fall apart or be out of style in a few years; but you crave authenticity and are too smart to fall for that Madison Avenue stuff (your neighbors may not be). Above all, consumer culture fosters conventions that are repressive and unfulfilling; but with the help of hip trends you can smash through those, create a new world in which

> people can be themselves, pretense has vanished, and
> healthy appetites are liberated from the stultifying
> mores of the past. (1997, 136)

In other words, consumer culture presented consumption as a solution to its own problems.

The generally accepted story of the relation between the 1960s counterculture and consumer culture is that the latter co-opted the former. In the beginning, the story goes, there was an authentic counterculture that was in opposition to capitalism and corporate culture. However, this authentic movement either sold out or was effectively mimicked by a mass-produced counterfeit culture of groovy, psychedelic products that captured the youth market and subverted the real counterculture's threat. Frank contends that the mass-produced counterfeit culture was "not so much evidence of co-optation, but rather evidence of the counterculture's roots in consumer culture" (1997, 27).

Of course, few would deny the connection between the counterculture and the popular music and "rebel" celebrities of consumer culture. Furthermore, the role of television and popular magazines in advertising the "summer of love" and the entire hippie phenomena is unquestioned. Frank's argument goes further than this to claim that it was in the heart of the beast, in advertising itself, that the first changes occurred that triggered the counterculture and the hippie movement: "The changes here were, if anything, even more remarkable, more significant, and took place slightly earlier than those in music and youth culture" (1997, 27).

Frank's study of advertisers in the late 1950s and early 1960s shows that they were developing their own counterculture. A new generation of advertisers was growing tired of the repetitive, "scientific" advertisements of the 1950s and was finding success with advertisements that were ironic, rebellious, and that attacked or made fun of consumer culture itself.

In 1960, the advertising company Doyle Dane Bernbach launched a campaign that was to define hip consumerism (see profile of William Bernbach in chapter 6). It was for the Volkswagen beetle (see description of Volkswagen Beetle in chapter 6). It is no accident that the commodity most identified with the 1960s counterculture is the Volkswagen.

Most car advertising before the 1960s consisted of beautiful fantasies of some sort: a verdant green countryside, elegantly dressed models, and gleaming metal; or a racetrack, skimpily dressed models, and more gleaming metal. Its photography grabbed you, and its text labored powerfully to extol the virtues of the car. The Volkswagen advertisement, in contrast, was simple, not flashy; self-deprecating, not self-congratulatory; and funny, not serious. It was the opposite of the advertising that everyone was used to. One of the first advertisements was a full page of mostly white space with a small picture of the car in the upper corner, a small headline toward the bottom saying "Think Small," and a couple of paragraphs that described how strange the car was.

Most significantly, the Volkswagen advertisements made fun of the product, of advertising, and of consumer culture. It was the advertisements that first called the car a "beetle" and said that the station wagon "looked like a shoebox." But it was at consumer culture itself that the advertisements aimed their sharpest barbs. They ridiculed the use of cars as status symbols. They poked fun at dealers' sales tactics. They pilloried the faddishness and planned obsolescence of the fashionable commodity.

These new advertisements were extremely successful and initiated a revolt in advertising against the hard sell that still dominated the industry. In this "revolution," the new generation of advertisers saw the emerging counterculture "not as an enemy to be undermined or a threat to consumer culture but as a hopeful sign, a symbolic ally in their own struggles against the mountains of dead-weight procedure and hierarchy that had accumulated over the years" (Frank 1997, 9). This partnership changed consumer culture.

> Almost no American car manufacturers were still using the idealized, white-family-at-play motif by that year [1965]. And with the exception of luxury lines (Cadillac, Lincoln, Chrysler), virtually every car being marketed in America introduced its 1966 model year as an implement of nonconformity, of instant youthfulness, of mockery toward traditional Detroit-suckers, or of distinction from the mass society herd.... The critique of mass society, leveled by the American automakers was noticeably different from that of Volkswagen and Volvo. The ads of the Big Three automakers were not concerned with evading planned obsolescence, but with discovering for annual style changes a more compelling meaning. Where Volkswagen and Volvo emphasized authenticity and durability, Detroit stressed escape, excitement, carnival,

> nonconformity, and individualism. It is a cleavage that goes to the heart of the commercial revolution of the sixties: every brand claimed to be bored, disgusted, and alienated, but for some these meant the never-changing Volkswagen and blue jeans; they steered others toward the Pontiac Breakaway and the Peacock Revolution [see description of Peacock Revolution in chapter 6]. (Frank 1997, 156–157)

What we see then is not the emergence of a movement that opposed consumer culture and was then co-opted and defeated by it, but rather a change within consumer culture itself. In the 1960s, consumer culture entered a new phase that Frank calls "hip consumerism." It is now more resistant to criticisms, because it is able to transform those very criticisms into reasons to consume. Hip consumerism uses the ambivalence, the contradictions, and the disappointments due to advertising's constantly broken promises as further inducements to buy more. The protests against manipulation, conformity, and loss of meaning are transformed into reasons to consume. Disgust with consumerism is turned into the fuel that feeds consumerism because we express our disgust with consumer culture through consumption.

Advertising no longer sells a commodity so much as a rebellious stance. For example, Benetton advertisements have not used pictures of its products since 1989. Instead, their advertisements feature shocking images of AIDS victims, racism, war, and death-row inmates. Oliviero Toscani, Benetton's head of advertising, sees these advertisements as a criticism of consumer culture: "The advertising industry has corrupted society. It persuades people that they are respected for what they consume, that they are only worth what they possess" (Ticnic 1997, 9). This is not the head of the politburo speaking, but the head of advertising at a major international company.

Hip consumers are anticonsumption, but they have been taught to express their attitudes through what they buy. They are rebels, but they have been taught to rebel against last year's fashions and especially to rebel against the old-fashioned Puritanism and frugality of their parents. They crave traditions and are willing to buy the latest tradition. They want authenticity and will pay for its simulation.

> What changed during the sixties, it now seems, were the strategies of consumerism, the ideology by which

business explained its domination of the national life. Now products existed to facilitate our rebellion against the soul-deadening world of products, to put us in touch with our authentic selves, to distinguish us from the mass-produced herd, to express our outrage at the stifling world of economic necessity. (Frank 1997, 229)

Hip consumerism has become the latest and strongest version of consumer culture. Both the critique of consumption and the solution to the problems of consumption are now contained within consumer culture. In other words, consumer culture presents itself as a problem that only more consumption can solve. Advertisements that incorporate ironic attacks on consumer culture are themselves protected from those attacks because they have positioned themselves on the side of the skeptical viewer.

Advertisements that promote rebellion, mock authority, and promise a mass-produced nonconformity are now ubiquitous. For example, one of the main targets of the counterculture's and of feminists' critique of consumer culture was the cosmetics industry, which was taken to be the epitome of artificiality and conformity to mass-produced standards of beauty. However, hip consumerism has revamped these commodities as signs of ironic artificiality, defiance, and nonconformity. A case in point, one company, significantly named Urban Decay, offers cosmetics with names like Plague, Demise, Rat, Roach, and Asphyxia.

New Age Consumerism

In addition to buying to express nonconformity and rebellion, consumers also buy to express an interest in living a simple life, a concern about the environment, and as a declaration of spirituality. For instance, those who seek the simple life can choose among more than 100 models of sleeping bags. They can peruse the advertisements in *Real Simple*, "the magazine devoted to simplifying your life." They can buy an SUV to get off-road and closer to nature. They can furnish their home with the latest craze in traditional crafts. They can, if they possess the money, have custom-made, one-of-a-kind clothes fashioned for them out of hand-spun fabric.

We can call this variant of the hip consumer the New Age consumer. A forthcoming article by Sam Binkley discusses the *Whole*

Earth Catalog, one of the most important documents of the change from hip consumption to New Age consumption. This strange mix of a Sears Roebuck catalog and opinionated *Consumer Reports* put together by dropouts from the counterculture used its lists of commodities to carry the 1960s rebellious spirit into the spiritual environmentalism that characterizes the New Age consumer.

The hip consumer responds to the contradictions of consumer culture through consumption that emphasizes artifice, irony, and nonconformity. The New Age consumer responds to these same contradictions also with consumption, but they prefer commodities that represent a noncommercial and more spiritual life. The New Age consumer prefers boutiques to national chains, gentrified neighborhood centers to shopping malls. However, even the mall-based chain store can be sold to the New Age consumer if it is properly marketed, as Anita Roddick proved when she introduced the environmentally friendly, politically correct chain, The Body Shop.

New Age consumers demonstrate through their consumption that they are earth-friendly, socially responsible, enlightened global citizens in tune with nature. They prefer natural wood, natural fibers, natural ingredients, organic food, and herbal body-care products. All of these are sold as remedies for the problems of consumer culture.

Kimberly Lau provides an interesting case of New Age consumerism in her study of *New Age Capitalism* (2000). She covers a number of examples including the spread of yoga and macrobiotic diets, but most germane is her examination of the marketing of aromatherapy. In the marketing of aromatherapy, we see many of the attributes of hip consumption that Frank described, but with a New Age twist.

Horst Rechelbacher, the founder of Aveda, introduced aromatherapy to the American public in 1978. Since Aveda's success, others have followed suit, including specialty stores such as The Body Shop, Garden Botanika, and H2O. In addition, noncosmetic but hip retailers such as The Gap, The Limited, Eddie Bauer, Urban Outfitters, Banana Republic, Pier 1 Imports, and The Nature Company have all introduced aromatherapy products. Lau estimates the annual sale of aromatherapy products to be $300 to $500 million, with an annual growth rate of approximately 30 percent (2000, 34).

Lau describes three characteristics of the aromatherapy advertising campaign that appeals to the New Age consumer: (1) it is presented as ecofriendly; (2) it is a remedy for the psychic ills of modern civilization; and (3) it is able to function as a hip consumer's status symbol.

As Lau informs us, "everyone from aromatherapists to essential oil suppliers and aroma researchers praises the earth-friendly nature of aromatherapy, but no one articulates the precise nature of its environmentalism" (2000, 39–40). Finding no evidence for its ecological beneficence, Lau can only surmise the following formula: "The association seems as simple as plants=green=earth-friendly" (2000, 40).

In addition, aromatherapy is associated with ancient and contemporary cultures that are portrayed as unsullied by the problems of modern consumer culture. It is variously associated with the ancient practices of Egypt, Greece, Rome, India, and China. In addition, Aveda advertises that some of its ingredients are obtained from the Yawanawa, who live in the rain forests of western Brazil. Lau sees this identification of aromatherapy with ancient and nonindustrialized cultures as "part of an attempt to counter modernity and the techno-industrial capitalist system it signifies" (2000, 30). In other words, advertising positions this product outside of consumer culture, as an alternative and even an antidote.[1]

Of course, this alternative to consumer culture can only be consumed by those able to afford it. This allows Aveda products, like most hip commodities, to function both as a status symbol and as an antistatus symbol. It represents both the material resources to buy expensive body-care products and a criticism of Western materialism.

> Aveda makes available for purchase the idea of participating in cultural critique, of living according to ancient philosophies, of living an alternative lifestyle. . . . Consumption becomes a mode of addressing social, political, and cultural disenchantment, although the very processes enabling consumption are what characterize modernity, itself the cause of the disenchantment being critiqued. (Lau 2000, 133)

Furthermore, all of the New Age commodities discussed by Lau claim to remedy the fragmentation that Daniel Bell, in *The Cultural Contradictions of Capitalism*, predicted would destroy consumer culture. Reconnecting mind, body, and spirit is a primary theme of these products. They are all, at least in name, holistic.

Here, too, the contradictions of our consumer culture function as another reason to consume.

Not only do these products turn anticonsumption into a reason for more consumption, but it is arguable that they co-opt any real opposition to consumer culture.

> Each product comes with a tag, an address, a lifestyle. The act of purchase locates the individual within a tribe, and in this way, fashion functions to regulate lifestyles and produce the belief that every consumer choice is a free choice, a way in which individuals invent themselves. Such practices can co-opt self-identifying groups into the consumer cycle, even those who may be politically and ethically opposed to it— for example, those targeted by the new niche markets in anti-fashions, eco-sensitive clothing, and products from recycled materials. (Finkelstein 1995, 232)

Cheesy Consumerism

For those unable to believe any longer in consumer culture's promises of nostalgic simplicity or ancient spirituality, there is yet another variant of the hip consumer, the "antihip" or the cheesy consumer. The hip consumer responds to the contradictions of consumer culture by stressing artifice and nonconformity. The New Age consumer responds by "buying" into a fantasy of nostalgic simplicity. This new variation, the cheesy consumer, stresses the artifice of the fantasy of nostalgic simplicity.

We see the cheesy sensibility in the popularity of reruns of *Gilligan's Island* and *The Brady Bunch.* One cable company is running these with faux retro commercials, but we can see such cheesy advertisements throughout our consumer culture. Old Navy seems to specialize in them, and cheese is the motif in Britney Spears's retro Pepsi commercials. David Letterman and especially his fake-hipster bandleader, Paul Schafer, is the epitome of cheese.

Cheese is a kind of manufactured camp (see chapter 4 for a discussion of camp). However, while camp aficionados must rummage through the near past for marginal figures, cheese is ready-made. Also, while camp has a subversive bite to it, the cheese attitude is simply sarcastic.

Michiko Kakutani (1992) explains the appeal of cheese to the jaded consumer. According to Kakutani, the current generation is one that "grew up suspicious of sincerity; wary of making emotional, political, or artistic commitments; and whose cynical, defensive mantra is, 'Hey, I'm cool, you're cool, and we won't endanger our coolness by ever admitting to a genuine emotion or serious ambition'" (C1).

The cheesy consumer wants to believe in families like the Brady Bunch and, of course, all of the consumer products that made them the happy family that they were, but he cannot. Cheese is a way to indulge in the fantasy, but now in a skeptical, ironic mode. Cheesy commercials allow the viewer to both enjoy the fantasy and feel smugly superior to it. In addition, they position the advertiser on the side of the skeptical consumer so that both can smirk at consumer culture even as they indulge in it.

Consumption as an International Social Problem

The hip comsumer, the New Age consumer, and the chees consumer have all been described previously as primarily American and European phenomena. However, consumer culture has become a global phenomenon and, consequently, a global problem. Here, too, more consumption is offered as a solution to consumer culture.

A global consumer culture is connected to the international flow of products, money, people, information, and services, which has been called *globalization*. There can be little doubt that the world is becoming increasingly interconnected and that this has enormous cultural implications. It is not only that countries are economically interdependent, but that they are also culturally interdependent. The political, social, and cultural borders that once separated cutlures have become permeable. Clearly, there are multiple forces at work in globalization—economic, political, institutional, technological—but undoubtedly the most obvious form that globalization assumes is as a global consumer culture.

> Few expressions of globalization are so visible, widespread and pervasive as the worldwide proliferation of internationally traded consumer brands, the global ascendancy of popular cultural icons and artifacts, and the simultaneous communication of events by satellite broadcasts to hundreds of millions of people at a time

> on all continents. The most public symbols of global-
> ization consist of Coca-Cola, Madonna and the news
> on CNN. (Held et al. 1999, 327)

Steger cites as examples of globalization the appearance of Nike sneakers on Amazonian Indians, Texaco baseball caps on sub-Saharan youths, and Chicago Bulls sweatshirts on Palestinians (2002, 36). In such examples, it is easy to see a homogenized—even Americanized—consumer culture spreading throughout the world by creating standardized tastes and desires. And, in fact, this homogenized world is often precisely what the advertising for consumption promises, as in the McDonald's advertisement, "It's what everyone around the world keeps saying—It's MacTime," or when Coke wants to teach the world to sing in perfect harmony.

Although some see globalization as an Americanized homogeneity, others see it as leading to the creating of heterogeneous, diverse, and plural local cultures. In other words, people in a small American town might be exposed to Japanese movies, African music, and French fashions, and each person in the town can create their own individual and unique lifestyle from these world sources.

The question whether globalization increases cultural homogeneity and sameness by establishing common codes and practices or whether it increases a heterogeneity of newly emerging differences seems now, to many analysts, to have been answered. Globalization does both. Globalization appears to make people more different but in a similar way. It creates a mixed system, where people are homogenized into similar individuals, ethnicities, and nations who want different things. It creates what Roland Robertson has called "glocalization" (1995).

Glocalization

According to Robertson, "globalization is not an all-encompassing process of homogenization but a complex mixture of homogenization and heterogenization" (2001, 462). There is an interpenetration of the global and the local that creates a difference-within-sameness. The local is not opposed to the global, rather it is an aspect of the global. Consequently, the homogeneity of global cultural flows will be matched by the heterogeneity of their reception, appropriation, and response. Everybody is exposed to McDonald's, Coke, and Levis, but people do different things with them. It is this that characterizes glocalization.

Glocalization is related to "delocalization." The defining characteristic of our global culture is that relations between people are no longer dependent on a particular location. The distance between people and the borders separating them mean less and less. We now inhabit a new global space along with the local space. The idea of glocalization is that our relation to the local is changed by the global context. Global forces undermine our bond to a fixed local culture, its unquestioned traditions, and stable identities. Through television, the Internet, advertising, trade, and travel, people are more exposed to the world and therefore freer from the constraints of the local.

Not only is delocalization caused by global forces, but people themselves are more mobile and prone to cross borders. Many of a locale's residents did not grow up in that locality, and these newcomers bring other traditions to this new place. In addition, indigenous locals travel, interact, and return, thereby transforming their cultures. These processes are so prevalent that a number of cities are dominated by cosmopolitan elites and immigrant neighborhoods. Sassen describes these as global cities (1991).

These processes lead to a cultural form that is referred to as "hybridization" (Pieterse 1995). Zwingle describes "sitting in a coffee shop in London drinking Italian espresso served by an Algerian waiter to the strains of the Beach Boys singing 'I wish they all could be California girls'" (2000, 153). Pieterse describes "Thai boxing by Moroccan girls in Amsterdam, Asian rap in London, Irish bagels, Chinese tacos and Mardi Gras Indians in the United States" (1995, 53). We regularly see these hybrids in music, novels, restaurants, paintings, crafts, and so on. The hybrid form pervades both high and popular culture and even "traditional" culture. In fact, much of what we take to be local and traditional is a hybrid. All around the world, we see the re-creation of local rituals for the tourist trade. Glocalization is connected to delocalization through the creation or re-creation of the local traditions in a way that conforms to global forces.

There is a similarity between glocalization and the niche markets created by consumer culture. This should not be a surprise since the very term *glocalization* began as "one of the main marketing buzzwords of the beginning of the nineties" (Tulloch 1991, 134). Global culture seems to be precisely tracking the trend among consumer goods that marketers have already recognized. Although there are some global brands, one business analyst observed that this "does not mean that there is a global consumer for companies to target. International cultural differences are by no means disappearing and, in the late twentieth century, individualism is as strong a world force as internationalism. Consumer goods are becoming more, rather than less, focused on the individual" (Fitzgerald 1997, 742). However, the individuals focused on by global marketing are, as one business leader put it, "heteroconsumers": "People who've become increasingly alike and indistinct from one another, and yet have simultaneously varied and multiple preferences" (Levitt 1988, 8).

Thus, there is indeed greater heterogeneity, but it is in the context of and, to a large extent, in response to the homogeneity of a consumer culture. What appears to be disorder is really systematic. Global consumer culture creates what Wilk calls "global systems of common difference" (1995). Again, this seems to be recognized by consumer advertising. An AT&T advertisement says, "What makes us all the same is that we're all different."

McDonaldization as Heterogeneity and Homogeneity

George Ritzer (2000) coined the term "McDonaldization" to describe the way in which more and more of our life is being run like a fast food restaurant. Because McDonaldization has become a widely used term for the globalization of consumer culture, it is useful to employ it to examine the interplay of heterogeneity and homogeneity. First, however, it is necessary to clearly define what is meant by McDonaldization. It is not simply the spread of a particular restaurant chain. Instead it is the spread of the processes of efficiency, calculability, predictability, and control, which McDonald's successfully introduced into consumption (see profile of Ray Kroc, founder of McDonald's, in chapter 6). Fast food restaurants provide food efficiently rather than providing good food. The fast food restaurant is able to calculate how many hamburgers have been served, how many seconds it takes to fill a cup, the exact profit margin of each sale, and so forth. Each hamburger, no matter when or where it is bought, is predictably the same. In order to achieve this efficiency, calculability, and predictability, people must be controlled. The idea of McDonaldization is that these processes are coming to dominate more economic and cultural sectors as well as spreading globally.

Although McDonaldization refers to much more than the

restaurant chain, it is instructive to begin with a focus on the heterogenizing aspects of McDonald's itself. We see within the homogeneity of McDonald's (the vanguard of McDonaldization) four types of heterogeneity.

First, McDonald's in a non-American setting provides a cheap and easily accessible tourist experience. Stephenson describes the experience of Dutch patrons where a local McDonald's provides "a kind of instant emigration that occurs the moment one walks through the doors, where Dutch rules rather obviously don't apply and where there are few adults around to enforce any that might" (1989, 227).

Second, when McDonald's is accepted as a local institution, it creates a new heterogeneous hybrid locality. The literature is rife with descriptions of tourists to the United States from other countries who are surprised to see a McDonald's here. Watson's (1997) collection is full of descriptions of the acceptance of McDonald's as a local phenomena in East Asian countries. This is indicative not of the power of the local, but of the power of McDonald's to re-create the local. As Ritzer points out, "Its impact is far greater if it infiltrates a local culture and becomes a part of it than if it remains perceived as an American phenomenon superimposed on a local setting" (2001, 171).

Third, the chain varies its menu to adapt to particular localities. In India, McDonald's outlets serve Vegetable McNuggets and Maharaja Macs made with mutton. In Turkey, they offer a chilled yogurt drink. In Italy, espresso and cold pasta. Teriyaki burgers are on the menu in Japan, Taiwan, and Hong Kong (along with red bean sundaes). The main sandwich in the Netherlands is a vegetarian burger; in Norway, it is McLaks (a grilled salmon sandwich); in Germany, frankfurters; in Uruguay, a poached egg hamburger called the McHuevo.

Finally, the process of McDonaldization is adopted by indigenous competitors of McDonald's to create a local variety of fast food. Ritzer mentions Russkoye Bistro in Russia, Ronghua Chicken and Xiangfei Roast Chicken in China, Mos Burger in Japan, and Uncle Joe's Hamburger in Korea (2001). Ritzer writes that "it is not the existence of American chains (and other new means of consumption) in other countries that is the most important indicator of the spread of McDonaldization, but rather the existence of indigenous clones of those McDonaldized enterprises" (2001, 170).

We see then that, on the one hand, McDonald's itself becomes more heterogeneous by adapting to the local, and, on the other hand, McDonaldization promotes heterogeneity in the locality by creating a tourist experience, a hybrid local, and by promoting McDonaldized local competitors. Nevertheless, as glocalization would predict, along with this increased heterogeneity of product and locality comes an increased homogeneity of process—of calculability, efficiency, predictability, and control.

The Contradictions of Global Consumer Culture

We see in global consumer culture the same contradictions that we outlined previously. Of course, as capitalism has spread, we see also the spread of its contradiction between a calculating, rational, frugal producer and an impulsive, irrational, prodigal consumer. In addition, even though many of these countries don't have a Protestant tradition or a bourgeois culture, we nevertheless see a contradiction between their traditional ethos and the impulses of a consumer culture. This often takes the form of a generational difference in developing countries.

> In each nation, there remains a significant population segment who have lived through underdevelopment, whose collective memories of material deprivation and thrifty ways are still fresh. Their moral/ideological position on savings has made them resistant to the rapid expansion of consumerism. In addition, this group often sees the arrival of consumerist culture as the consequence of the penetration and contamination of traditional cultural practices by "Western," particularly American, cultures. Thus, the moral debate on consumption has often been characterized as a "generational conflict," supposedly between the deprived generation who embody thrift as a traditional value and the affluent and fast-spending, "Westernised" generation. (Beng-Huat 2000, 8)

We also see the same contradictory view of the consumer. On the one hand, the spread of consumer culture is driven primarily by the choices made by those who live in the invaded territory. The consumer is the sovereign director of globalizing consumer culture. On the other hand, as Wilk writes, "it is clear that people are not making completely free choices about goods. They are not merely absorbing foreign goods into their existing modes of consumption, and making free strategic choices in the global marketplace. Third world consumers are subject to various forms of coercion, both economic and ideological" (1994, 81).

These contradictions of global consumer culture are also resolved through the consumption of anticonsumption. Just as in Western culture, others are encouraged to consume in order to represent their belief in anticonsumption traditions, their disdain of advertisers' attempts to control them or their rebellion.

We certainly see some of the same aspects of hip consumerism in response to the globalization of consumer culture. For example, marketers in Eastern Europe have introduced a new product labeled "Ordinary Laundry Detergent" as a hip response to the heavy promotion of Tide as cleaning " better than ordinary laundry detergent" (Money and Colton 2000, 190). However, most characteristic of the response to the contradictions of global consumption has been what Robertson calls a "willful nostalgia" (1992). Woodruff and Drake report, for example, that "Czech-made" soft drinks promise to relieve the stress of the urban, cosmopolitan life that is associated with such global products as Coke and Pepsi (1998). The cosmetics company Shiseido emphasizes its Japanese origins even outside of Japan and advertises an image of Japanese mystique and exoticism (Schutte and Ciarlante 1998). The makers of French chocolates emphasize a nostalgic "Other" of tropical jungles, but also the craft tradition of handmade chocolates (Terrio 1996).

We even see this willful nostalgia being used by McDonald's itself. The McDonald's in Singapore offers a "kampong" burger. Beng-Huat tells us that "kampong refers to the villages in which most Singaporeans lived prior to being resettled into high-rise public housing estates, a time which is remembered nostalgically as the 'good old days' when life was much more relaxed and community more organic than today's high-stress living in a globalised economy" (2000, 195–196).

Along with these familiar contradictions, we see also the highlighting of a new one, the contradiction outlined previously between heterogeneity and homogeneity. In reaction to the new contradiction, people are encouraged to consume in order to resist a homogenizing globalization, which is usually and most effectively presented as Americanization.

The Consumption of Anti-Americanization

Before we describe the way in which anti-Americanization is used to spur consumption, we should point out that the United States first spurred consumption as a symbol for rebellion rather than as a symbol of homogenous conformity. Schutte and Ciarlante describe Coca-Cola, Levis, and Marlboro as symbols of individualism and freedom (1998, 195). Yoshimi describes American consumer goods as "symbols of 'emancipation' and 'resistance'" (2000, 202). According to Beng-Huat, "American products have been used to express resistance to local repressions" (2000, 16). Humphrey says that Western consumer goods represented "resistance to the regime" in the Soviet Union (1995, 57), and this continued in post-Communist Russia with Chevrolet successfully selling cars to Russians with a "Born in the U.S.A." campaign (Money and Colton 2000, 189).

Despite the use of images portraying American products as symbols of emancipation and resistance, quite the opposite symbolization has often occurred. This has emerged naturally enough from the contradictions of global consumer culture listed previously. There has been a condemnation of the unbridled consumer both as not rational enough and as not traditional enough (Sacks 1998). Furthermore, the image of the sovereign consumer, which consumer culture introduced, has often been used as the basis for criticizing the manipulated consumer. It was not long before both nations and local entrepreneurs saw the advantage to be gained in portraying globalization, or more usually Americanization, as the enemy. Appadurai notes the benefits of "posing global commoditization (or capitalism, or some other such external enemy) as more real than the threat of its own hegemonic strategies" (1996, 32). Beng-Huat describes the "moral panic" created by the South Korean government and media against an Americanized consumer culture (2000).

Of course, these moral crusades have not diminished consumption in South Korea or in any other culture. Instead, as we will describe later, these antiglobalization attitudes function like the anticonsumption attitudes described in the first part of this chapter. They fuel more consumption. This might be suspected since, as many analysts have noted, the United States is "the home of opposition and resistance to globalization, in spite of the widely held view that globalization is an American project. In fact, it has by now become appropriate to talk of the globalization of anti-globalism" (Robertson 2001, 459).

McDonaldization in France

Let us return again to McDonald's and look at its reception in France as an exemplary case of the consumption of anti-Americanization. McDonald's was, for the French, identified with the United States, and the French relation with American culture has been, to say the least, ambiguous. France is well known for having rejected American culture in the 1960s and 1970s, only to embrace it by the mid-1980s (Kuisel 1993). Even though McDonald's was introduced into France in 1972 in the period of supposed American rejection, it nevertheless benefited from this American association because many saw McDonald's as a kind of "reverse snobbery" (Fantasia 1995, 227). This view existed even among the upper class, as evidenced by the fact that a haute couture fashion show served a buffet of McDonald's food during this period.

Along with McDonald's, there was an accompanying spread of McDonaldization among the French food industry. In the beginning, these French fast food restaurants tried to benefit from the association of fast food with the United States, by using such names as Magic Burger, B'Burger, Manhattan Burger, Katy's Burger, Love Burger, and Kiss Burger. In addition, their look and food products were copied from the American model. Indeed, Fantasia reports that French-owned hamburger places far outnumbered American-owned ones (1995, 206). More important than the food and the look, the restaurants copied the processes of McDonaldization: its efficiency, calculability, predictability, and control.

Of course, McDonald's identification with the United States has not been solely to its benefit. The very thing that has made McDonald's so popular has also made it the target of antiglobalization activists. French McDonald's have been sites of protest as well as of vandalism and bombing. The case of Jose Bove who destroyed a half-built McDonald's in protest of a World Trade Organization (WTO) ruling has become a cause célèbre with support from tens of thousands of protestors as well as political leaders (see description of World Trade Organization (WTO) in chapter 6). More recently, those protesting the invasion/liberation of Iraq have burned a Ronald McDonald statue in Ecuador, smashed McDonald's windows in Paris, and scaled a McDonald's sign in South Korea.

Nevertheless, despite the opposition to McDonald's, Mc-Donaldization has continued apace and increasingly acquired a French twist. French fast food restuarants quickly moved from American food and look to traditional French foods such as croissants and sandwiches on brioche or baguettes. Despite their now identifiably French names, products, and looks, these food outlets follow the same standardized, mechanized, and efficient practices that McDonald's introduced. However, they market themselves as a French (i.e., non-American) fast food. In a minor reverse incursion, a few of these French fast food places (e.g., Pret à Manger) have invaded the United States, drawing upon the French identification with fine food to help sell their McDonaldized products.

More important than this reverse incursion is the fact that the French fast food places have used the rejection of McDonald's and of Americanization to sell their own products. In other words, the rejection of McDonald's has been used to promote the spread of McDonaldization. France provides us with a clear example of the increase in heterogeneity—of products, look, and national identification—along with the increased homogenization of process.

This is not merely an economic phenomena. As Chua Beng-Huat describes in the case of Singapore, the state is deeply involved.

> Consumption expansion thus tends to lead to some level of global homogenization of culture among consumers, an effect that gives rise to negative responses to globalisation. As consumer goods are always also cultural goods, expansion of consumption of imported products and services often gives rise to an exaggerated sense of "panic," of cultural "invasion" which, supposedly, if left unchecked will result in the demise of the local culture. Critics, including the state, thus inveigh against specific "foreign" targets, such as "Americanisation" or "Japanisation," and take upon themselves to promote "local" culture as ballast against the "foreign" cultural invasions. The desire of the state to involve itself in such ideological critique is obvious. Homogenisation of culture globally is antithetical to the idea of the "uniqueness" of nationalist sentiments and, therefore, is potentially threatening to

the hold of the nation-state on its citizens. Emphasising the "national" as "local" differences is in the interests of the nation-state as an act of self-preservation. Hence, existing alongside embracing the arrival of capital is a cultural/moral critique of both the commodification of social life and the "cultural imperialism" of the countries from which the goods originate. (2000, 183–184)

We see a similar effect in the marketing of such soft drinks as Mecca Cola and Qibla Cola, which target the European Muslim community and position themselves as an expression of anti-Americanization (Hundley 2003). The idea is that individuals are to express their contempt for the United States and its associated consumer society through the consumption of products that are produced, packaged, and marketed in a way that is deeply dependent on American consumer culture. In addition, although not so strongly anti-American, the Japanese create a national identity that is presented as distinct from others, especially Americans, and which is tied to what Yoshino (1999) calls a cultural marketplace. Likewise, Foster describes the people of Papau New Guinea as using consumption to create a local identity in opposition to the identity attached to global brands (2002). One final example, Johnston describes an advertisement for a flavored milk drink in New Zealand that is strongly critical of American culture, but which uses a musical rap form to express it (2001). In these and many other cases, the spread of consumer culture is supported by the rejection of consumer culture represented as Americanization.

Conclusion

As discussed in the first part of this chapter, we have been encouraged to buy in order to establish our individuality in a mass-produced culture, to express our disgust with consumption by more consumption, to purchase the latest improved traditions. In the context of globalization, the consumption of anticonsumption is given a new twist. Now people are encouraged to buy to express their rejection of homogenized Americanization. Our disgust with the homogenized Americanization of McDonald's is used to expand the underlying process of McDonaldization. Our disgust with global consumer culture is used to strengthen and spread it.

Far from creating a crisis, the problems of consumer culture have made it more resilient. This is because our dissatisfaction with the culture is expressed through more consumption. Consumption has become our model for dissent, our model for freedom, our model for political activity. All alternatives to consumer culture—the simple life, the spiritual, the traditional, the local—become variant consumer fantasies. Consumption is a social problem and it is offered as its own solution.

Note

1. It is not necessary to invoke ancient and nonindustrialized cultures to position a product outside of consumer culture. Passamai describes how New Age consumers invoke science fiction and fantasy stories to position commodities outside of consumer culture (2002).

References

Appadurai, Arjun. 1996. *Modernity at Large: Cultural Dimensions of Globalization.* Minneapolis, MN: University of Minnesota Press.

Bell, Daniel. 1976. *The Cultural Contradictions of Capitalism.* New York: Basic Books.

Beng-Huat, Chua. 2000. "Consuming Asians: Ideas and Issues." In C. Beng-Huat, ed., *Consumption in Asian Lifestyles and Identities,* 1–34. New York: Routledge.

———. 2000. "Singaporeans Ingesting McDonalds." In C. Beng-Huat, ed., *Consumption in Asian Lifestyles and Identities,* 183–201. New York: Routledge.

Binkley, Sam. Forthcoming. "The Seers of Menlo Park: The Discourse of Heroic Consumption in the *Whole Earth Catalog.*" *Journal of Consumer Culture.*

Dominguez, Joe, and Vicki Robin. 1993. *Your Money or Your Life: Transforming Your Relationship with Money and Achieving Financial Independence.* 2d ed. New York: Penguin.

EcoFuture. 2003. *All-Consuming Passion: Waking Up from the American Dream.* http://www.ecofuture.org/pk/pkar9506.html.

Ewen, Stuart. 1976. *Captains of Consciousness: Advertising and the Social Roots of the Consumer Culture.* New York: McGraw-Hill.

Fantasia, Rick. 1995. "Fast Food in France." *Theory and Society* 24: 201–243.

Finkelstein, Joanne. 1995. "The Anemic World of the High Consumer: Fashion and Cultural Formation." In D. Miller, ed., *Worlds Apart: Modernity Through the Prism of the Local*, 227–245. New York: Routledge.

Fitzgerald, Niall. 1997. "Harnessing the Potential of Globalization for the Consumer and Citizen." *International Affairs* 73: 739–746.

Foster, Robert. 2002. *Materializing the Nation: Commodities, Consumption, and Media in Papua New Guinea*. Bloomington: Indiana University Press.

Frank, Thomas. 1997. *The Conquest of Cool: Business Culture, Counterculture, and the Rise of Hip Consumerism*. Chicago: University of Chicago Press.

Held, David, Anthony McGrew, David Goldblatt, and Jonathan Perraton. 1999. *Global Transformations: Politics, Economics, and Culture*. Stanford, CA: Stanford University Press.

Humphrey, Caroline. 1995. "Creating a Culture of Disillusionment: Consumption in Moscow, a Chronicle of Changing Times." In D. Miller, ed., *Worlds Apart: Modernity through the Prism of the Local*, 43–68. New York: Routledge.

Hundley, Tom. 2003. "Foreign Cola Knockoffs Offer Anti-American Political Flavor." *Chicago Tribune*, 5 February, B1.

Johnston, Jessica. 2001. "The Battle for Local Identity: An Ethnographic Description of Local/Global Tensions in a New Zealand Advertisement." *Journal of Popular Culture* 35: 193–205.

Kakutani, Michiko. 1992. "First There Was Camp; Now There's Cheese." *New York Times*, 7 August, C1.

Kuisel, Richard. 1993. *Seducing the French: The Dilemma of Americanization*. Berkeley, CA: University of California Press.

Lau, Kimberly. 2000. *New Age Capitalism: Making Money East of Eden*. Philadelphia: University of Pennsylvania Press.

Levitt, Theodore. 1988. "The Pluralization of Consumption." *Harvard Business Review* 2: 7–8.

Miller, Jim. 1987. "Port Huron Statement." In J. Miller, ed., *Democracy Is in the Streets: From Port Huron to the Siege of Chicago*, 329–374. New York: Simon and Schuster.

Money, R. Bruce, and Deborah Colton. 2000. "Global Advertising." *Journal of World Business* 35: 189–205.

New Road Map Foundation. http://www.cn.org/zpg/acpmain.htm.

Passamai, Adam. 2002. "Cultural Consumption of History and Popular Culture in Alternative Spiritualities." *Journal of Consumer Culture* 2: 197–218.

Pieterse, Jan N. 1995. "Globalization as Hybridization." In M. Featherstone, S. Lash, and R. Robertson, eds., *Global Modernities*, 45–68. London: Sage.

Ritzer, George. 2000. *The McDonaldization of Society.* New Century ed. Thousand Oaks, CA: Pine Forge.

———. 2001. "Globalization Theory: Lessons from the Exportation of McDonaldization and the New Means of Consumption." In G. Ritzer, ed., *Explorations in the Sociology of Consumption: Fast Food, Credit Cards and Casinos*, 160–180. Thousand Oaks, CA: Sage.

Robertson, Roland. 1992. *Globalization: Social Theory and Global Culture.* London: Sage.

———. 1995. "Glocalization: Time-Space and Homogeneity-Heterogeneity." In M. Featherstone, S. Lash, and R. Robertson, eds., *Global Modernities*, 25–44. London: Sage.

———. 2001. "Globalization Theory 2000+: Major Problematics." In G. Ritzer and B. Smart, eds., *Handbook of Social Theory*, 458–471. London: Sage.

Sacks, Jeffrey. 1998. "Unlocking the Mysteries of Globalization." *Foreign Policy* 110: 58–64.

Sassen, Saskia. 1991. *The Global City: New York, London, Tokyo.* Princeton, NJ: Princeton University Press.

Schutte, Hellmut, and Deanna Ciarlante. 1998. *Consumer Behavior in Asia.* New York: New York University Press.

Steger, Manfred. 2002. *Globalism: The New Market Ideology.* Lanham, MD: Rowman and Littlefield.

Stephenson, Peter H. 1989. "Going to McDonald's in Leiden: Reflections on the Concept of Self and Society in the Netherlands." *ETHOS: Journal of the Society for Psychological Anthropology* 17: 226–247.

Terrio, Susan J. 1996. "Crafting *Grand Cru* Chocolates in Contemporary France." *American Anthropologist* 98: 67–79.

Ticnic, Serra. 1997. "United Colors and United Meetings: Benetton and the Commodification of Social Issues." *Journal of Communication* 47: 3–25.

Tulloch, Sara, comp. 1991. *The Oxford Dictionary of New Words.* Oxford: Oxford University Press.

Watson, James. 1997. *Golden Arches East: McDonald's in East Asia.* Stanford, CA: Stanford University Press.

Wilk, Richard. 1994. "Consumer Goods as Dialogue about Development." *Culture and History* 7: 79–100.

———. 1995. "Learning to Be Local in Belize: Global Systems of Common Difference." In D. Miller, ed., *Worlds Apart: Modernity through the Prism of the Local*, 110–133. New York: Routledge.

Woodruff, David, and James Drake. 1998. "Ready to Shop Until They Drop." *Business Week* (22 June): 104.

Yoshimi, Shunya. 2000. "Consuming 'America': From Symbol to System." In C. Beng-Huat, ed., *Consumption in Asian Lifestyles and Identities*, 111–134. New York: Routledge.

Yoshino, Kosaku. 1999. "Rethinking Theories of Nationalism: Japan's Nationalism in a Marketplace Perspective." In K. Yoshino, ed., *Consuming Ethnicity and Nationalism: Asian Experiences*, 8–28. Honolulu: University of Hawaii Press.

Zwingle, Erla. 2000. "A World Together." In K. Sjursen, ed., *Globalization*, 153–164. New York: H. W. Wilson.

4

Stigmatizing Inequality
in Consumer Culture

Leon Wynter starts his book, *American Skin*, by talking about the relation between race and shoes. In New York in 1965, white boys wore U.S. Keds sneakers. If a child had on Converse All-Stars, he was a "Negro or one of the tiny handful of Puerto Ricans" (Wynter 2002, 1). There was one white boy who regularly wore Converse and nobody knew what to make of him. Today, Wynter reports, you can tell little about someone's race by looking at what a person wears. "Whites and nonwhites are still mostly segregated within their neighborhoods in the Bronx. But everyone—young and old, working and upper middle class, college and high school graduates—wears the same sneakers, baseball caps, jeans, boots, and designer names" (Wynter 2002, 4). In a generation, the role of consumer objects in the American system of inequality has completely changed. Whereas consumer objects were one of the most important markers of segregation and inequality, they have now become signs of integration and homogeneity. In this chapter, we will try to understand how this has happened.

Inequality is present in practically all societies. Orwell showed us that even in *Animal Farm*'s utopia of equality, "some animals are more equal than others." Skin color, caste, gender, age, religion, sexual orientation, citizenship—these are only the most obvious forms of inequality. Despite being practically universal, inequality takes a unique form in different cultures. As you would expect, inequality takes a different form in a consumer culture. We actually should say that inequality takes two forms:One is obvious and the other is much more difficult to perceive.

In the next two chapters, we will look at the two ways that inequality functions in a consumer culture. In this chapter, we will look at the first type of inequality—one that we actually experience in a direct, less ambiguous, and more transparent manner. This type of inequality can be called stigmatizing inequality because it treats people as though there is something wrong with them—at the very least, as though they are not our equal.

The second type of inequality—which we will not discuss until the next chapter—is anonymous, indirect, and not resulting from our intention. We will call this anonymous inequality. In general, this kind of inequality is not stigmatizing because it doesn't involve people we personally know. I may, in fact, very much admire (from afar, or a tourist's admiration) the people being oppressed in this second type of inequality, but the inequality is created even without my intention, although certainly not without my action.

Consumer objects are involved in both types of inequality, and in this chapter we will look at how consumer objects are used in stigmatizing inequality. Consumer objects are one of the main ways in which we communicate who we are to others. It is not just that our T-shirts have messages, but that they—like all of our clothes, like all of our possessions—are messages. The things we consume are expressions of ourselves, and whether or not we consciously intend a message, others will read it as such.

Such messages can be about many things—including messages about our own individuality and idiosyncrasies—however, the messages are often about our class, race, gender, sexual orientation, and so forth. In other words, they are messages about where we rank in a system of inequality. And even messages about our individuality are often set against the background of systems of inequality. We are individuals in comparison to the stereotypes that make up the system of inequality. Sometimes we consume to indicate membership in a group, sometimes to indicate nonmembership, and sometimes as ironic comments on any system of membership.

The attempt to work out the contradictions of consumer culture discussed in the previous chapter typically takes place within the system of stigmatizing inequality that the individual inherits. So, for example, hip, "anticonsumer" consumption is often pursued in relation to real or perceived inequality—sometimes a rejection of the inequality, occasionally a retro reproduction of it, and, more usually, an ironic comment on it. We will see later that antiracism and antisexism have become important parts of the rebellious attitude of the hip consumer. Similarly, nostalgic, authentic, or spiritual consumption is usually expressed in terms of the particular—usually stigmatized—group that one grew up in. The nostalgic authenticity of an African American is different from that of an Italian American. The same is true of cheesy consumption, since what is marginal or mainstream differs from subculture to subculture.

We see then that even as consumer culture appears to be increasingly homogeneous and as various processes and trends converge, many consumer practices remain embedded in historically specific social contexts. Perhaps the most important social context is the existing system of stigmatizing inequality. In our consumer culture, we can identify six important types of stigmatizing inequality: race, gender, sexual orientation, class, age, and poverty. Each will be discussed in this chapter, but first we will make some general remarks on how stigmatizing inequality is taken up and transformed by a consumer culture.

It is as wrong to suppose that consumer culture simply eradicates social inequality as it would be to suppose that these inequalities persist without being transformed by consumer culture. Consumer culture does not simply replace inherited systems of inequality, rather it uses, transforms, and, to some degree, subverts their power to stigmatize by changing the signs of stigma into fashion statements.

Inequality is both perpetuated by a consumer culture and simultaneously subverted. Consumption perpetuates inequality by enhancing its visibility. For example, markers of gender inequality are taken up by a consumer culture, enhanced, and reinterpreted as signs of sexuality. Even though the marker of inequality is even more on display, it now may serve a different purpose. Rather than marking the person for discriminatory treatment, it may serve as a self-assertion on the part of the formerly stigmatized individual.

The transformation of stigmatizing signs into fashion statements is a general trend in consumer culture, but the extent of that transformation and the form that it takes depend heavily upon the particular history of that system of inequality in that particular culture. Consequently, we shall see that despite important similarities in each of the types of inequality discussed in this chapter, there are also significant differences.

Race and Ethnicity

In looking at inequality based on race and ethnicity, we can start with the history of people of African descent in American consumer culture. In the early years of the United States, most African Americans were slaves and therefore had limited opportunities to participate in a consumer culture. But even those who were never slaves were and still are harmed by the stigmatizing inequality of racial discrimination. Their opportunities for consumption have been affected by this discrimination, since there have been separate and, of course, far from equal access to commodities.

In the struggle for civil rights, consumption became the black community's most effective tool (see description of Civil Rights Boycotts in chapter 6). Robert Weems describes consumer activism as "the most potent nonviolent strategy employed by African Americans during this period of civil rights activity" (1998, 56). Even before the famous consumer boycotts of busses and the lunch counter sit-ins, African Americans had organized boycotts to protest racist violence, humiliating treatment, demeaning images, and discriminatory hiring practices. For example, the 1930s saw various "Don't Buy Where You Can't Work" campaigns.

Furthermore, Weems documents another way in which consumption promoted civil rights: through the activity of those businesses who targeted the black consumer (1998, 70–79). Weems convincingly argues that, more than any ethical commitment, it was the profit potential of an expanded consumer market that was a primary motivation for the recognition of racial equality.

Because African Americans before the twentieth century were predominantly poor and rural, not many marketing campaigns were directed at them. They did figure in some advertising, but mostly as servile or humorous representations that appealed to whites. As early as the 1930s, a few companies began to target African American consumers. Except for musical recordings and personal grooming products, these marketing campaigns simply tried to sell standard "white" products to a new group of consumers who just happened to be of African descent.

However, as the Civil Rights Movement progressed in the 1960s and 1970s and businesses became more attuned to the demands of the African American consumer, marketers moved away from assuming a desegregated market and began to promote consumption as an expression of racial pride.

> The 1960s graphically demonstrated the elasticity of American capitalism. Corporate marketers began the decade by developing advertisements that catered to African Americans' perceived interest in racial desegregation. By decade's end, as African Americans moved politically from a more passive to a more confrontational stance, U.S. corporations promoted the "soul" market, which extolled black culture and customs, to retain the allegiance of black consumers. (Weems 1998, 70)

For example, in the late 1960s, one widely used advertisement for cigarettes featured a dashiki-wearing black man with copy that read, "Bold Cold Newport . . . a whole new bag of menthol smoking." By the 1970s, so-called blaxploitation films such as *Superfly* and *Shaft* became hugely successful by portraying the continuing inequality, the depravity of the white-controlled system, and the capacity of a black man (and in a few cases, such as *Foxy Brown*, a black woman) to attain a version of personal integrity despite the corrupt system. Far from being suppressed or censored, rich, white producers lined up to produce more of them. The most important color to the producers was clearly green.

Consumption was used as a vehicle for claiming the respect that was still denied African Americans in the realm of employment and production. Paul Gilroy, writing about British popular culture of the 1970s and 1980s, argued that for minority communities, "consumption is turned outwards; no longer a private, passive or individual process it becomes a procedure of collective affirmation and protest in which a new authentic public sphere is brought into being" (1987, 210).

To a large degree, race- and ethnic-based consumption dovetails with the hip consumerism discussed in the previous chapter. Consumer objects, such as the African dashiki featured in the Newport advertisement, are seen to represent a nostalgic or exotic alternative to consumer culture. Consumption, in this case, is used in an attempt to retrieve some of the socially cohesive elements destroyed in the real or imagined traditional culture. African Americans are different than other ethnic groups because of the large-scale disruption of living traditions during slavery, but it is a difference of degrees rather than kind, since all traditions become mediated by images in consumer culture.

The theme of black pride and standing up to racism has also been used to attract consumers of European descent. Hip-hop and rap became the preferred music of millions of white teenagers. Benetton ran a series of advertisements that featured the theme of racism. One of the first such advertisements pictured black and white hands handcuffed together. The Timberland Company ran an advertising campaign urging consumers to "Give Racism the Boot."

Companies wanted so much to be able to identify with the popular criticism of racism that at least one advertising campaign featured fabricated instances of racism. Nike had Tiger Woods saying, "There are still courses in the United States that I am not allowed to play because of the color of my skin." After the advertisement ran, both Nike and Tiger Woods admitted that he could play on any course that he wanted to.

We are in the strange position that many consumer objects—clothes, music, food—are more race identified than ever, and yet this in no way restricts their consumption. African Americans eat Mexican food; whites listen to black music; Hispanics watch Oprah. Racial identity, according to the author of *American Skin*, is "now just a label, a fashion" (Wynter 2002, 5).

We see that barriers to consumption based on race are eradicated much more quickly than barriers in other areas, such as employment. This is not to say that racial issues simply disappear from consumer culture (see table 4.1). Rather, signs of race that support systems of inequality are often used in a consumer culture for a different function. Segregation continues, but now as a segmentation of the consumer market. For example, marketing research tells us that affluent African Americans are more likely than whites to buy convertibles, expensive stereos, and sailboats (O'Hare 1989). Businesses will continue to discriminate, but now in order to better sell to that market segment, whether sailboats to rich African Americans or malt liquor to destitute African Americans.[1]

We see a similar evolution in the ethnic market. Consumer markets that once discriminated against some ethnicities tried at first to market to a "melting pot." However, just as discussed in connection with African Americans, segmentation reemerged as marketers became more attuned to the demands of the ethnic groups.

One significant part of the ethnic market has been unacculturated (usually first-generation) immigrants. Marketing aimed at these immigrants both validates and perpetuates the foreign culture right in the middle of the United States. Even though immigrants may be ignored in mainstream media and political discus-

Table 4.1   Ethnic Differences in Product Usage and Store Patronage

Product Usage or Store Patronage	Anglos/ Whites	African Americans	U.S. Latinos	Asian Americans
Number of different types of electronics owned (1996)				
	13.6	19.9	41.9	24.6
Percentage of group owning individual electronic products				
Television	97.0	99.0	99.0	93.0
VCR	78	78	62	75
Microwave	86	73	57	70
Camera	75	60	49	66
Compact disc player	34	43	48	52
Answering machine	48.4	43	22	43
Video game player	35.7	36	33	30
Dishwasher	46.5	21	9	21
Personal computer	26.8	23	9	41
Camcorder	21.7	16	17	25
Beeper	12.7	31	19	21
Cellular phone	15.3	19	8	19
Store shopped at most often (1994) as percentage of ethnic group				
J.C. Penney	15.1	18.5	18.5	16.2
Sears	12.8	21.7	22.2	17.3
Kmart	17.2	17.6	21.1	21.8
Wal-Mart	28.1	7.8	9.1	4.7
Other	26.7	34.2	29.0	39.9
Total	**99.9**	**99.8**	**99.9**	**99.9**
Hamburger place visited in the last four weeks (1996) as percentage of ethnic group				
McDonald's	46.4	44.6	46.7	56.4
Burger King	25.9	22.8	35.2	31.4
Wendy's	9.8	12.9	8.1	6.4
Other	17.8	8.6	9.9	5.8
Total	**99.9**	**99.9**	**99.9**	**100.0**

Source: Marye C. Tharpe. 2001. *Marketing and Consumer Identity in Multicultural America.* Thousand Oaks, CA: Sage, 44–45.

sions, they have been recognized as consumers and are sought after by marketers. Marketers offer specially tailored merchandise and services that support the continuation of foreign cultural forms while at the same time providing the vehicle through which the newcomers are introduced to the mainstream consumer world. As one marketing executive for Pepsi said, "It's funny because I was an international business major in my undergraduate studies, and I often feel like I am doing international marketing in the domestic environment" (Rossman 1994, 155).

Of even more interest is the ethnic market that is aimed at the fully acculturated. This is a phenomena sometimes called symbolic ethnicity (Gans 1979), in which ethnicity is manifest through forms of leisure activity—such as festivals, ethnic music, and other cultural spectacles—as well as through consumption. As segregated ethnic communities recede, people tend to use their consumption of ethnic goods and services to signal their ethnic identity. Halter observes that "shopping for an ethnic identity has become big business for contemporary consumer society" (2000, 8). Halter's explanation of the popularity of this type of consumption is analogous to the explanation for hip consumption discussed in chapter 3.

> My research suggests that although the impetus to reclaim roots often stems from disdain for commercial interests, paradoxically, consumers look to the marketplace to revive and re-identify with ethnic values. Though a crucial component of the rationale for the creation of ethnic pride groups and related culture-specific practices may be to protest against the ills of consumer society, the new ethnics demonstrate that they are nonetheless deeply tied to consumerist practices. (2000, 13–14)

As Halter reports, whites are seeing themselves more frequently as an ethnic group and are looking to consume products indicating, for instance, Irish or Scandinavian pride (2000, 11). In addition, the hip consumer may use consumer objects to make ironic comments on their own traditions. For instance, the white wedding dress, a symbol of sexual purity in European traditions, may be redesigned today as a sexual fetish costume. This ironic costume may still be used in a hip wedding or as a fashion in a Manhattan nightclub. Of course, the amount of symbolic importance attached to an object by a community will differ, and this variance will affect the extent to which individual style and irony are allowed without being punished.

Just as in racial marketing, the audience includes many more than just members of the particular ethnic group. For example, one of the fastest-growing segments of the recording industry is world music, which sells the latest in authentically traditional music to jaded American consumers. And alongside Hallmark's cards aimed at African Americans (Mahogany line), Hispanics (Primor), and Jews (Tree of Life), there is also a line of cards (Common Threads) filled with traditional sayings and images from a multitude of traditional cultures that is sold primarily to those of European descent.

Here we see the same contradiction—that is, consumer culture presents itself as a problem that only more consumption can solve—but the form is somewhat different. Rather than rebellion and nonconformity, consumption represents a search for the authenticity of a folk culture presumably unsullied by the corruption of consumer culture. People are ready to buy the latest fad in representations of an unchanging tradition.

Gender: The Feminine

Whereas inequality based on race and ethnicity has tended to become market segmentation, gender inequality has taken a somewhat different course in consumer culture. One reason for this difference is that, from the very start, consumer culture was intimately related to gender issues. We have already seen that consumer culture carries a contradiction in its view of the consumer as both rational and impulsive. As signs of gender are taken up by the system of consumption, this contradiction is accentuated so that women are represented both as the ultimate in consumer impulsiveness and as the rational consumer of mundane, non-symbolic goods such as groceries.

In the historical development of consumer culture, the binary division male/female has lined up with other divisions such as work/leisure, production/consumption, public/private, rational/impulsive. Men were seen as workers, producers, in the public sphere, and rational. Women were seen as having more leisure, consuming, in the private sphere, and impulsive. These differing characterizations are related to the social changes that accompanied the emergence of a consumer culture. First, the change from a basically agrarian to an industrial society meant that the household was divided from the workplace, and this change, as we know, was gendered, so that men went to the factories for the paid labor of production, while women stayed in the private home and took over the unpaid labor of provisioning the family.

This change was accompanied by a related change in the political sphere. As local traditions and inherited authorities lost their legitimacy, they were replaced by decisions made through discussions in certain formal and informal institutions, ranging from legislative bodies to coffeehouses. These discussions were governed by rules of order that required that contributions be rationally articulated. Just as with the public sphere of production, this political public was identified with and exclusive to men. Consequently, men became identified with rational demands that could be accommodated by a political system, while women were identified with impulsive, frivolous demands that disrupted political systems.

In both cases, women became identified with consumption— on the one hand, the mundane, necessarily economical consumption related to provisioning the household and, on the other, the frivolous consumption derived from irrational, impulsive demands (see tables 4.2 and 4.3). This is why critics of consumer culture regularly complained that the culture was being feminized (e.g., Hoggart 1957).

Furthermore, the passive attractiveness of the consumer object was easily related to the traditional role of the woman in sexual courting. Indeed, a common theme of advertising from the earliest placards to the latest Internet pop-up is the association of a commodity with an eroticized woman. And it makes very little difference whether the target consumer is male or female. The barely dressed female model has been used to sell everything from women's hats to power tools.

Reacting to the relation between women and consumer culture, analysts have tended to one extreme or another. One side asserts that consumer culture victimizes women. For example, in the groundbreaking feminist work *The Feminine Mystique* (1963),

Table 4.2 Women's Expenditure as a Percentage of Total Expenditure

Items	Percentage of Total Expenditure
Women's Clothes	90
Children's Clothes	85
Food	80
Educational Courses	79
Child Care/School Expenses	78
Medical/Dental	59
Household Goods	51
Tobacco	43
Recreation	42
Men's Clothes	40
Holidays	36
Gambling	35
Meals Out	34
Repairs to House	33
Motor Vehicles	31
Alcohol	27

Source: Adapted from Jan Pahl. 2000. "The Gendering of Spending within Households." *Radical Statistics,* no. 75 (autumn): 38–48.

Table 4.3   Mean Spending by Men and Women over a Two-Week Period to the Nearest Dollar

	Both in Full-Time Employment		Male in Full-Time Employment; Female in Unpaid Work	
	Men's Mean Spending in Dollars	Women's Mean Spending in Dollars	Men's Mean Spending in Dollars	Women's Mean Spending in Dollars
Food	38	117	26	132
Household goods	39	57	36	38
Holidays	111	108	200	53
Men's Clothes	35	26	33	20
Repairs to House	183	138	59	72
Meals Out	32	20	27	9
Motor Vehicles	92	57	75	47
Gambling	9	6	9	3

Source: Adapted from Jan Pahl. 2000. "The Gendering of Spending within Households." *Radical Statistics,* no. 75 (autumn): 38–48.

Betty Friedan lambastes advertising for implanting false needs and using overly sexualized images of women. Consumption is portrayed there as the realm of female enslavement. The other side argues that consumer culture liberates women by opening up a public sphere in which they could be active participants. We saw in chapter 1 that the department store is the concrete historical example of this access to the public sphere. Not only did women dominate this public space as shoppers, but the consumer industries provided some of the first opportunities for female employees. If one effect of consumer culture has been to portray women as sexualized commodities, another has been to open economic opportunities and a new public sphere that allowed women to become aware of their commonalities.

In addition, although consumer culture exploited the image of women as sexualized commodities, it did not invent it. And there is a sense in which the prominent display and commercial use of this image has subverted its power. The bikinied model draped over the car is more obviously artificial and patently exploitive than the romantic archetype of women of the previous age. Even as the sexualized image of the feminine was used to sell products, its sense of naturalness was undermined.

We see the undermining of this sense of naturalness in the cosmetics industry where the image of the sexualized woman reigned supreme. For example, in the 1930s, the cosmetics firm, Volupte, marketed two new lipsticks. One was aimed at the elegant gentlewoman and the other was aimed at those who liked to be shocking. The name of the first was Lady and the second, Hussy. *Mademoiselle* magazine described the choice between the two as follows: "Each of these two categories being as much a matter of mood as a matter of fact, we leave you to decide which you prefer to be" (quoted in Peiss 1996, 311). That cosmetic firm, of course, did not make up the categories of Lady and Hussy; it simply used them to market a commodity. However, in the process, it transformed these categories into a matter of mood rather than a fixed identity. They were an individual decision rather than a degrading social judgment.

In addition, women gained some power through their role of the mundane provisioner for the household. Most of the early consumer movements were organized by women (Furlough 1991). In her study of World War I consumer movements in Germany, Belinda Davis notes the privileged status of women as consumers: "It was when women appeared to act in the role of wronged consumers that their disruption of order in the street was accepted and even condoned. And it seems that only women were accorded the privilege of responding in that fashion" (1996, 299).

Stigmatizing inequality around gender has not simply become a form of marketing segmentation. It has persisted and even become more ubiquitous, because it is intertwined with the growth of consumer culture. Nevertheless, to some degree this form of inequality has become more obviously artificial and has opened up a public space for women. Consequently, stigmatizing inequality has been subverted by consumer culture.

Sexual Orientation and Camp

Many of the systems of inequality in consumer culture are similar in the sense that we see a working out of the central contradictions of consumer culture discussed in chapter 2. Nevertheless, they are all different because they have different histories and different social contexts. We see this mix of similarity and difference when we turn to sexual orientation in consumer culture.

On the one hand, like racial discrimination, consumer culture at first ignored the gay and lesbian consumer, until it was seen that there was money to be made (see table 4.4). Then, consumer-oriented and popular-culture businesses led the way in accepting different orientations. We have danced to the Village People, Roseanne has been kissed by a lesbian on national television, Greg Louganis's book has become a number one best-seller, Martina Navratilova has sold us computers, Ellen has come out,

Table 4.4 Marketing to Gays and Lesbians

1979	Anheuser-Busch (Bud Light) and Absolut vodka ensure their advertisements are inclusive of the gay community.
1980s	Few companies pursue gay marketing. This has been attributed to the AIDS crisis, which peaked in the mid-1980s.
1994	American Airlines establishes a unit focused on the gay and lesbian market.
	IKEA makes the first prime-time television spot featuring a gay couple shopping for furniture.
1995	Automaker Subaru runs a series of advertisements with the caption "It's Not a Choice. It's the Way We're Built" to appeal to the gay and lesbian community.
2000	Office Max advertises on http://gay.com.
2001	JP Morgan Chase sets up marketing programs focusing exclusively on the gay market.
2002	Jaguar North America launches marketing and advertising campaign to specifically reach gay, lesbian, bisexual, and transgender (GLBT) consumers.
	Procter and Gamble markets its "Whitestrips" (a tooth-whitening product) using "The Smile Team," a group of handsome, athletic men with great smiles, who appeared at gay pride and gay film festivals.
	American Express builds an entire program around the gay consumer, including the development of gay-specific copy for its advertising campaigns.

and gay marriage has been featured on the cover of the most conservative newspapers.

On the other hand, like women, the gay and lesbian consumer tends to be represented in an overly sexual way. Furthermore, like both racial communities and women, consumer boycotts have been a primary way for gays and lesbians to exert influence, most notably through the boycott of Florida's citrus products sparked by singer/spokesperson Anita Bryant's campaign against homosexuals in the late 1970s.

However, sexual orientation has a special relation to consumption because, unlike gender or many aspects of race and ethnicity, sexual orientation is not easily recognized without the props of dress or mannerisms. Consequently, there has always been a greater concern with fashion and conspicuous consumption in the gay and lesbian community. It should be noted that this concern is strongly gendered. Lesbians have tended to exhibit a kind of antifashion because of fashion's connection to traditional femininity, while gay men have seen fashion as both a personal and political statement.

At first, advertisers had to use coded messages to sell to the gay and lesbian community. Advertisements with same-sex imagery were used, but they were usually ambiguous. The couples shown might be close, and perhaps overly playful, friends or they might be lovers. The precise relationship was left to the imagination of the viewer. Even when homoerotic images became more accepted, advertisers realized that they could use this ambiguity to aim the same advertisement at married, single, gay, or straight viewers. Each group could decode the advertisement to fit their particular inclination. In addition, this coding had another effect that became even more significant for consumer culture, because it was out of this milieu that "camp" emerged.

When something that is fundamental to the formation of a person's identity is at variance with what most people in a society believe is normal, it has an effect on the way that one approaches the normal. Consequently, homosexuals tend to have a very skeptical and ironic view of what passes for normal, not just in sexuality, but in all things. This ironic sense is heightened by a social pressure to obscure any self-expression behind a code because of a fear of being "outed." It is this ironic view of normality and sensitivity to codes that is the basis for camp.

Camp comes from the French *camper*, to pose in an exaggerated fashion. It refers to a sensibility that favors exaggeration and artifice. The act that is by definition camp is the drag performance. In drag, gay men (and in a few cases, women) dress up as the opposite sex in an exaggerated manner. The drag performance simultaneously applauds and mocks normal gender roles. In general, the woman who is portrayed by the drag artist is already an exaggeration of the gender role (e.g., Mae West), and the performance tends to heighten that exaggeration almost to the point of parody. The drag performance denaturalizes the normal heterosexual roles and suggests that all masculinity and femininity is a performance.

Camp has come to mean not so much the drag performance itself as those types of celebrities that make for good drag. Camp refers to those cultural products that have exaggerated elements that tend to denaturalize and almost parody the very categories that they represent. Just as Mae West exaggerated and almost parodied femininity, camp aficionados prefer such cultural products as 1950s Japanese monster movies that exaggerate and almost parody the attempt to manipulate the emotional reactions of the audience.

Camp is not found in the products themselves so much as in the attitude with which they are consumed. Almost anything can be camp, but in general, camp items are out-of-fashion commodities that were originally aimed at a popular audience, but which were, for various reasons, never completely successful. Camp items are usually marginal, exaggerated, passé. For instance, flamingo lawn ornaments, an exaggerated piece of exotic nature on the suburban lawn, became more popular as a camp item—see John Water's movie *Pink Flamingos*—than they ever were in the 1950s.

A seminal essay on camp by Susan Sontag describes it as apolitical (1966). Sontag writes that "the whole point of Camp is to dethrone the serious. Camp is playful, anti-serious. More precisely, Camp involves a new, more complex relation to 'the serious.' One can be serious about the frivolous, frivolous about the serious" (288). This is true, but there is, nevertheless, a political dimension to camp. Through its exaggerations, camp subverts the categories that divide people up into normal and not normal and that divide things and feelings into natural and artificial. Scott Long stresses the political dimension of camp by reminding us of how the Stonewall riots that led to the modern gay rights movement started: "It is no coincidence that the first acts of homosexual liberation were undertaken by drag queens" (1993, 80).

The camp sensibility has escaped from the homosexual ghetto and now pervades our consumer culture. Camp has become ubiquitous in advertising and popular culture because it fits so well with the ironic tone favored by the hip consumer discussed in chapter 3. In one of the first printed discussions of the subject, Christopher Isherwood has a character in his novel, *The World in the Evening*, predict the importance of camp to the modern attitude: "You'll find yourself wanting to use the word whenever you discuss aesthetics or philosophy or almost anything. I never can understand how critics managed to do without it" (1956, 106).

Camp has indeed become indispensable in consumer culture. First, it manages to reinstate a kind of hierarchy of taste even within the trash of popular culture. There are those who get it and those who do not, those who are in and those who are out. Second, it allows even those who are skeptical of consumer culture to indulge in its pleasure, albeit ironically. The child who secretly watched the ersatz hippy *Partridge Family,* can now proudly carry his or her lunch box to work as an ironic comment. Most importantly, camp led to "cheese," a manufactured, prepackaged campiness discussed in chapter 3. Both camp and cheese emphasize exaggeration and artifice. Both require an ironic sense. However, whereas Sontag noted that one can say something is "not marginal enough" to be camp (1966, 287), cheese usually involves the best-known phenomena of consumer culture.

Camp is in tension with consumer culture. The people who recognize camp are those who society sees as abnormal. What is most campy are those products that tried so hard to be normal, to be mainstream, but failed. Camp celebrates the failures and therefore criticizes the criteria by which mainstream success is judged. Cheese, however, celebrates the successes of consumer culture and brings them back for an ironic rerun. The cheese attitude smugly laughs at these products, but it does not subvert them.

Class

Perhaps the most studied aspect of the intersection of consumption and inequality has had to do with class. We must note that for sociologists, class means much more than just the amount of money that one makes. Class, in its broadest sense, means a group with a common relation to what they need in order to make a living. Let us look at the difference between the owner of a family business, the owner of a factory (a capitalist), and someone who works at the factory. In the small business, the person who owns the tools and other means of making a living also does the work. However, with the factory, the person who owns the means of making a living is not the person who does the work. In addition, the small-business owner probably owns the products that he makes until he sells them, but the factory worker never owns what she makes, because the products made by the factory worker are owned by the capitalist who owns the factory.

It is assumed that the people in each group share similar opportunities in life—for example, that the children of the capitalist are more likely to go to a good preschool than the children of the workers. At each step of their lives, the members of different classes would have somewhat different opportunities and choices. Of course, the amount of money that one makes would be an important part of those opportunities, but class means more than that. The bankrupt capitalist, for example, may have made bad choices and ignored crucial opportunities, but that is different than the worker who never had those choices and opportunities in the first place.

As we saw in chapter 1, consumer culture was, from its very inception, a class-based phenomena. It was intertwined with the rise of the middle class. The middle class was, for the most part, bourgeois, but it also included the growing number of office workers and bureaucrats. As class position was defined increasingly by consumption practices, these groups had common opportunities and choices, even though they had very different relations to what they needed to make a living.

In the beginning of consumer culture, fashions were defined by those above the middle class. In the eighteenth century, fashion flowed from the court to the rest of the aristocracy and then to the bourgeois. By the nineteenth century, the bourgeois upper class took on more of the role of leaders, and fashion flowed from them to the rest of the middle class. At least in this early stage of consumer culture, the lower class simply followed the upper class. This is often called a trickle down effect.

One sociologist who studied this early stage of consumer culture was Thorstein Veblen. In *The Theory of the Leisure Class*, Veblen focuses on the need of people to make distinctions between themselves through the display of consumer objects (see profile of Thorstein Veblen in chapter 6). Specifically, Veblen examines the efforts of the lower class to use consumer objects to pass themselves off as members of the upper class and the efforts of the upper class to maintain their distinction from the lower classes (1899).

Veblen assumes that there are two motives for consumption: (1) the creation of distinctions and (2) emulation. According to Veblen, all classes seek to distinguish themselves from those situated below them in the social hierarchy. But, classes also attempt to emulate those that rank above them. So, each time an upper class finds a way to distinguish itself, the lower class will attempt to emulate it (ibid.).

Veblen used the term "conspicuous consumption" to describe how status objects are ostentatiously displayed to symbolize class membership. The upper class determines the consumer object that is to be conspicuously consumed, and the lower class attempts to imitate. However, once the lower class successfully imitates the status objects of the upper class, the upper class abandons the objects and declares new objects that distinguish them from those below. This, according to Veblen, is what drives fashion's constant pursuit of the latest novelty. Every time the lower class copies the latest fashion, the upper class must create a newer one (ibid.).

There are reasons to question both the trickle down theory and the premise that emulation is the force driving modern consumption. For one thing, many elite consumer objects, fashions, or styles have actually originated from lower classes. Jeans, Doc Marten shoes, cargo pants, peasant blouses, Harley Davidson motorcycles, punk styles, and jazz music are all objects of consumption that have "trickled up" from lower social groups to the elite. Indeed, the previous discussion on camp and sexual orientation suggests that it was precisely the low status of homosexuals that made them creatively use fashion to produce a recognizable community.

Take, for example, the T-shirt. Two generations ago, it was part of working-class garb. Today, it is assuredly a part of the upper class, and, indeed, one upper-class designer describes the T-shirt as something that is now beyond class. In the introduction to a fashion book, Giorgio Armani said, "I love the T-shirt as an anti-status symbol, putting rich and poor on the same level in a sheath of white cotton that cancels the distinctions of caste" (1966, 13). Of course, we can hardly take Armani seriously on his sense of equality between rich and poor. Nevertheless, it is clear that consumer culture operates in a more complex fashion than just a trickle from rich down to poor. Certainly, most products travel the established path from the high to the lower, but those cases where products do not are significant to our understanding of consumer culture.

The sociologist Herbert Blumer (1969a) found that approaches that focused on class are too narrow to encompass the truly dynamic diffusion of consumer objects. Rather than a vertical movement of consumer goods that trickle down a class hierarchy, Blumer argued that fashion often moves horizontally across a variety of social groups simultaneously.

> Styles which start life on the streetcorner have a way of ending up on the backs of top models on the world's most prestigious fashion catwalks. This shouldn't surprise us because, as we have seen, the authenticity which streetstyle is deemed to represent is a precious commodity. Everyone wants a piece of it. But it is more than the price tag which distinguishes the genuine article from its chic reinterpretation. It's a question of

> context. And when fashion sticks its metaphorical gilt frame around a leather motorbike jacket, a Hippy kaftan, a pair of trainers, or a Ragga girl's batty-riders, it transforms an emblem of subcultural identity into something which anyone with enough money can acquire and wear with pride. (Polhemus 1994, 8)

Class is by definition tied to production. Class still functions in a consumer culture, because, of course, all consumer cultures also produce. However, like other inequalities, class functions differently in consumer culture. Class in consumer culture is increasingly a style, a fashion statement. Wearing jeans and a bowling shirt no more indicates your class position than does wearing an evening gown or a suit. The former may be worn by practically anyone and the latter by those with the money to buy them. Class is not the issue, only money. To the extent that class is distinct from money, it is only a style, a matter of dressing up or dressing down.

Style as an Individual Expression

What we see in our analysis of inequality is that consumer society does not eliminate preexisting racial, gender, sexual orientation, or class divisions; rather, the objects and signs associated with inequality tend to be used as part of a style. Style is the way that people express their individuality in consumer culture. Sociologists have long believed that our individuality is not solely a matter of the individual, but that it is also shaped by the culture. Not only must others be able to recognize our expressions of individuality, but others also evaluate these expressions, and this recognition and evaluation by others influences our self-evaluation and our self-esteem.

In consumer culture, it is not what you produce that defines your individuality, but what you buy. Our individuality is expressed through what we consume and display. This means that we create a sense of individuality by selecting from what other people have made. Our clothes, food, drink, home, car, and so forth are regarded as indicators of our taste and sense of style, even though, in most cases, they are made by someone else.

Another one of the contradictions of consumer culture has to do with our freedom to express our individuality through a consumption style. On the one hand, if someone is making the product, there is little to keep us from using it as part of our style. One need not be virginal (or even a bride) to wear a white wedding dress, Italian to eat Italian food, Christian to wear a crucifix, male to wear a tie, or a princess to wear a tiara. Neither do we need any of the skills necessary to produce these items. In this sense, we have much more freedom to express our individuality than ever before. On the other hand, we can only consume what is offered in the market. We must create our personal style out of those items that are available. Not only does this restrict our freedom, but it does so in a way that makes the expression of individuality especially difficult, because the availability of an item in a consumer market invariably means that many others are purchasing this same item, and it is likely that it is purchased as an expression of their individuality.

This limited availability of truly one-of-a-kind items is why a style means more than simply purchasing and wearing an item. What makes a style is the creative organization of different items into a coherent and distinctive ensemble. One cannot really buy a style. One can only buy the items that are then creatively combined to form the individual style. One sociologist points out the Scylla and Charybdis of navigating a style, explaining: "If the room of a contemporary house consisted only of items representing a single style, it would create a very sterile impression and the individual would not find any natural place in it. It would be an equally big mistake for a person to try to produce all the furniture totally according to his own private taste in order to create a private style of his own. Only a genius . . . could succeed in such an effort (Gronow 1997, 99).

Our individuality finds its expression somewhere in between the manufactured style of the producers and the uniqueness of the creative genius. This makes our attempts to express our individuality in consumer culture difficult and precarious. We must find a way to use other people's products—in most cases, meant for a mass market—to express our individuality. Furthermore, our identity in modern culture is increasingly tied to what is individual about us instead of the social position that we are born into. People living in a modern society are relatively free to choose and, at the same time, almost forced to construct their own identity. Such a situation is bound to create a great deal of anxiety and to produce ways to deal with it. Of course, the way to deal with it is, as always, through more consumption. This is best seen by looking at Martha Stewart.

Martha Stewart is the founder and CEO of Martha Stewart

Living Omnimedia. At the time this book is being written, Martha Stewart has resigned from her position as CEO because of an investment scandal. In 1996, she was named one of "America's Twenty-Five Most Influential People" by *Time* magazine. She produces a popular magazine, a television show, and a website, as well as authoring numerous books. She sells—on her website, through her catalog, and through K-Mart—hundreds of items for home and garden. But, undoubtedly, her most important product is her style. This girl from an impoverished family of Polish immigrants is currently the most influential authority on style in America.

In one sense, Martha Stewart is only the latest in a long line of domestic advisers that date from the eighteenth century, when women's identity was firmly tied to their management of the bourgeois household. Some of the more notable domestic advisers were Isabella Beeton in England and, in the United States, Catharine Beecher, a sister of Harriet Beecher Stowe. There are, however, a number of characteristics that are unique to Martha Stewart and that place her squarely within consumer culture.

First, Martha Stewart is much more about consumption than any previous domestic adviser. Of course, all of the domestic advisers that we remember wrote and sold their books, but no other created a consumer empire around their advice. The Home Furnishing Network remarks that Stewart has "successfully translated that personal style from her books, magazine, and television show into affordable products that allow average Americans to live a little more stylishly and elegantly" (quoted in Smith 2000, 337).

Second, Martha Stewart's advice is much more about individual choice rather than following social norms and rules. Previous books of domestic advice were, as one early book described itself, aimed at "those whose 'gentle' minds lead them to wish to do what is expected of them, and that which may be considered the right thing" (Troubridge 1931). Martha Stewart also describes what is expected and right—not as a prescription but as a template to improvise on. For example, on her website, she presents for weddings "some traditional guidelines for seating arrangements, procession, ceremony formation, and recession." However, she quickly adds, "You can choose to conduct your ceremony in a different way."

Finally, Martha Stewart emphasizes her educational rather than prescriptive role. She does not tell people what they should do, she only teaches them skills. Columns in her magazine *Martha*

Stewart Living such as "Wedding 101," and "Field Trip" emphasize that this is an educational endeavor. She describes her role as follows: "I'm less mother than teacher . . . hardly anybody I know thinks of me as a mother" (Lippert 1995, 26).

Despite Martha Stewart's reputation as the "queen of WASPs," she uses ethnicity and race as part of her style. Her magazine, television show, and website include quite a bit of information about Jewish traditions and ceremonies. She offers numerous recipes from a "Mess O' Greens" to fish tacos that are derived from, or identified with, minority groups. In one of her Thanksgiving issues, she featured an African American family and their traditional recipes. In the December issue of her magazine, she offers tips on how to have a very Martha Christmas, Hanukkah, and Kwanzaa. In addition, she will sometimes emphasize her own ethnicity, for example, by having her very Polish mother make pierogi on her show.

We see in Martha Stewart all of the styles discussed above. She has become a favorite of female impersonators. She presents high-, middle-, and working-class ideas and recipes as the occasion demands. But it is in terms of gender role as a style that Martha Stewart has made her greatest contribution. Her success can be traced to her ability to present traditional, back-to-the-kitchen femininity as a lifestyle choice. Staging femininity as a style, she has transformed domesticity into big business.

However, as with so much of consumer culture, this style is a fantasy. "You lie in bed, nestled among your uncoordinated sheets, eating a Lean Cuisine. . . . You flip through the pages of a Martha book or magazine and you dream. You don't cook" (Lavin 1996, 51). And it is a fantasy that leads directly to more consumption. As one journalist admitted, "I did not create an outdoor canopy, I purchased a patio umbrella. I did not make my own gift wrap with gold enamel paint, I bought it in bulk" (Mallick 1995, D1).

Inequality Based on Age

Style is the way that people express their individuality in consumer culture. For the most part, stigmatizing inequality just becomes part of our style, part of our expression of individuality. Race, ethnicity, gender, and sexual orientation allow marketers to divide us into groups, but these groups are not necessarily unequal in terms of consumption. These inequalities still function in the realm of production to give people different access to money, but once people have the money, these inequalities have little effect on people's ability to consume. There are, however, two kinds of inequality that still persist in consumer culture and arguably grow even stronger. They are inequality based on age and on money. We will deal with age first.

The young have a disproportionate influence on consumer culture in comparison to other age groups and especially in comparison to the elderly. Youths are important to consumer culture in three ways: (1) as a profitable current market, (2) as a potential future market, and (3) as a group that influences other markets. We will briefly discuss each of these.

In the 1960s, American children spent about $2 billion a year. By the end of the 1980s, this figure had risen to $6 billion. By the mid-1990s, it was around $9 billion. Tootelian and Gaedeke (1992) found that despite a 15 percent decline in the number of American teenagers in the 1980s, this group's aggregate spending power increased by nearly 25 percent. In addition to the amount they spend directly, it is estimated that children directly influence $130 billion of parental purchases (Gunter and Furnham 1998).

Recognizing the growing importance of the young consumer, American companies spent $500 million in 1990 marketing to it, five times more than was spent in 1980 (Durning 1992, 122). But this investment was intended to affect more than their current consumption. Marketers were also trying to influence what children would purchase throughout the rest of their lives. The very young are especially susceptible to advertising since many of them do not fully recognize the commercial nature of advertisements (Gunter and Furnham 1998). Studies have shown that a number of consumer preferences are established in youth and then remain fairly stable into adulthood. Some preferences, such as cigarettes and beer, are established years before any actual consumption occurs.

Marketing to children is, in this sense, marketing to the future. In addition, if we believe that consumer culture will inevitably spread to the rest of the world, then there is another sense in which marketing to children is marketing to the future. The spread of consumer culture occurs most rapidly among the young of other cultures.

> Before there is a geographic culture there is a children's culture; that children are very much alike around the

> industrialized world. The result is that they very much want the same things; that they generally translate their needs into similar wants that tend to transcend culture. Therefore, it appears that fairly standardized multinational marketing strategies to children around the globe are viable. (McNeal 1992, 250)

Finally, children are important in consumer culture because of the influence that they have over other groups. For one thing, children tend to be leaders in using new products. Because of the rapid pace of change, younger consumers are usually more knowledgeable about new commodities than older consumers. Thus, parents are often forced to consult their children not only about what is in fashion, but even about the basic function of newer high-tech gadgets.

However, the youth market is even more influential as a symbolic market, because this market includes not only those who actually are young, but the vastly greater number of those who want to feel young. For example, the Pepsi generation has no age limit; instead, it symbolically attaches a youthful attitude to the product. One important trend in marketing has been the use of campaigns developed for children to sell a childlike experience to adults. Disney has been particularly effective with this strategy.

The direct focus on youth is fairly recent. Advertising campaigns specifically targeting young consumers did not really begin until the mid-1950s (Kline 1998). Before this, the youth market was usually reached through parents. Department stores that sold to the middle-class family also included children's items. By the late 1920s, Macy's began to advertise that it had the largest toy department in the world. Dolls, stuffed animals, balls, and sport equipment became hot commodities. Slowly, items began to be promoted not only for parents to buy for children, but also for children to buy themselves. Department stores produced their own radio programs for children and put on elaborate shows. Some items, such as cheap, sensationalist "dime novels" and comic books, became popular despite, or possibly because of, parents' disapproval.

In our consumer culture, children's first experiences with consumption generally occur in the first few years of their lives. It will often involve a shopping trip with some sort of commentary provided by the parent on choosing and buying items. The child may be allowed to select items off of a shelf and to hand money to the cashier. By the age of four or five, most children in the United States have already made an independent purchase, usually a gift for a parent with some minimal help from the other parent or a relative. By the age of ten, they have been found in the United States to make over 250 purchase visits a year to a variety of different kinds of stores (McNeal 1992).

Recently, marketers have targeted increasingly younger consumers. A *Wall Street Journal* article quoted an expert in marketing who declared that "two-year-olds are concerned about their brand of clothes, and by the age of six are full-out consumers" (quoted in Schiller 1989). Children's cartoons have become basically one long advertisement. Dolls come equipped with brand-name clothes. Many companies that specialize in children's products have formed company-sponsored marketing groups, which they call "clubs." Children who join these clubs enroll in a program of serial advertising.

As children have become the direct target of marketers, parents have tended to be seen as "gatekeepers," whose efforts to protect their children from commercial pressures must be circumvented so that those children, in the rather chilling terms used by the marketers, can be "captured, owned, and branded" (de Graaf et al. 2001, 53). John de Graaf, who produced the PBS documentary "Affluenza," reported that "speaker after speaker revealed the strategy: Portray parents as fools and fuddyduddies who aren't smart enough to realize their children's need for the products being sold. It's a proven technique for neutralizing parental influence in the marketer/child relationship" (2001, 53–54).

With the focus on youth, the consumption of the middle-aged and elderly has progressively less influence on the market (see table 4.5). For example, few movies, electronics, and fashions are designed for the older consumer. This undoubtedly widens the divide between the young who enjoy consumption and feel well served and the elderly who feel there is something morally wrong with consumer culture and who are ill-served by it.

The Poor

Another type of inequality built into consumer culture is based on poverty. Being poor in a consumer culture is, to paraphrase Dickens, the best and worst of times. On the one hand, poverty is the one thing that can keep you from participating in consumer culture. As we have seen, racial and ethnic minorities, women,

Table 4.5 Typical Spending in Family Life Cycle Stages

Stage	Typical Items of Expenditure
Young, single adult	Clothing, entertainment, car
Unmarried couples	Low-cost furniture, budget travel
Newly married, no children	Furniture, appliances, entertainment
Married, no children	Designer furniture, entertainment, smaller homes, sports cars, career clothing
Family, with young children at home	Insurance, medical expenses, children's clothing, toys, larger homes
Family, with older children at home	Personal electronic items, holidays, family-size packages of food and household goods, larger homes
Single parents	Low-cost housing, discount food, inexpensive clothing
Divorced without children	Apartments, small packages of food and household goods, dating service, clubs
Family, children left home (empty nest)	Travel, hobbies, home improvement
Family, main breadwinner retired	Medical expenses, retirement homes, cosmetics, jewelry
Solitary survivor	Medical expenses, restaurants, apartments

Source: Adapted from Gerrit Antonides and W. Fred Van Raaij. 1998. *Consumer Behaviour: A European Perspective.* New York: John Wiley and Sons, 312.

gay men and lesbians, and the working classes are not necessarily excluded from consumer society, while white Westerners, men, heterosexuals, and the bourgeois are not necessarily included. There is, then, a very real sense in which consumer culture cares only about one thing—whether you have money.

On the other hand, our poor are certainly the least materially impoverished of any culture in history (see table 4.6). The progress in just our lifetime is generally unrecognized, but nevertheless, astounding. It is common to measure a country's success against poverty by looking at its poorest one-fifth. Currently, the poorest one-fifth of the U.S. population buys more than the average one-fifth did in 1955 (Twitchell 2001, 18).

It may be true, as Jesus said, that the poor are always with us, but the poor are not always the same. In particular, our stereotype, our image of the poor, is different in different cultures. In a culture based around production, the poor are imagined to be those who do not produce, that is, the unemployed. Poverty, in the cultural imagination of consumer culture, is tied less to being a failed worker than to being a failed consumer. Those who are visibly poor, who beg on our streets and fill our homeless shel-

Table 4.6 Standard of Living of All American Families (1900) and Poor American Families (1970)

Percent of Families Having Amenities	All Families in 1900	Poor Families in 1970*
Flush toilet	15	99
Running water	24†	92
Central heating	1	58
One (or fewer) persons per room	48	96
Electricity	3	99
Refrigeration	18 (ice)	99 (mechanical)
Automobiles	1‡	41

Source: Stanley Lebergott. 1976. *The American Economy: Income, Wealth, and Want.* Princeton, NJ: Princeton University Press, 8.

Notes:
* Family incomes under $4,000
† Data are for 1890
‡ Data are for 1910

ters, are assumed to consume the wrong thing, usually the wrong drug, or to consume some substance to excess.

The poor are also more or less visible depending on the culture. In a consumer culture, they are not very visible. Except for those few beggars that are encountered in the urban centers, the poor are difficult to recognize. You rarely see people wearing rags. You rarely see people starving. Although many suffer from less manifest mental illnesses, few have obvious physical problems that are in need of immediate attention.

Furthermore, the poor do not form groups in a consumer society. Previously, geographical location, or sometimes dislocation, brought the poor into contact with each other, so that a community could form. For example, in this country, there were huge tracts of Appalachia that were essentially a community of poor. Similarly, there were large parts of urban cities made up of immigrants or minority races who were almost all poor, but who formed a tight community. Today's poor tend to be mobile individuals. At most, they will seek therapy rather than community. They dream of winning the lottery rather than a new form of society.

The poor in consumer culture, despite being materially better off, are not able to fully participate in this culture because they have less disposable income after basic necessities are acquired (see table 4.7). Poverty is not just the inability to buy things; it is also the inability to engage in the central practice of our culture. A culture that is directed by the decisions of consumers in the market pays no attention to the truly poor. The quirks and caprices of

Table 4.7 Average Annual Food Expenditures, 2000: Household by Pretax Income

Item	Annual Pretax Income								
	Less than $5,000	$5,000–$9,999	$10,000–$14,999	$15,000–$19,999	$20,000–$29,999	$30,000–$39,999	$40,000–$49,999	$50,000–$69,000	$70,000 and Over
Average Total Spent on Food	$2,627	$2,462	$2,984	$3,743	$4,507	$5,118	$6,228	$6,557	$8,665
Meat/Poultry /Fish/Eggs	$437	$451	$581	$695	$800	$803	$938	$898	$1,095
Dairy Products	$151	$189	$234	$273	$305	$338	$376	$401	$472
Fruits and Vegetables	$268	$324	$372	$455	$519	$508	$595	$580	$785
Average Percent of Pretax Income Spent on Food	133%	32%	24%	22%	18%	15%	14%	11%	8%

Source: Adapted from U.S. Department of Labor, Bureau of Labor Statistics. 2000. *2000 Consumer Expenditure Survey.* http://www.bls.gov/CEX (accessed 2 July 2003).

the rich cause extensive changes in what our society produces, while the urgent needs of the poor have little effect. The poor are left to select from choices that have been determined by those with more money and other interests.

In addition, since individuality is expressed through consumption, the poor are greatly disadvantaged in expressing their own individuality. An individual style cannot be reduced to money, but there is no question that it is easier to be stylish with than without money. Usually the poor must express their individuality with products made for millions of others, while the rich can express theirs with products that are one-of-a-kind. It is clear that individuality is easier to express in the second case than in the first.

Of course, there is a sense in which it is possible to consume without actually buying. Stores and malls are open to those who simply wish to look, desire, and fantasize. Indeed, this is often what we mean when we use the term *shopping*. Nevertheless, it is one thing to decide not to buy and another to not be able to. The poor experience shopping as a locked door with a window through which they are invited to admire.

In a culture where consuming means so much, not having money is a profound social disability. For parents faced with the desires of their children, the failure can feel overwhelming. This is why economists have defined poverty in terms of a social norm rather than in any absolute sense. Indeed, the very term "standard of living" suggests the point: The standard is a social norm.

As one *New Yorker* cartoon expressed it, "I was sad because I had no onboard fax until I saw a man who had no mobile phone."

James Duesenberry popularized the phrase "keeping up with the Joneses" (1952). He argued that the preservation of human dignity and self-esteem required that we match our neighbors in the purchase of dishwashers, televisions, second cars, and the like. What we buy, and, more importantly, what we want to buy is determined by what is possessed by those we see around us. However, recent research indicates that what the poor see around them has drastically changed.

Traditionally, people have measured their own consumption by comparing themselves to what sociologists call a reference group—a comparison group located nearby in the social hierarchy. For instance, people living in working-class neighborhoods generally saw and wanted what other working-class neighbors had. Of course, there has always been a tendency to copy those in the next-higher income level, but there was also a strong social pressure not to "put on pretensions," to be "true to your roots," and true to some core nonconsumer values such as community and family.

This dedication to nonconsumer values now appears to be less true. People still measure themselves against a reference group, but it is no longer composed of their neighbors. It is now composed of those they see in television programs and advertising. People do not measure their well-being against their friends, but against the television show *Friends*. According to Juliet Schor (1998), the reference for a large number of Americans are the upper-middle-class individuals and families that dominate the shows and advertisements on television. These shows depict incomes that are typically three to five times the income of average viewers. This is why Schor's research shows that increased consumption is related to watching more television. Each additional hour of television watched in a week was correlated with an additional $208 of annual spending (1998, 81–82).

It is easier to see the lifestyle of a television family than it is to see that of one's own neighbors. This inflates the viewer's perceptions of what others have, and consequently what one feels deprived without. Even the poor compare themselves to the upper-middle-class people who populate television programs and commercials. If a poor person watches the Super Bowl on television, he or she will see advertisements for Macintosh computers, $60,000 SUVs, and investment companies. Schor believes that this explains why "the level of income needed to fulfill one's dreams doubled between 1986 and 1994, and is currently more than twice the median household income" (2000, 10).

Despite this inequality, the poor have found a way to participate in consumer culture through accumulating debt. Early in their history, revolving-credit plans were provided by many department stores. Instead of needing to save before making a large purchase, the consumer could spend without any rational planning. Instead, a rational plan to pay off the purchase in monthly installments would be calculated and enforced by the department store.

By the 1920s, such companies as gas and hotel chains provided credit cards to customers for purchases made at company outlets. The use of credit cards quickly expanded after World War II. In 1950, Diners Club issued the first "universal" credit card to 200 customers who could use it at twenty-seven restaurants in New York (see description of Diners Club Card in chapter 6). In a few years, credit card use by traveling salesmen helped to expand the system to other parts of the country and to a variety of establishments. This was quickly followed by bank credit cards. The first national plan was BankAmericard (now VISA), begun in California in 1959 and licensed in other states in 1966. Since then, credit cards have spread to all parts of the world (Ritzer 1995).

In 1968, when the federal government first began to track credit card debt, it was reported to be $1,316,770,000, about 1 percent of total consumer debt. By 2002, the figure for credit card debt was $712,190,720,000 or 42 percent of total consumer debt. This was occurring at a time when consumer debt itself was expanding. In the 1990s alone, consumer credit increased by 70 percent after adjusting for inflation. Table 4.8 shows a similar in-

Table 4.8 Household Indebtedness as a Percentage of Disposable Income

Country[ies]	Liabilities	
	1983	*1993*
USA	74	97
Canada	75	101
UK	74	110
Japan	85	112
France	58	79
Italy	8	32

Source: Adapted from Gerrit Antonides and W. Fred Van Raaij. 1998. *Consumer Behavior: A European Perspective.* New York: John Wiley and Sons, 450.

crease in most developed countries. For the rich, credit cards are financial tools that allow them to keep track of spending and avoid carrying large amounts of cash. However, for the poor trying to live like those they see on television, credit cards mean record levels of debt and bankruptcy.

Conclusion

Each of the systems of inequality in consumer culture is different, because each has different histories and different social contexts. Nevertheless, there are strong similarities among many of them. We see in most cases that the system of inequality is transformed into a fashion statement regarding the individuality of the consumer. Furthermore, we see that consumer culture makes the signs of inequality more visible and makes them appear more arbitrary. In this sense, consumer culture subverts stigmatizing systems of inequality.

Nevertheless, we should be clear about four things. The first point—to repeat what has been said previously—is that there are at least two systems of inequality—based on age and poverty—which have grown stronger in consumer culture. Consumer culture may promote diversity, but only if it is a marketable diversity. If diversity can be sold, then it is less likely to become the basis of inequality. If it cannot be sold, then it disappears from our radar screen, creating a stronger inequality because it is now invisible.

The second point is that even though a system of inequality has been transformed into a fashion statement, the effects of the inequality can be the same. It really makes little difference whether stigmatized individuals live in a deteriorating community and engage in self-destructive behavior because they are forced to or because they choose to as part of their self-affirmation. In either case, segregation and inequality continue.

Third, even if systems of inequality are subverted by trends in consumer culture, there are many other trends in our society, not the least of which are systems of production that have long supported forms of inequality that are able to provide cheap labor by paying certain races and ethnic groups less, by requiring one gender to provide free domestic labor, and by privileging the heterosexual family that is able to supply cheap labor for the future.

The final point, which will be the main focus of the next chapter, is that even as stigmatizing inequality is subverted by its transformation into a fashion system, it strengthens a different kind of inequality, which is anonymous, indirect, and not resulting from our intention. This inequality occurs not because we stigmatize people, but as a result of our participation in consumer culture.

Note

1. One notable exception is in housing, where the removal of the barriers to consumption required legal intervention. Some have argued that barriers in the consumption-related area of borrowing also remain; however, differences in credit histories and savings complicate this issue.

References

Antonides, Gerrit, and W. Fred Van Raaij. 1998. *Consumer Behaviour: A European Perspective.* New York: John Wiley and Sons.

Armani, Giorgio. 1966. "Introduction." In A. Harris, *The White T,* 1–15. New York: Harper Style.

Blumer, Herbert. 1969a. "Fashion: From Class Differentiation to Collective Selection." *Sociological Quarterly* 10: 275–291.

———. 1969b. *Symbolic Interactionism: Perspective and Method.* Englewood Cliffs, NJ: Prentice-Hall.

Davis, Belinda. 1996. "Food Scarcity and the Female Consumer." In V. de Grazia and E. Furlough, eds., *The Sex of Things: Gender and Consumption in Historical Perspective,* 287–310. Berkeley, CA: University of California Press.

de Graaf, John, David Wann, and Thomas Naylor. 2001. *Affluenza: The All-Consuming Epidemic.* San Francisco: Berrett-Koehler.

Duesenberry, James S. 1952. *Income, Saving, and the Theory of Consumer Behavior.* Cambridge, MA: Harvard University Press.

Durning, Alan. 1992. *How Much Is Enough?: The Consumer Society and the Future of the Earth.* New York: Norton.

Friedan, Betty. 1963. *The Feminine Mystique.* New York: Norton.

Furlough, Ellen. 1991. *Consumer Cooperation in France: The Politics of Consumption, 1834–1930.* Ithaca, NY: Cornell University Press.

Gans, Herbert. 1979. "Symbolic Ethnicity: The Future of Ethnic Groups and Cultures in America." *Ethnic and Racial Studies* 2: 1–20.

Gilroy, Paul. 1987. *"There Ain't No Black in the Union Jack": The Cultural Politics of Race and Nation.* London: Hutchinson.

Gronow, Jukka. 1997. *The Sociology of Taste.* New York: Routledge.

Gunter, Barrie, and Adrian Furnham. 1998. *Children as Consumers: A Psychological Analysis of the Young People's Market.* New York: Routledge.

Halter, Marilyn. 2000. *Shopping for Identity: The Marketing of Ethnicity.* New York: Schocken.

Hoggart, Richard. 1957. *The Uses of Literacy: Aspects of Working Class Life with Special Reference to Publications and Entertainments.* London: Chatto and Windus.

Isherwood, Christopher. 1956. *The World in the Evening.* New York: Avon.

Kline, Stephen. 1998. "Toys, Socialization, and the Commodification of Play." In S. Strasser, C. McGovern, and M. Judt, eds, *Getting and Spending,* 339–358. New York: Cambridge University Press.

Lavin, Cheryl. 1996. "The House of Stewart." *Chicago Tribune* (15 February): 51.

Lebergott, Stanley. 1976. *The American Economy: Income, Wealth, and Want.* Princeton, NJ: Princeton University Press.

Lippert, Barbara. 1995. "Our Martha, Ourselves." *New York Times,* 15 May, 26–35.

Long, Scott. 1993. "The Loneliness of Camp in Camp Grounds: Style and Homosexuality." In D. Begman, ed., *Camp Grounds: Style and Homosexuality,* 78–91. Amherst, MA: University of Massachusetts Press.

Mallick, Heather. 1995. "We Worship Martha Stewart, Our Lady of Lifestyle. But Why?" *Toronto Sun,* 18 June, D1.

McNeal, James. 1992. *Kids as Customers: A Handbook of Marketing to Children.* New York: Lexington Books.

O'Hare, William. 1989. "In the Black: Affluent Blacks Are a Rapidly Growing Market." *American Demographics* 11: 24–26.

Pahl, Jan. 2000. "The Gendering of Spending within Households." *Radical Statistics,* no. 75 (autumn): 38–48.

Peiss, Kathy. 1996. "Making Up, Making Over: Cosmetics, Consumer Culture, and Women's Identity." In V. de Grazia and E. Furlough, eds., *Sex of Things: Gender and Consumption in Historical Perspective,* 311–336. Berkeley, CA: University of California Press.

Polhemus, Ted. 1994. *Streetstyle: From Sidewalk to Catwalk.* New York: Thames and Hudson.

Ritzer, George. 1995. *Expressing America: A Critique of the Global Credit Card Society.* Thousand Oaks, CA: Pine Forge.

Rossman, Marlene. 1994. *Multicultural Marketing: Selling to a Diverse America.* New York: AMACOM.

Schiller, Herbert I. 1989. *Culture, Inc.* New York: Oxford University Press.

Schor, Juliet. 1998. *The Overspent American: Upscaling, Downshifting, and the New Consumer.* New York: Basic Books.

———. 2000. "The New Politics of Consumption." In J. Schor, ed., *Do Americans Shop Too Much?*, 3–36. Boston: Beacon Press.

Smith, Cynthia Duquette. 2000. "Discipline—It's a 'Good Thing': Rhetorical Constitution and Martha Stewart Living Omnimedia." *Women's Studies in Communication* 23: 337–366.

Sontag, Susan. 1966. *Against Interpretation, and Other Essays.* New York: Farrar, Straus & Giroux.

Stewart, Martha. N.d. *Bride 101.* http://www.marthastewart.com/page.jhtml?type=content&id=channel1582&catid=cat457 [2 March 2003].

Tharpe, Marye C. 2001. *Marketing and Consumer Identity in Multicultural America.* Thousand Oaks, CA: Sage.

Tootelian, D., and R. Gaedeke. 1992. "The Teen Market: An Expolratory Analysis of Income, Spending, and Shopping Patterns." *Journal of Consumer Marketing* 9: 35–45.

Troubridge, Laura. 1931. *The Book of Etiquette.* Kingswood, UK: The World's Work.

Twitchell, James. 2001. *Living It Up: Our Love Affair with Luxury.* New York: Columbia University Press.

U.S. Department of Labor, Bureau of Labor Statistics. 2000. *2000 Consumer Expenditure Survey.* http://www.bls.gov/cex [2 July 2003].

Veblen, Thorstein. 1899. *The Theory of the Leisure Class.* London: Routledge.

Weems, Robert. 1998. *Desegregating the Dollar: African American Consumerism in the Twentieth Century.* New York: New York University Press.

Wynter, Leon. 2002. *American Skin: Pop Culture, Big Business, and the End of White America.* New York: Crown.

5

Anonymous Inequality in Global Consumer Culture

For four days in late 1999, the city of Seattle was paralyzed. Police patrolled the streets in riot gear. Almost 600 people were arrested. The scent of tear gas filled the air. Mixed with the chants of peaceful protesters were the sounds of smashing windows. It was the first mass demonstration in decades to capture the attention of the nation, and it was the last of the millennium.

The primary target of this protest was the World Trade Organization (WTO). If there had been questions about the WTO before the Seattle protest, the main one would have been, what is it? And the answer, that it is an international organization established in 1995 to reduce trade barriers, would have brought a yawn to most listeners. But it was opposition to this organization of trade experts proposed by Canada, based in Geneva, and representing 135 countries that set into motion these extraordinary events.

Rallying around the cry "Shut Down the WTO!" thousands of protesters blocked Seattle's streets and made it impossible for delegates to enter the meeting. Anarchists, trade unions, environmentalists, and various groups more difficult to categorize (with such names as ACME Collective, Bananarchy Movement, Portland Spuds, and STARC Naked) combined to confront an organization whose primary mission is to allow consumer goods to move more easily around the world.

Self-described anarchists recruited students from local Seattle campuses. They joined steelworkers and dockworkers, farmers and fishers. The protesters had different and often conflicting concerns: some about cheap labor in developing countries, some about the environment, some about genetically engineered food, many about the spreading power of transnational corporations. People came outfitted in giant condoms, carrying inflatable dolphins, dressed as sea turtles, sporting fluorescent orange hard hats. There were cardboard puppets, waving ears of corn, reverberating five-gallon-bucket drums, and posters representing every political stripe and color.

The protesters' explicit complaints about the WTO were frequently muddled by the multitude of voices, and, even when clear, they often did not stand up to closer inspection. For example, probably the clearest criticism made by the protesters was against the WTO ruling that overturned a U.S. ban on the sale of Asian shrimp whose catch endangers sea turtles. However, none of the protesters' literature, websites, or speakers took into account the WTO claim that the ruling was about discrimination, not environmental protection. The suit was brought before the WTO by Asian countries (India, Malaysia, Pakistan, and Thailand) who successfully argued that the United States discriminated because it provided favored Caribbean countries with technical and financial assistance and longer transition periods for their fishers to start using turtle-excluder devices. The WTO ruling clearly stated that the United States can pursue the protection of endangered turtles, but that this *difference* in treatment could not be justified. According to the WTO, the goal of this and other rulings is to encourage countries to respect the nondiscrimination provisions of the multilateral trading treaties that the countries themselves have negotiated (Ruggiero 2000). These rules allow the protection of species, the environment, and scarce resources so long as the protection is applied without arbitrary or unjustifiable bias and is not just a cover for discriminatory treatment.

Nevertheless, the specific facts of the complaints are not really relevant either to the protesters or to our theme of consumption. The protesters did not need to engage the WTO's explanation because the WTO was primarily a symbol of the larger forces that constitute a spreading consumer culture. It could be argued that like market forces, the WTO is remote and mysterious, powerful and unaccountable—that like consumer culture, it is concerned with commodities and markets rather than jobs, health, the environment, development, and national sovereignty. It was not a particular ruling or even a particular organization that was being targeted, but the spread of consumer culture around the world. As one of the attendees, former British Columbia premier Glen Clark, said, "There is a real backlash against globalization. People are starting to question the genuflecting at the altar of the free market" (Howard 2000, 94). More than the WTO, the protesters seemed to be expressing rage about being dominated by corporations like Starbucks, McDonald's, and Nike. And, indeed, more than the WTO meeting, these stores bore the brunt of the damage.

Early on the first day of the protest, small groups began breaking windows of retail stores, such as Nike and Starbucks, that depend heavily on global trade to furnish consumer products. The downtown Starbucks café was looted, and soon twenty-five other Starbucks were closed (see description of Starbucks in chapter 6). By the end of the four days, downtown businesses claim to have lost $20 million in sales and property damage (Brunner 2000, A1). Ironically, many of the businesses targeted by the protesters were seen by local community leaders as glowing examples of downtown's rebirth.

According to some, these multinational businesses and free trade in general will, in the long run, be beneficial for the very issues that the protesters point to. By boosting the economy as a whole, global trade may create resources that could be used to train workers for more valuable jobs. As living standards rise, people may demand a cleaner environment, and they could insist that their country's new riches be invested in people's health. In addition, there is reason to believe that free trade will help close the gap between rich and poor countries. In the last twelve years, as the free trade mantra has dominated global relations, developing countries' share in world trade has risen from one-fifth to more than one-quarter, and their share of trade in manufactured products has doubled. It could be argued that the problems associated with free trade have less to do with trade than with a lack of political will to justly use the riches that trade produces, but, as we will argue near the end of this chapter, even this lack of political will may be traceable to a spreading consumer culture.

Starbucks and Anonymous Inequality

Both the advantages and disadvantages of global trade can be examined by looking closely at Starbucks. Starbucks seems to be everywhere. By 2005, Starbucks predicts that they will have a total of 10,000 locations in sixty countries (Dukcevich 2002).

Starbucks began as a roaster of high-quality coffee, but what spurred their growth and created the mass-market, specialty coffee industry was the decision by Howard Schultz to open European-style coffee bars instead of just selling coffee beans to restaurants. With that, Starbucks became much more than a cup of coffee. It became a brand. Along with over two dozen varieties of beans, an assortment of mugs, teapots, and coffee-making equipment, they sell their own cookbook and even a Starbucks compact disc. You can also buy a bottled Starbucks Frappuccino either in Starbucks cafés or in many grocery stores, where you will also find their six different Starbucks coffee ice creams.

With this success has come a notoriety that is at first puzzling. In a recent popular movie, *Austin Powers 2: The Spy Who Shagged Me*, Starbucks was portrayed as a front for the evil empire of the megalomaniac villain. On the one-year anniversary of the WTO protest, vandals attacked nine Starbucks stores. In addition, Starbucks became the target of a sustained protest over the inequities of the international coffee-trading system.

Nobody denies that Starbucks is exemplary in their treatment of their own workers. Even part-timers at Starbucks are entitled to medical benefits and participation in the stock-option plan. Furthermore, Starbucks had been strongly involved in local charities and even set up its own philanthropic foundation. It is the company's effect on workers in other parts of the world, who do not have any formal relation with Starbucks, and its unintended effects on entire geographic regions that are at issue.

We will call what is at issue here anonymous inequality. Unlike the stigmatizing inequality discussed in the previous chapter, anonymous inequality is created without anyone intending it. This idea of a result without intention may seem paradoxical. For many sociologists, it is useful to think of such relations as if they involved some gigantic mechanical device. This is the image that most have in mind when they refer to these relations as a system. The capitalist market is just such a system. It can be thought of as a "virtual" mechanical device that takes consumer actions as input and distributes scarce resources as its output. Even though the consumer only means to buy a cup of coffee, the system takes this action as an input and uses it to distribute resources. In many cases, this distribution is unequal.

In table 5.1, we have listed the difference between stigmatizing inequality, which was discussed in chapter 4, and anonymous inequality. The key difference is the different way that people in-

Table 5.1 Stigmatizing versus Anonymous Inequality

	Stigmatizing Inequality	Anonymous Inequality
Relations between people	Often know each other, at least recognize each other	Unknown to each other Very difficult to establish personal relation or recognition
Involvement of individual's intentions	Must be intentional or habitual	Usually is not intentional
Political effects	Intimately involved with politics either to enforce the inequality or to rectify past inequality	Difficult to see direct political effects Possible to have a political effect through boycotts
Use of consumer objects	To mark people as different	To connect people through a market system
Consumer culture's effect on inequality	Tends to make more obvious, turn into a fashion statement, and, ultimately, subvert	Gives greater scope for a globalized system of anonymous inequality

volved in the inequality are related to each other. In stigmatizing inequality, the people often know each other, or they at least are able to recognize each other. For example, in a racially based system of inequality, stigmatizing inequality would be in effect only if certain races were considered for higher-paying positions. In many cases, those eligible for the position and those excluded from it know each other personally. At the very least, they are able to recognize each other as members of different races.

In anonymous inequality, the different people need not know each other and usually do not. For instance, we will look at the effect of the coffee trade on a system of global inequality. The buyer of a cup of coffee does not know the plantation worker who grew the particular beans used to brew the coffee, nevertheless the two may be involved in a system of inequality. Indeed, if the buyer of the coffee becomes concerned about his or her involvement in the system of inequality, it is very difficult for the buyer to discover who exactly is being disadvantaged by the system.

The second difference is that in stigmatizing inequality, the inequality is either intended or part of ingrained habits. One of the important trends of modern culture is that inequality based on ingrained habits is disappearing, so that most stigmatizing inequality is now entirely intentional. Previously, people might have gone to segregated churches and restaurants simply because that is what they were used to and comfortable with. Today, most segregation and discrimination is a conscious decision. In stigmatizing inequality today, people are not hired for jobs, are not served in certain establishments, are not allowed in specified areas because other people actively intend to discriminate against them.

In anonymous inequality, the intention is not necessary. The coffee consumer does not intend to hurt the plantation worker. In fact, the buyer of the coffee may actually admire plantation workers in an abstract, romanticized way. The consumer simply wants consistently good coffee for a reasonable price. But, even without any intention, it is still the actions of the consumer that cause the inequality. The consumer may be surprised or even appalled at the result of their action, but that makes the inequality no less real.

The third distinction is based on political effects. Because stigmatizing inequality involves people we know and because it is intentional, it has direct political effects. The creation and perpetuation of such a system of inequality usually involves political decisions. Furthermore, the dismantling of such a system also involves political decisions. Laws barring discrimination are passed, affirmative action programs are put into place, and so forth.

Anonymous inequality also involves political decisions, but in a less straightforward way, because anonymous inequality often appears to be simply the workings of an economic system. As we will discuss later, the economic system of international trade requires political decisions regarding, for example, tariffs and so on. It also has political effects such as supporting political regimes that will protect large landholders. Nevertheless, these political decisions appear to be just background to the workings of the economic system.

This peculiar mix of economic and political systems makes political action against anonymous inequality particularly difficult. For stigmatizing inequality, laws can be demanded and government programs can be instituted, but since anonymous inequality is set into motion by the unintended actions of the consumer, political remedies are more difficult. Because it appears to be an economic problem, economic solutions, such as boycotts, are commonly proposed. As we will discuss later, there is a long history of boycotts and consumer action in relation to both stigmatizing and anonymous inequality. However, such consumer actions against anonymous inequality are problematic mainly because consumer action is also one of the prime causes of the inequality, even though it may not be perceived as such.

A fourth difference between stigmatizing inequality and anonymous inequality is the way in which consumer objects are used. Consumer objects are involved in both types of inequality, because such objects are one of our primary means of relating to each other. With stigmatizing inequality, what we buy is displayed to different groups of people in different ways. If, for example, we purchase a white sheet and create a hooded robe out of it to wear, the object functions as a sign in a system of stigmatizing inequality. We buy certain things or keep others from buying certain things in order to display our difference. For example, one race may not be able to buy a meal at a nice restaurant. Instead, they are forced to consume meals in a manner that marks them as different.

However, it is also true that the purchase of a consumer product relates us in an anonymous way with all of those who worked to produce and supply this product. Furthermore, all of those who worked to supply us with these products are connected in an economic system that takes our consumption as one input and that produces inequality. Think, for example, of the cup of coffee that you might have bought before sitting down to read this text. In that simple transaction, you entered into a relationship with hundreds of others: the waitperson, the owner of the coffee shop, the people working at the roaster, the importer, the truck driver, the dockworkers, all of the people on the ship that brought the beans, the coffee plantation owner, the pickers, and so on. In addition, you supported a particular trading relation between countries, a particular form of government in the grower's country that has been historically shaped by the coffee trade, a particular relation between the plantation owner and the worker, and many other social relations. You did all of this by exchanging money for a cup of coffee. In the relation between these objects lies hidden all of these social relations between people.

Finally, the growth of consumer culture has had different effects on these two types of inequality. We argued in chapter 4 that stigmatizing inequality tends to be subverted by consumer culture because the stigmatizing signs of difference simply become part of a fashion system. In addition, the stigmatized people tend to become market segments. This happens to different degrees with different kinds of stigmatizing inequality, and also it happens less to the stigmatization of the elderly and the poor. Even so, consumer cultures tend to have less stigmatizing inequality than other types of cultures.

The effect is quite the opposite with anonymous inequality. We will argue in this chapter that anonymous inequality is one of the main effects of the growth of consumer culture.

Coffee and Capitalism

Starbucks aside, coffee is an important commodity to examine in trying to understand the anonymous inequality of modern consumer culture and its global dimensions. Michael Jimenez calls coffee "the paramount beverage of that emergent consumer society" (1995, 53). Chapter 1 already discussed the importance of coffee, along with sugar, cocoa, and tea, in spurring the changes toward a consumer culture in seventeenth-century Europe. Coffee was one of the first commodities to go from a luxury of the elite to an everyday necessity for the middle class (see table 5.2). It was also one of the first common products to be tied to a global market.

Furthermore, it is generally accepted that the idea of equal democratic participation in political decisions without regard to wealth and status found one of its first expressions in eighteenth-century coffeehouses (Habermas 1989). It has been claimed that one of the attractions of the Starbucks phenomena is that it harkens back to these earlier coffeehouses. Starbucks has designed their shops to suggest a place for conversation and community rather than simply a place to purchase coffee.

Aside from coffee's historical role, its intrinsic properties seem particularly well suited to capitalism. Early in its promotion, coffee marketers sponsored research documenting the rela-

Table 5.2 World Coffee Production, 1950–1990

	Production (metric tons)					Percent Change
1950	1960	1970	1980	1990	1950–1990
2,222,000	4,268,000	4,262,000	5,039,000	6,282,000	183

Source: Robert A. Rice and Justin R. Ward. 1996. *Coffee, Conservation, and Commerce in the Western Hemisphere.* Washington, DC: Smithsonian Migratory Bird Center and Natural Resources Defense Council, table 2, p. 39.

tion between coffee and productivity. People were particularly encouraged to use coffee to overcome the body's natural rhythms of a mid-morning and late afternoon slowdown. As the middle class grew and office routines replaced more invigorating activities, the coffee break became an accepted feature of the workplace. Even beyond the enhancement of productivity, coffee also became an important part of leisure time in the emerging consumer culture. Housewives met for a cup of coffee. Coffee was regularly served to guests. It also became the beverage of choice for dining out. As Gregory Dicum and Nina Luttinger claim, "In a society that combines buzzing overstimulation with soul-aching meaninglessness, coffee and its associated rituals are, for many of us, the lubricants that make it possible to go on" (1999, ix).

The acceptance of coffee as the beverage of the middle class was motivated by several changes in the way it was produced, marketed, and consumed. In production, economies of scale and technological improvements reduced costs significantly, so that even the lower end of the middle class could afford it. In marketing, coffee was one of the first products to move from a bulk, unbranded grocers' item to a prepackaged, brand-name item. In fact, the introduction of the vacuum-packed can made coffee one of the few products that was actually improved by its being prepackaged. In addition, there were some important changes in the technology of consuming coffee. For example, the automatic electric coffeemaker was invented in 1906, and there was a batch of technological developments in household grinders, improved coffeepots, and filters that stimulated greater household usage. However, most significant were the changes in advertising coffee.

A conglomerate of roasters and marketers called the Joint Coffee Publicity Committee was formed in the early decades of the twentieth century to promote the use of coffee. They took advantage of the new media such as radio and cinema, as well as billboards, newspapers, and magazines to promote coffee drinking. By the 1920s, this marketing included an educational program aimed at housewives on the importance of coffee. These campaigns attempted to tie women's self-esteem to their ability to make a good cup of coffee. One "subtle" advertisement said that "Mrs. Bradley surprised her husband" with a good cup of coffee and "they lived happily ever after" (cited in Jimenez 1995, 50). Another focus of the campaign was on advertising the medical benefits of coffee in medical journals.

Thanks to these changes, coffee became a staple of the new consumer culture. By the 1930s, coffee was accepted as the pre-eminent adult beverage. Most adults drank it. Few households were unprepared to offer it to guests. It was available in nearly all public spaces.

This demand for coffee created a national market for a standardized product. What had been a patchwork of local roasters with different-tasting products became a homogenous national product. Regional roasters quickly went national and were soon bought out by food conglomerates. These changes placed more emphasis on standardization and price than on taste and quality. Consequently, coffee quality decreased. As advertising increasingly focused on the brand, Ponte tells us that "the product itself became of secondary importance. . . . By competing almost exclusively on advertising, the major roasters stripped coffee of most of its charm and appeal" (2002, 1110).

Whatever has happened to its charm and appeal, coffee embodies the significance of anonymous global connections in a consumer culture. For most of the last century, coffee has been the world's most valuable (legally) traded commodity after oil. By examining coffee, we see the far-flung and unintended social effects of the vast network of market relations in a global consumer culture. Although most coffee is consumed in developed countries, it is primarily grown in developing countries. It is the perfect example of a commodity that depends on international trade, and it exemplifies the way that inequality works in our global consumer culture.

The coffee trade has profoundly shaped the societies of the countries that produce it. The history of the trade in coffee begins in the colonial era for which it was an ideal crop since it grew only in the colonies, was easily shipped, and had a ready market in Europe. As the colonial era faded, coffee was the primary commodity that allowed (or forced) the newly liberated countries to be outwardly focused.

Because the United States was not really a colonial power, its relation to the coffee trade was somewhat different. People from the United States never owned or even managed the coffee plantations. They were simply the main buyers. Nevertheless, the effects on the coffee-growing countries were the same.

In most of these coffee-producing countries, the cultivation of coffee transformed the geographic and demographic landscape. The replacement of tropical forests with coffee estates was equated with development. New towns, roads, and railroads were built to service the increased coffee production. The natural environment, the people's pattern of settlement, and even the region's identity were all deeply affected by the coffee trade. In addition, coffee has shaped the politics of these regions. In most coffee-growing countries, production was concentrated into huge plantations with a few rich owners and many poor workers. In most cases, this promoted repressive authoritarian governments to protect the rich landowners from the impoverished workers.

A historian of Brazil observed that "the economic dominance of coffee was unquestionable. Among the property-owning sectors of society the right of the planters to control the political system was unquestioned, and the mass of working people—slaves, freedmen, native Brazilian peasants, and immigrants—had no political voice. The government of Sao Paulo was itself the instrument of the coffee planters" (Holloway 1980, 39).

Most importantly, the production of coffee tied the local economy to an international economic system. The effect of this is especially evident with coffee because coffee prices have always been subject to significant price fluctuations in the international market. Coffee's production is tied to tropical weather patterns that are inherently unstable and unpredictable. If production were limited to one region, this would not matter because bad weather would cause a shortage *and* higher prices, thereby recompensing the region affected. However, since coffee production is spread all over the tropical regions of the world, a drought in Africa could happen at the same time as a bumper year in Latin America. This would mean that African growers would have both low harvest and low prices. The important point here is that the detrimental effect on the producing country is made worse by being part of an international system.

In addition, changes in consumption because of such events as economic booms and busts in consuming countries can be responded to only very slowly in producing countries, because the coffee shrub generally takes five years to produce a mature crop. For example, new areas might be planted in response to an increase in demand that may be gone or have found alternative sources by the time the first bean is produced. Furthermore, once that five-year investment has been made by a grower, he or she is very loathe to pull up the plant in response to a market glut.

The governments of coffee-producing countries have historically tried to restrain these international fluctuations. In fact, coffee was one of the first international commodities that the producing countries attempted to control. Most of these attempts were spearheaded by Brazil, which has been the largest producer of coffee. Despite Brazil's dominance, the presence of Pacific and African producers and the increasing demand for Colombian and other Central American varieties created a global trading structure that was very difficult to unify into a trading bloc.

Brazil was able to bring some stability to coffee prices in the early decades of the twentieth century, but this was quickly met with resistance in the consumer counties, especially in the United States. Public outrage over the "foreign" control of coffee prices led to political debates over what came to be called the "coffee question." It was suggested that coffee importers should be prosecuted for conspiracy to gouge consumers. Boycotts and a trade war were threatened.

Economic Cosmopolitanism

In response to these threats, coffee producers and other groups began an advertising and lobbying campaign to bring greater awareness of the effects of international trade. According to Jimenez, this campaign laid "the foundations for a new vision of the international order" (1995, 55). Coffee producers convinced politicians and even the general public that price fluctuations threatened the stability of governments that were important to the United States. This was a surprisingly effective argument in the 1940s and 1950s because of the fear of communist influence in Latin America. It was argued that unstable economies would produce unstable governments vulnerable to communist takeover. All of this brought increased awareness of the implications of being part of a global economy. Rather than considering only the local effects of price controls, Americans started to look at the global implications. Jiminez calls this way of looking at the world "economic cosmopolitanism," and he argues that the coffee trade was "a singularly appropriate vehicle" for introducing this viewpoint into the United States (1995, 52).

Starting during World War II, economic cosmopolitanism led to a series of international agreements involving both producing and consuming countries in order to stabilize prices. The setting of prices moved out of the marketplace and into the back rooms of international trade meetings. This culminated in an international coffee agreement (ICA) establishing a global cartel that assigned quotas to both producing and consuming countries, thereby creating a relatively stable pricing system from 1962 to 1989.

After 1989, when communism no longer appeared to be a threat, the U.S. promotion of an ideology of free trade caused the collapse of the ICA and once again exposed coffee-producing countries to the fluctuations of international trade. There was an immediate plunge in coffee prices to historic lows as power shifted to consuming countries. One analyst describes the change as follows:

> The end of the ICA regime has profoundly affected the balance of power in the coffee chain. From a fairly balanced contest between producers and consumers within the politics of the commodity agreement, market relations shifted to a dominance of consuming country–based operators (including their agents based in producing countries) over farmers, local traders and producing country governments. This has been accompanied by lower and more volatile coffee prices, a higher proportion of the income generated in the chain retained in consuming countries, and a declining level of producer-held stocks. (Ponte 2002, 1105)

It is quite correct to say that power has shifted to the consumer countries, but it is equally true to say that it has shifted to the consumer. In a sense, the free market ideology has meant that the governments of both the consumer and producer countries have been bypassed for a more market-driven relation between producers and consumers. When a consumer buys a cup of coffee, it has geographic, demographic, and political effects in the producer country. A complex, global network connects those who produce coffee in tropical, developing countries to coffee consumers in wealthy, temperate countries. Intertwined with the economic relation are particular political relations. In buying coffee, you support the free trade relation that prevents states from trying to control devastating price fluctuations. You support repressive regimes in coffee-growing countries. You support an economic system that entails disparity between the owners of the land and those who tend the crops. In other words, you support an international inequality between producer and consumer countries and the inequality involved in the production of coffee. And, as we have argued, you do all of this anonymously, without knowing the people affected and without intending it.

Starting in the 1960s and building throughout the 1980s and 1990s, a new environmental damage was added to the social, political, and economic effects of the international coffee trade. Driven by increased demand and the desire to boost yields, coffee plantations switched from growing coffee under the shade of a tree canopy to sun coffee farming. This change produced a dramatic increase in both yields and environmental degradation (Wille 1994). Growing coffee under direct sunlight required a significant increase in the use of fertilizers, herbicides, fungicides, and insecticides. The cutting down of the shade trees also eliminated a vibrant habitat for wildlife. Furthermore, buyers get a less expensive product and consumers get a product of more consistent quality. Consequently, shade coffee requires a commitment to priorities other than making money or providing consumers with an inexpensive and consistent product.

In a very real sense, this social and ecological devastation is also caused by the coffee consumer. However, because of an international trading system, this damage is never seen by the consumer. One way to redress this problem would be to convince consumers to buy shade-grown coffee. However, shade-grown coffee is more expensive, the quality is not as consistent, and there are no health benefits to the consumer because the pesticides used to grow sun coffee are purged during roasting. What is required is for consumers to become aware of the anonymous effects of their consumption and to make consumer decisions based on the people involved rather than the product's quality and price. This is where we return to Starbucks.

The Latte Revolution and Fair Trade

Recent years have seen a surge in consumer demand for specialty coffees. The change in consumer taste cannot be understood without looking at Starbucks. Starbucks was founded in 1971 in Seattle and spent most of the 1980s "educating" consumers on the qualities of fine coffees. However, the company did not really take off until it designed a reproducible café-type environment for the coffee consumer. It was Starbucks the milieu, rather than Starbucks the coffee, that triggered the company's growth and spread. Howard Schultz, the CEO of Starbucks, described it this way: "We would take something old and tired and common—coffee—and weave a sense of romance and community around it. We would rediscover the mystique and charm that had swirled around coffee throughout the centuries" (quoted in Dicum and Luttinger 1999, 115). Ponte calls this the "latte revolution" and claims that "coffee bar chains sell an ambience and a social positioning more than just 'good' coffee" (2002, 1111). Furthermore, he connects this change with a more general change in consumer culture.

> This happened at the same time as other consumer products moved from mass-production and marketing to being recast as more authentic, flavorful and healthy (micro-brewed beer, specialty breads, organic vegetables). By combining "ambience" consumption and the possibility for consumers to choose type, origin, roast, and grind, Starbucks managed to de-commoditize coffee. It sold coffee pre-packaged with lifestyle signifiers. (ibid.)

This decommodification of coffee—the transformation of coffee from just the product of anonymous producers to a sign of a *lifestyle*—provided an opportunity for a new relation between the consumer and the producer. Consumers became interested not just in the quality and price of the coffee, but in what the purchase of coffee said about the consumer's values. This opened up the possibility for a change in the anonymous inequality of global consumer culture. Coffee has been one of the first commodities where this new possibility has begun to express itself.

The growth of "lifestyle" coffee consumption has been accompanied by consumer interest in organic coffee, shade-grown coffee, and "Fair Trade" coffee. Fair Trade refers to a movement that aims to achieve a fair price for small coffee growers. Beginning in 1988 from a small Dutch organization, the Fair Trade movement became international in 1997 with the establishment of the Fair Trade Labeling Organizations International. Its founders hoped to offset the effects of global economic forces on poor countries by establishing a minimum price for coffee. It includes a distribution system based on small, democratically run cooperatives with shared profits. Despite the fact that Fair Trade coffee is more expensive, does not taste better, and provides no direct benefit to the consumer, it is one of the fastest-growing specialty coffees, although it still makes up only about 2 percent of the market.

Just as Starbucks has been at the center of re-creating coffee as a lifestyle commodity, it has also been at the center of the Fair Trade controversy. In both cases, Starbucks's role is primarily symbolic. Starbucks created itself as a brand and a milieu and has now become a symbol of the anonymous inequality of a consumer culture.

In the fall of 1999, groups in favor of Fair Trade began to organize protests, letter-writing campaigns, and boycotts against Starbucks, not because Starbucks was particularly egregious, but because it was such a potent symbol. At first, Starbucks resisted the protestors' demand to sell Fair Trade coffee because those beans were not as consistently high quality as sun-grown coffee. However, realizing its dependence on symbols of lifestyle and its vulnerability to such protests, Starbucks soon capitulated and began to offer Fair Trade coffee in its stores as well as developing worker and consumer education programs. It was not long before Starbucks positioned itself as a leader in this movement. Its literature now stresses its role in conservation, workers' welfare, and development in coffee-growing countries.

When we look at Starbucks, we do not see an evil empire, just as any fair look at the WTO will not see a cabal of multinationals out to wreak environmental havoc. What we see instead are mainly contradictions: a progressive company, treating their workers well, responding to organized social demands, trying to provide their customers with inexpensive consistent quality, *and* contributing to ecological damage in developing countries. With the WTO, we see an international organization trying to address trade disputes *and* ending up harming endangered species. Similarly, we see contradictions in the response to global consumer culture, for example, people who smash the windows of Starbucks and Nike while wearing clothing from The Gap.

These are the sort of contradictions that we get with anonymous inequality. Here, the people being treated unequally are not stigmatized. In fact, they may be very much admired, as the Starbucks coffee drinker may admire the people who work on the coffee plantations. But, the actions of the Starbucks drinker nevertheless harm those who work on the coffee plantation. Because they are the result of a global system of anonymous inequality, these harms are extremely difficult to see.

Distance between Producers and Consumers

It may be possible through research to discover some of the damage, as well as the good, done to a producer country through our consumption. However, this information is not immediately available at the point of purchase. When we are deciding on our purchase, we normally have only two sources of information. The first is the product itself, which is often on display, but even when it is not displayed, we can inspect the product after our purchase and it can inform subsequent consumption.

The second source of information is the price. For most consumers, this information is either related to what can be afforded or used to contrast with comparable objects. The price, in fact, contains much more information. In the price is contained information about the growing season in the producer country, shipping costs, marketing strategies, government policies, and so forth. All of these are reflected in the price, but it is not an easy task to untangle all of this information from the pure numbers of the price.

Other kinds of information are next to impossible to factor into the price or they may show up in an inverted way. For example, while economic costs usually show up in the price, social and ecological costs usually do not. Economic costs such as broken-down factories, outmoded equipment, and inefficient workers are reflected in the higher price of the product. In making their selection, the consumer usually will not buy higher-priced, lower-quality goods, and therefore the producers who have created these economic costs are punished. However, many social and political costs actually lower the price, and consequently producers who add to those costs may be rewarded. In the case of coffee, we have seen that sun-grown coffee causes more environmental damage, and yet it lowers the price of the coffee. Going only on price and product, consumers will tend to buy sun-grown coffee, even though it causes environmental damage.

We can assume that at least some consumers would be willing to buy more expensive coffee that causes less environmental damage, however it is not easy for consumers to know which coffee causes more or less environmental damage. This is particularly true in cases where there is a "distance" between the producer and the consumer. In other words, when the producer is next door, we are more able and willing to include the social and environmental costs in our consumption decision, but when the consumer is across the globe, it is more difficult to see the social and environmental costs, and we are less motivated to take them into consideration.

The idea of distance is discussed by Thomas Princen (2002). He defines distance as the separation between decisions about production and decisions about consumption. Princen analyzes distance along four dimensions, three of which are important for our discussion here: geography, culture, and agency. Distance along any of these dimensions makes it difficult to get any information that is not contained in the product or the price.

The first dimension of distance, geography, is the easiest to understand. It is the actual physical distance between the producer and the consumer. Social and political damage that many would object to in their own locale can be tolerated when it occurs thousands of miles away. Even if the consumer is concerned about what happens in these faraway countries, the geographic distance makes it difficult to get the information necessary to make an informed choice.

The second dimension is cultural distance. We often know very little about the culture in which our products are produced. I may, for example, be able to find out how much a worker is paid, but I still might not know what the amount means in that culture. A dollar a day sounds meager to someone living in the United States, but it may or may not be a fair wage in Brazil. Furthermore, I have no idea whether production decisions are being forced on the people through coercion and poverty or whether these people have knowingly traded environmental damage for economic benefit. To make matters worse, this cultural distance allows those who benefit from these practices to misrepresent the culture that is being damaged. Geographic distance can be overcome simply by travel, but cultural distance requires someone who will explain what things mean to those involved, and those who do the explaining may have their own agenda.

The third dimension is the distance created by the chain of agents—people and organizations—that connect the producer and the consumer (see figure 5.1). International commodities, such as coffee, must pass along a chain made up of workers, landowners, government inspectors, wholesale buyers, shippers, roasters, and so forth, all of the way to the consumer. It is important to remember two things about this chain of agents. First, each

Figure 5.1 Global Coffee Network: Web of Agents

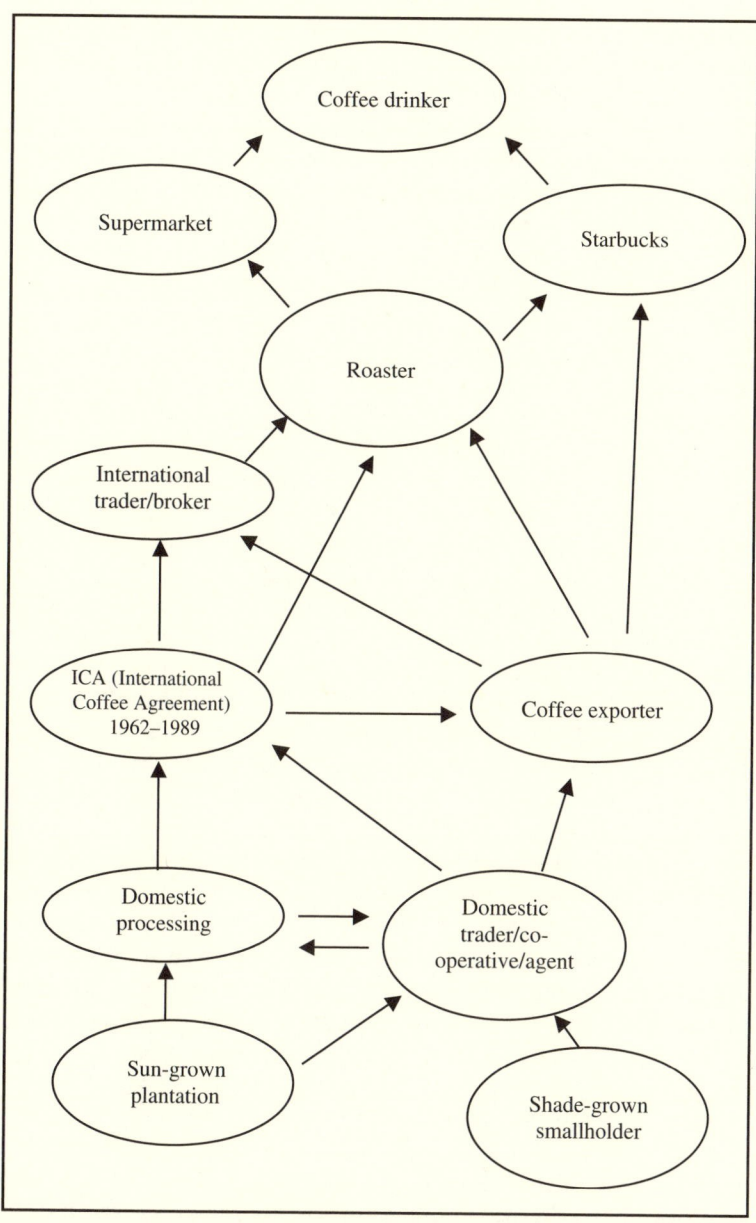

Source: Adapted from Gregory Dicum and Nina Luttinger. 1999. *The Coffee Book: Anatomy of an Industry from the Crop to the Last Drop.* New York: The New Press, 107.

person and organization along the line has its own particular interests that may or may not coincide with the producers or the consumers. Second, every exchange along that chain is liable to be unequal in the power that the agents have in the transaction. This imbalance is especially strong in international exchange because agents from rich countries might have many more choices about who to buy from than the choices that poorer countries have on who to sell to. In addition, the economics of processing and shipping require huge capital investments in such things as factories and cargo ships, so that those agents are likely to be much more powerful than such agents as workers.

Because of this chain of agents, information about the ecological and social damage of production may not be passed from producer to consumer even in cases where both ends of the chain want that information to be shared. Every link in the chain typically involves two agents, and if either of those agents want to suppress the information, it will most likely be stopped at that point.

The greater the distance along any of these dimensions, the more difficult it is for the consumer to have any effect on the production of the commodity. This will happen even where both producers and consumers are honest and concerned about social and environmental damage, but it is especially likely where it is in the interest of some party to manipulate the flow of information in order to continue with practices that cause social and environmental damage. In particular, this will happen where those who benefit have access to advertising campaigns or lobbying.

It is our belief that much of the harm done by consumer society is due to this distance. Environments are destroyed, people are displaced, inequality is allowed to increase because of the distance that exists in the anonymous relations of global capitalism.

There are basically two ways that this problem of distance can be addressed. First, one can attempt to decrease the distance by doing such things as buying local to decrease geographic distance, traveling to and learning about other cultures to decrease cultural distance, and encouraging producer or consumer cooperatives to decrease agency distance. Where these measures are not feasible, the only alternative is a more organized response that attempts to bridge the difference with the express interest of minimizing environmental and social damage. There are different ways of organizing this response—political protest, governmental regulations, import laws, or international bodies—but perhaps the most popular in our consumer society has been the boycott.

Boycott Movements

Because the environmental damage and anonymous inequality seem to be caused by consumer culture, it makes sense to many to attempt to fix it through consumption. We have seen previously that a consumer boycott was used against Starbucks. This was only the latest in a long history of consumer boycotts (see table 5.3). They all have in common an interest in turning consumer choice into a political force. A boycott is an attempt to achieve objectives by urging individual consumers to refrain from making selected purchases. It mobilizes the defining practice of consumer culture usually in order to achieve goals that are against the tendencies of consumer culture, that is, for noneconomic goals.

The term *boycott* originated in a movement by Irish peasants to ostracize an English land agent, Captain Boycott, in the 1880s, but the practice started long before this. One of the more famous is the American boycott of English products dramatized by the Boston Tea Party, which led up to the American Revolutionary War. During the 1760s, numerous political groups organized consumer boycotts of British goods, especially those, such as tea, that were heavily taxed. The list of boycotted goods also included silks, velvets, clocks, watches, and coaches. Tim Breen describes how these consumer boycotts helped to create a national identity: "Americans discovered political ideology through a discussion of the meanings of goods, through observances of non-consumption that forced ordinary men and women to declare exactly where they stood on the great constitutional issues of the day" (1993, 250).

At about the same time as the American boycott of British goods, a campaign developed with many similarities to the case of coffee discussed previously: the boycott of slave-grown sugar (Sussman 2000). Religious groups and other abolitionists began a boycott in England and America against sugar grown in the West Indies. It was argued that the apparently harmless practice of eating sugar supported slavery through a world trade network.

Boycotts also were successfully used as a supplement to labor strikes. Unions had a difficult time carrying out effective strikes in the early twentieth century because it was relatively easy for employers to replace striking workers. Early labor leaders saw the boycott as a consumer counterpart to the strike. This practice continues, but its last notable success was in the 1970s

Table 5.3 Historical Time Line of Consumer Boycotts

1300s	The practice of boycotting is documented as far back as the fourteenth century.a
1766	Religious groups and other abolitionists begin a boycott in England and America against slave sugar grown in the West Indies.
	Americans *boycott* British goods. The most prominent boycott is the Boston Tea Party, an event that led to the American Revolutionary War.
1880	The term *boycott* originates in 1880 with the ostracism of Captain C. C. Boycott, an Irish land agent, over his treatment of his tenants.
1902	A meat boycott is initiated largely by women on New York's Lower East Side who protest sharp price increases, which they blame on oligarchic control over the beef industry.
1930s	The "Don't Buy Where You Can't Work" campaign encourages African Americans, particularly women, to support African American businesses.
1947	Ghandi promotes Satyagraha (nonviolent political protest) by organizing boycotts of British salt and cloth as part of a strategy of nonviolent protest that ultimately leads to Indian independence.
1955	Rosa Parks refuses to give up her seat on a city bus to a white man, triggering the Montgomery bus boycott, a pivotal event in the Civil Rights Movement.
Late 1960s	Boycott of Dow Chemical's Saran Wrap in response to the company's manufacture of napalm in the Vietnam War.
	The California grape, celery, and grapefruit boycott, spearheaded by Cesar Chavez, unionizes farmworkers. This forces concessions from the growers by the early 1970s.
1970s	Nestlé, the world's largest baby food manufacturer, is boycotted between 1974 and 1984. The boycott is reinstated in 1998 after the World Health authority determines that information contained in its advertisements for baby formula is either misleading or incorrect.b
	Gay rights groups boycott Florida citrus products in response to antigay rhetoric by singer Anita Bryant, which leads Florida citrus commissioners to end an endorsement contract with the singer.
1980s	1984, the Urban Alliance on Race Relations launches a mail-back campaign whereby every catalog or flyer that does not reflect the multiracial composition of the local population is mailed back to the respective corporations with a note to the president and advertising director explaining why.c
	1986, Barclays Bank withdraws from South Africa, despite being the largest bank in the country, primarily as a result of a consumer boycott against South African apartheid. The boycott of companies doing business in South Africa becomes a global movement, critical in the eventual downfall of apartheid.d

Table 5.3 Historical Time Line of Consumer Boycotts *(continued)*

1990s	European boycott of Shell over its plan to dump the Brent Spar oil platform at sea and reports of environmental harm as a result of its operations in Ogoniland, Nigeria.
	Boycotts of Texaco in the United States over alleged racial remarks by senior management.
	Boycotts of Mitsubishi over alleged sexual harassment in the workplace and, according to the Rainforest Action Network, for environmental degradation around its manufacturing plants.
	A multicountry boycott of Nike over alleged sweatshop conditions at Asian suppliers.
	Avon's recognizable sign, "Avon calling," is replaced with "Avon killing" in media spoofs protesting animal testing. Benetton and Revlon are similarly targeted.
	McDonald's is consistently attacked for environmental practices such as deforestation, as a result of its need for cattle pasture, and because it is viewed as a stalwart of American imperialism (and thus boycotted across Europe after the United States invades Iraq in 2003). In 1999, French antiglobalization farmer Jose Bove destroyed the building site of a McDonald's restaurant in the southern French town of Millau. A McDonald's restaurant was blown up in Athens in 1999 by an anarchist group, and others are blown up in Brittany, France, in 2000 by revolutionary separatist groups and in China in December 2001 by a Muslim group.
	Heinz and Bumble Bee Seafoods are boycotted for using nets for catching tuna that also capture and kill dolphins.
	General Electric is boycotted for manufacturing military weapons.
2000–	In 2003, Starbucks is boycotted by antiwar protesters in Lebanon and criticized by New Zealand advocates seeking higher coffee prices for farmers.

Source Notes:
a Jill Gabrielle Klein, N. Craig Smith, and Andrew John. 2002. *Why We Boycott: Consumer Motivations for Boycott Participation and Marketer Responses.* London Business School Centre for Marketing: Working Paper No. 02-701, June.
b N. Craig Smith. 1990. *Morality and the Market: Consumer Pressure for Corporate Accountability.* New York: Routledge.
c Carol Tator. 1984. "Mail-Back Campaign." *Currents* (summer): 15–18.
d Kenneth Rodman. 1994. "Public and Private Sanctions against South Africa." *Political Science Quarterly* 101, no. 2: 313–334.

with the boycott of celery, grapes, and grapefruit spearheaded by Cesar Chavez, which was able to unionize farmworkers when all previous efforts and methods had failed.

Even outside the labor movement, most early boycotts had economic motivations. For example, the 1902 meat boycotts were sparked by sharp increases in retail meat prices orchestrated by a cartel of meatpackers. These boycotts typically involved the poor, often recent immigrants to America. Similarly motivated by economic concerns were consumer leagues, which also threatened boycotts in order to protest high prices. These leagues generally involved women activists. The earliest such organization, the National Consumer League, was founded in 1899. Another important group was the National Association of Housewives' Leagues, established in 1912.

Some of these consumer leagues went beyond economic issues to address social concerns. Florence Kelley, the founding executive director of the National Consumer League, proclaimed that the aim of the organization was to "moralize" the power of the consumer so that workers received fair living wages, goods were produced under sanitary conditions, and the interests of the community were promoted (Kelley 1986; see profile of Florence Kelley in chapter 6).

In addition to boycotts aimed as specific products, there is also a history of boycotts aimed at new types of consumption. There were campaigns against department stores, against chain stores, and against mail-order shopping. These boycotts were usually led by independent shopkeepers who were threatened by the changes in marketing, but they often found a resonance in those who saw that the changes threatened not just a particular merchant, but a way of life.

Furthermore, there has been a history of boycotts by African Americans, such as the "Don't Buy Where You Can't Work" campaign in the 1930s. The idea behind this campaign was summarized by W. E. B. Du Bois, "If we once make a religion of our determination to spend our meagre income so far as possible only in such ways as will bring us employment consideration and opportunity, the possibilities before us are enormous" (1985, 147). This and similar calls led to the formation of such consumer groups as the Housewives' League of Detroit, which had 10,000 members in 1934 and encouraged African American women to support African American businesses.

Of course, the effectiveness of these boycotts depended on there already being some economic integration. Cities where African Americans bought mainly from African Americans were largely unaffected by boycotts. This is why boycotts in Atlanta were ineffective in the 1960s, while the boycotts in Nashville and Birmingham, where white business depended heavily on African American purchasing, were highly effective (Wirmark 1974, 124).

Here, we see that the boycott has been used to confront both anonymous and stigmatizing inequality. Such boycotts still continue addressing inequality based on race, ethnicity, gender, and sexual orientation, as well as other forms of inequality.

Most of the boycotts discussed thus far were aimed at hurting the sales of the targeted company. The loss of consumer sales was believed to be the means for gaining concessions from the targeted firms. However, as consumption has become more of a symbolic activity, consumer boycotts have also become more symbolic. Friedman (1995) makes a useful distinction between "market" boycotts and "media" boycotts. It is media boycotts that have become increasingly important in our consumer culture.

Friedman illustrates the difference between market and media boycotts by pointing to the typical site that a boycott group would pick for their protest. "A marketplace-oriented group would be likely to demonstrate in front of a store selling a boycotted product, urging consumers not to buy the item. A media-oriented boycott, on the other hand, would be more likely to select the target firm's headquarters, making sure that demonstrators were positioned in front of a company sign or logo, so that television cameras would be able to link these identifying visuals with the boycotters' publicity materials" (1995, 198).

Media boycotts are more likely to use celebrities, disrupt stockholder meetings, protest at the homes and offices of business executives, have press conferences featuring photogenic "victims" of the corporate practices, and organize protest activities in public places that are unrelated, or only symbolically related, to the firm. Rather than time-intensive picket lines, they use media-friendly humor and irony, such as replacing Avon's recognizable sign, "Avon calling," with "Avon killing" to protest animal testing. Friedman describes one particularly effective tactic: "Involving children as activists. Environmental groups have been particularly successful doing this in support of the tuna boycott and the tropical timber boycott. The human interest value of these stories of activist schoolchildren was clear to the news media, which gave the stories wide coverage" (1995, 197). Because the aim is symbolic rather than to directly hurt sales, the boycott could actually be a "buycott." For example, protest groups promoted a campaign in 1985 to buy products from New Zealand in support of that country's ban on ships carrying nuclear weapons.

Beyond the tactics, the objectives of the boycotts have also changed. The new media boycotts are less about economic self-interest and more about representing larger values. Instead of economic self-interest, media boycotts tend to aim at ethical or socially responsible actions. They include such issues as gender and racial inequality (e.g., tourism boycotts of Miami and Arizona), the environment (e.g., targeting Mitsubishi for their destruction of the rain forest), animal rights (e.g., Avon, Revlon, and Benetton for testing products on animals), and peace (e.g., General Electric for manufacturing military weapons).

Undoubtedly, the two most popular of these issues are animal rights and the environment. These two issues were absent from boycotts before the 1970s, but have become the major concerns of present-day media boycotts. Organizations such as People for the Ethical Treatment of Animals, Earth First!, and the Rainforest Action Network are now the major leaders in boycotts, even though the organizations did not exist twenty years ago. What these issues have in common is that they are intellectually simple and emotionally appealing. A picture of a dolphin entangled in a net or of a laboratory bunny quickly communicates a powerful symbolic message, as do many of the slogans associated with the movement such as "save the dolphins."

The fact that these media boycotts have larger ethical objectives also influences the targets of the boycotts. Marketplace boycotts trying to directly affect sales tended to target the most egregious of the companies. Media boycotts tend to target the most well known companies, regardless of the extent of their involvement in the objectionable activity. For example, in recent (2003) protests over the U.S. invasion of Iraq, McDonald's became a primary target of boycotts by European activists. A reporter for the *New York Times* explains why:

> The fact that protesters are drawn to the Golden Arches in their quest to gain attention is an interesting example of brand power working in reverse. Many marketing experts contend that "branding" is not a logical process, that the most successful brands make an emotional connection with consumers. This also seems to be true of brand backlashes. Under happier circumstances, the McDonald's name and imagery can stand as shorthand for a quick, dependable U.S.-style meal. Now, it can be seen as standing for something else: the policies of the United States and its place in the world. (Walker 2003, C1)

Media boycotts prefer companies and especially brands that are well known and easy to identify, and where consumer violation of the boycotts will be visible. They especially prefer global companies. In some ways, corporations like Disney, Wal-Mart, and Nike have helped make themselves vulnerable to consumer actions. Their success in diversifying interests, buying out local competition, and transferring production to cheap labor markets abroad has created an "interconnectedness" in the global economy, which gives activists a lot of avenues to pursue (Ferguson 1997, 44).

Many of these media boycotts have been very successful. For example, Avon, Neutrogena, Benetton, and a slew of other cosmetics companies stopped animal testing. The primary targets of a tuna boycott, Heinz and Bumble Bee Seafoods, agreed to catch fish in a way that would avoid harming dolphins. A number of these companies publicly attributed their changed policies to the boycott campaigns. Nevertheless, there are limits to what can be accomplished through these boycotts. Media boycotts around complex issues are difficult to organize. Many companies are not well known enough to become the target of boycotts. Some goals do not have celebrity support or are not associated with photogenic victims.

All of these boycott movements have three things in common. First, they represent a democratization of protest, since they allow anyone who consumes to protest—even if not old enough to vote, or not a citizen, or a former felon. This has been especially important when large segments of the population have been disenfranchised because they were women or colonized subjects. It should be noted, however, that economic differences become significant, since few care if the poor boycott a product.

Second, these movements attempt to bring to our attention the connection between the production of commodities and their consumption. The movements have argued that the buying of sugar was directly connected to the system of slavery that produced it, that the buying of clothes is connected to the sweatshops in developing countries, or that the buying of coffee is connected to ecological damage. The movements maintain that socioeconomic injustice and environmental damage, whether it happens around the world or around the corner, is enabled or hindered by the everyday purchases of the average consumer. At the same time, such movements recognize that the relation between producer and consumer is commodified and alienated. We are not encouraged to go to Colombia to work alongside the coffee producer; instead, we demonstrate our concern through what we do or do not buy.

Third, these movements depend on an image of the powerful consumer. To begin with, we should realize that these boycotts are less a protest against consumer culture and more an attempt to introduce different values into it. The consumer is seen as the most important agent for effecting this change in values. In the case of coffee, the farmers, the local governments, and, to an extent, even the coffee chains are seen as puppets controlled by the consumers' choices. The farmers must grow coffee in the most economical way, governments must allow or even encourage what is good for their gross national product, and coffee stores must sell what the consumer will buy. Only the consumer seems free to make choices between different values, for example, justice over profit or ecology over consistent taste. All other choices seem to be a chain of responses determined by the values of the consumer. This is another one of the contradictions of consumer culture. Those who engage in these boycotts believe more in the power of the consumer than does any advertising director or marketing executive.

Conclusion

The popularity of media boycotts signals a changed attitude to politics in our consumer culture. In chapter 2, we saw that the consumer has become the model for the citizen. Not only do people participate less as citizens—for instance, fewer and fewer people vote—but when people do participate they do so "in consumer mode" (Firat and Dholakia 1998, 103). Across the political spectrum, the figure of the consumer has become dominant. For conservatives, the government needs to get out of the way of the all-powerful and mostly beneficent capitalist economy that is run by and for the consumer. Liberals distrust the production side of the economy, but through the increasing popularity of boycotts, even liberals have pinned their hopes on the consumer. Rather than democracy representing the ability of people to form a common goal through open discussions, it has come to mean the ability to choose among prepackaged goals and candidates. In the widespread turn to boycotts, we see the culmination of the consumer model of the citizen. Zachary Lyons, editor of *Boycott Quarterly*, said the following: "People are recognizing that voting with their dollars has a lot more power than their political vote, because corporations actually have more power in Congress than the lawmakers supposedly in charge" (quoted in Ferguson 1997, 44).

We cannot forget the benefits of a consumer culture. Rational people want material goods and there is nothing ignoble about that. Despite all of the advertising, public-relations campaigns, and shady marketing, consumer culture truly is an expression of our freedom. A society driven by consumption has fed more people, clothed more people, and housed more people than any society in history. It has even, as we argued in chapter 4, subverted some important forms of inequality.

Nevertheless, we cannot ignore the disadvantages of a consumer society. The freedom of the individual consumer has limited the freedom of the community. The society that has fed, clothed, and housed people has also damaged the environment and created more trash than any other society in history. In place of stigmatizing inequality, a more incorrigible anonymous inequality has emerged.

Perhaps the most worrying aspect of consumer society is that our options for addressing its problems seem to be narrowing. Most people, for example, are deeply concerned about the ecological damage caused by consumption, but the response to it has been channeled into individual consumer choices. People do not agonize over different government and community-based solutions; instead, they agonize over whether they should use paper or plastic bags at the grocery store. The truth is that neither choice makes much difference given the current institutional structures, but the consumer approach to solving problems cannot change institutional structures or even talk about communal solutions. Consumer-based solutions involve recycling or buying a tree to plant or, as we discussed in chapter 3, buying commodities that symbolize our disgust with consumption. But no matter what its benefits, consumption cannot really solve its own problems. Perhaps we will consume our way out of a consumer culture, but it is more likely to be through a catastrophic destruction than by buying the simple life. The solution to the problems of consumer culture requires first an understanding of consumption's benefits and problems and second people that are able to act as citizens instead of just as consumers.

References

Breen, Tim. 1993. "The Meaning of Things: Interpreting the Consumer Economy in the Eighteenth Century." In J. Brewer and R. Porter, eds., *Consumption and the World of Goods*, 249–260. New York: Routledge.

Brunner, Jim. 2000. "$9.3 Million Bill from WTO Bound to Swell with Claims against City." *Seattle Times* (25 June): A1.

Dicum, Gregory, and Nina Luttinger. 1999. *The Coffee Book: Anatomy of an Industry from the Crop to the Last Drop*. New York: The New Press.

Du Bois, W. E. B. 1985. *Against Racism: Unpublished Essays, Papers, Addresses, 1887–1961*. Amherst: University of Massachesetts Press.

Dukcevich, Davide. 2002. "Starbucks' Flight to Latin America." *Forbes* 170, no. 4: 27–28.

Ferguson, Sarah. 1997. "Boycotts 'R' Us." *Village Voice* (8 July): 44–46.

Firat, A. Fuat, and Nikhilesh Dholakia. 1998. *Consuming People: From Political Economy to Theaters of Consumption*. New York: Routledge.

Friedman, Monroe. 1995. "On Promoting a Sustainable Future through Consumer Activism." *Journal of Social Issues* 51: 197–215.

Habermas, Jürgen. 1989. *The Structural Transformation of the Public Sphere*. Cambridge, MA: MIT Press.

Holloway, Thomas. 1980. *Immigrants on the Land: Coffee and Society in Sao Paulo, 1886–1934*. Chapel Hill: University of North Carolina Press.

Jimenez, Michael. 1995. "From Plantation to Cup: Coffee and Capitalism in the United States, 1830–1930." In W. Roseberry, L. Gundmundson, and M. Samper Kutschbach, eds., *Coffee, Society, and Power in Latin America*, 38–64. Baltimore, MD: Johns Hopkins University Press.

Kelley, Florence. 1986. *The Autobiography of Florence Kelley*. Chicago: Charles Kerr.

Klein, Jill Gabrielle, N. Craig Smith, and Andrew John. 2002. *Why We Boycott: Consumer Motivations for Boycott Participation and Marketer Responses*. London Business School Centre for Marketing: Working Paper No. 02–701, June.

Ponte, Stefano. 2002. "The 'Latte Revolution'?: Regulation, Markets and Consumption in the Global Coffee Chain." *World Development* 30: 1099–1122.

Princen, Thomas. 2002. "Distancing: Consumption and the Severing of Feedback." In T. Princen, M. Maniates, and K. Conca, eds., *Confronting Consumption*, 103–132. Cambridge, MA: MIT Press.

Rice, Robert A., and Justin R. Ward. 1996. *Coffee, Conservation, and Commerce in the Western Hemisphere*. Washington, DC: Smithsonian Migratory Bird Center and Natural Resources Defense Council.

Rodman, Kenneth. 1994. "Public and Private Sanctions against South Africa." *Political Science Quarterly* 101, no. 2: 313–334.

Ruggiero, Renato. 2000. "Foreword: Reflection from Seattle." In J. Schott, ed., *The WTO after Seattle*, xiii–xvii. Washington, DC: Institute for International Economics.

Smith, N. Craig. 1990. *Morality and the Market: Consumer Pressure for Corporate Accountability*. New York: Routledge.

Sussman, Charlotte. 2000. *Consuming Anxieties: Consumer Protest, Gender, and British Slavery, 1713–1833*. Stanford, CA: University of Stanford Press.

Tator, Carol. 1984. "Mail-Back Campaign." *Currents* (summer): 15–18.

Walker, Rob. 2003. "Anti-War Protests Give McDonald's a Taste of Brand-Power Backlash." *New York Times*, 30 March, C1.

Wille, Chris. 1994. "The Birds and the Beans." *Audubon* (November–December): 1–17.

Wirmark, Bo. 1974. "Nonviolent Methods and the American Civil Rights Movement, 1955–1965." *Journal of Peace Research* 11: 115–132.

6

People, Events, Trends, and Organizations

This is an idiosyncratic selection of people, events, trends, and organizations. The people include advertising executives, consumer activists, economists, sociologists, marketers, and business people. The events, trends, and organizations vary from large and important trends such as bourgeois culture to isolated events such as the introduction of the Volkswagen Beetle. Our primary criteria for selection was to provide an easy resource for those who wish to know more about the story presented in the previous five chapters.

People

Charlotte Beers (1935–)

Charlotte Beers is an important figure in the history of women in the advertising industry. Beers was the first female product manager for Uncle Ben's and eventually became the first female vice president ever at J. Walter Thompson. In her two years as CEO of Tatham-Laird & Kudner, Beers achieved profit margins double the average for the industry and tripled billings to $325 million. In 1992, Beers left Tatham-Laird & Kudner and joined Ogilvy & Mather, where she worked for four years and increased the billings to $2 billion during her tenure. Beers's reputation and success were recognized by *Fortune Magazine* when its first issue to highlight the most powerful women in the United States featured Beers on the cover.

In October 2001, President George W. Bush appointed Beers as the undersecretary of state for public diplomacy and public affairs. Beers's advertising experience was harnessed in order to promote a positive image of the United States abroad. In pursuit of such efforts, Beers considered purchasing airtime on the Arabic-language Al-Jazeera network in order to "pitch" the American message to a potentially hostile audience. Criticisms of Beers's efforts to "market" America to the rest of the world likened the information campaign of the U.S. government to the selling of products such as Uncle Ben's rice, for whom Beers worked for many years. As a result of such criticism, and for health reasons, Beers resigned the post of undersecretary of state for public diplomacy and public affairs in March 2003.

References

Douglas, William. 2001. "Bush Relies on Advertising Experts to Win over Muslims." 25 October. http://old.smh.com.au/news/0110/25/world/world10.html [30 April 2003].

U.S. Department of State. 2003. "Biography—Charlotte Beers." 13 March. http://www.state.gov/r/pa/ei/biog/5319.htm [30 April 2003].

William Bernbach (1911–1982)

By the time of his death from leukemia in October 1982, Bill Bernbach had established himself as an icon in both the world of advertising and mainstream popular culture. Bernbach was chosen by *Advertising Age* as number one on the magazine's twentieth-century honor roll of advertising's 100 most influential people, and he is widely recognized as the most influential creative force in advertising's history, serving as mentor to some of the most renowned figures in the advertising world.

Bernbach grew up in the Bronx in New York during the Great Depression. After receiving a bachelor's degree in English from New York University, Bernbach went to work for Schenley Industries, a distillery that relied heavily on advertising. At Schenley, Bernbach was exposed to the importance of marketing and began conceiving advertising ideas. After serving in World War II, Bernbach worked for Grey Advertising as a copywriter, but hoping for more autonomy and opportunities to be innovative, in 1949 Bernbach founded the firm Doyle Dane Bernbach (DDB) with Ned Doyle and Maxwell Dane. DDB was among the first advertising firms to introduce the idea that television commercials should appeal to the emotions, feelings, and desires of viewers. Bernbach was said to respect the intelligence of the public, and therefore saw advertising as a form of art that could reveal and unleash creative energies as well as deliver an honest message. DDB would eventually work on the advertising campaigns of many famous companies, including Volkswagen, Avis Rental Cars, Mobil, Heinz, American Airlines, and Sony. Bernbach worked for DDB for thirty-three years, and through his innovation and experimentation, he changed the nature and scope of advertising, and therefore consumer culture, in the United States.

References

Advertising Age. 1999. *The Advertising Century.* New York: Crain Communications.

Higgins, Denis, ed. 1986. *The Art of Writing Advertising: Conversations with William Bernbach, Leo Burnett, George Gribbin, David Ogilvy, Rosser Reeves.* New York: McGraw-Hill/Contemporary Books.

Young, James Webb, and William Bernbach. 1988. *Technique for Producing Ideas.* Reissue ed. New York: McGraw-Hill/Contemporary Books.

Aristide Boucicaut (1810–1877)

Aristide Boucicaut was born in the Orne region of France. After leaving for Paris in search of work, Boucicaut became a draper's assistant but lost his job as a result of the economic crisis and revolution that swept through France in 1848. In 1869, along with two acquaintances, the Videau brothers, with whom he had entered a partnership, Boucicaut expanded an existing market stall into a department store, which was named Le Bon Marché and completed in 1887. The store made an immediate impression and was described as "a cathedral of commerce for a congregation of customers" by French novelist and social critic, Émile Zola, in his book *The Ladies Paradise* (1883, 72). Due to favorable economic conditions in France during the 1870s and 1880s, Boucicaut succeeded in "seducing" consumers with a range of products that seemed irresistible compared to the selections of other stores at the time or of other markets in the past. Boucicaut is credited for introducing and refining what are now standard retail practices, including home delivery, a mail-order catalog, clearly marked and fixed prices, regular sales, promises of free merchandise, balloons for children, and discount coupons.

Long before the passage of welfare legislation aimed at improving workers' conditions, Boucicaut paid bonuses to his staff and provided a pension fund, free medical coverage, a staff library, free musical lessons, and the day off on Sundays. Boucicaut's philanthropy extended to those beyond his staff. For example, Boucicaut offered to divert surplus food from Bon Marché to injured soldiers fighting in the Franco-Prussian War, which began in 1870. Upon Boucicaut's death in 1877, Le Bon Marché had become the largest department store in the world.

References

History of Le Bon Marché. 2001. 10 October. http://www.bonmarche.fr/anglais/index.htm [30 April 2003].

Miller, Michael B. 1994. *The Bon Marché: Bourgeois Culture and the Department Store, 1869–1920.* Princeton, NJ: Princeton University Press.

Florence Kelley (1859–1932)

Kelley was a renowned and influential activist during the Progressive Era who spearheaded many efforts to enact labor legislation on behalf of women and children. Kelley was born in Philadelphia and graduated from Cornell University in 1882. Two years later, she married a doctor and socialist labor leader, Lazare Wishnieweski, but left him in 1891 and moved into Hull House, an activist organization in Chicago that was led by Jane Addams. In 1892, Kelley completed a law degree from Northwestern University Law School.

From 1899, Kelley served as director of the National Consumer's League (NCL), an organization committed to industrial reform through consumer pressure. The NCLA attached a white label to products made by employers with fair and safe labor practices while consumers were encouraged to boycott companies and goods that failed to earn the white label designation. In addition to writing several books on the topic of industrial reform—including *Ethical Gains through Legislation* (1905) and *Modern Industry in Relation to the Family, Health, Education, Morality* (1914)—Kelley was instrumental in the movement to abolish child labor, pass legislation for working women, establish the minimum wage, and provide maternal and child health services.

In 1894, Kelley was influential in getting child labor legislation passed in the Illinois state legislature, but in 1995 the law was repealed. Kelley supported many progressive causes, including women's suffrage and civil rights for African Americans, and helped to establish the National Association for the Advancement of Colored People (NAACP) in 1909 and the Women's International League for Peace and Freedom (WILPF) in 1915.

References

Goldmark, Josephine Clara. 1981. *Impatient Crusader.* Chicago: Greenwood.

Kelley, Florence. 1914. *Modern Industry in Relation to the Family, Health, Education, Morality.* New York: Longman.

Saller, Carol, and Ken Green. 1997. *Florence Kelley (On My Own Biographies).* Minneapolis, MN: Carolrhoda Books.

Sklar, Katherine Kish. 1986. *The Autobiography of Florence Kelley: Notes of Sixty Years.* Chicago: Charles H. Kerr.

———. 1997. *Florence Kelley and the Nation's Work.* New Haven, CT: Yale University Press.

John Maynard Keynes (1883–1946)

Keynes is among the most important figures in the history of economics. Born in Sussex, England, John Maynard Keynes was educated in Eton College and King's College at the University of Cambridge. After studying mathematics at Cambridge, Keynes took the civil service examinations and was placed in the India office. In 1909, Keynes returned to Cambridge to teach economics, but by 1915, Keynes was working for the British treasury. Keynes resigned from the treasury, however, in 1919 over his dismay over what he saw as the unfair and unfeasible reparations demands placed on Germany. In the 1930s, a period of economic depression in the West, Keynes wrote *The General Theory of Employment, Interest and Money* (1936), a book that would revolutionize the field of economics and greatly shape postwar public policy in Western capitalist countries.

The ideas expressed in *The General Theory of Employment, Interest and Money*, which gave rise to what became known collectively as "Keynesian economics," centered on the central role played by the state in combating unemployment and inflation through economic stimulation and the management of aggregate demand. Using the Great Depression as his prime example, Keynes argued that the unregulated markets promoted in the laissez-faire approach to economics failed to secure employment in the absence of some government regulation. Neoclassical economic policies that advocated nonintervention were therefore discredited, leading to a paradigmatic change in the way governments dealt with domestic spending and macroeconomic financial policy. In his final years, Keynes remained less active due to failing health, but nonetheless helped to set up the International Monetary Fund (IMF) and provide the rationale for such policies as compulsory savings and rationing to prevent price inflation.

References

Blaung, Mark. 1990. *John Maynard Keynes: Life, Ideas, Legacy.* London: Palgrave Macmillan.

"Keynes, John Maynard, 1st Baron Keynes of Tilton." 2003. *Microsoft Encarta Online Encyclopedia.* http://encarta.msn.com/encnet/refpages/RefArticle.aspx?refid=761569910 [30 April 2003].

Skidelsky, Robert. 1995. *John Maynard Keynes: The Economist as Savior 1920–1937: A Biography.* New York: Penguin.

Ray Kroc (1902–1984)

Ray Kroc was the founder of McDonald's Corporation, the world's largest fast food restaurant chain. In the early 1950s, Kroc sold milk shake machines to restaurants, one of which was a burger stand owned in San Bernardino by two brothers, Dick and Maurice "Mac" McDonald. Due to a growing demand among customers of the McDonald's for milk shakes, Kroc suggested that the brothers open more restaurants. In 1955, Kroc created the McDonald's Corporation and opened the first McDonald's franchise in Des Plaines, Illinois. After six years of operation, Kroc paid $2.7 million to buy out the McDonald brothers. In the years that followed, McDonald's grew rapidly, partly as a result of Kroc's active involvement in company management and insistence on standardization in both food preparation and the training of employees, the latter of which is done at "Hamburger University" in Elk Grove, Illinois. By 1963, 500 McDonald's restaurants had opened, and in 1967 McDonald's expanded outside the continental United States into Canada and Puerto Rico.

With more than 24,500 McDonald's locations in 115 countries, McDonald's remains a very visible symbol of Western fast food and has become large enough to influence the prices of certain commodities, such as beef and potatoes. Due to its size and its social influence—for example, see the discussion of McDonaldization in chapter 3—McDonald's has come under increasing criticism. Critics of McDonald's claim that the fast food chain has contributed to various global problems, including logging in rain forests to make room for beef cattle, encouraging obesity, and using child labor to make the toys that come with Happy Meals.

References

Kincheloe, Joe L. 2002. *The Sign of the Burger: McDonald's and the Culture of Power (Labor in Crisis)*. Philadelphia: Temple University Press.

Kroc, Ray, and Robert Anderson. 1990. *Grinding It Out: The Making of McDonald's*. New York: St. Martin's Press.

Love, John F. 1995. *McDonald's: Behind the Arches*. Chicago: Bantam.

Ralph Nader (1934–)

Born in Winsted, Connecticut, to Lebanese immigrants, Ralph Nader studied government and economics at the Woodrow Wilson School of International Affairs at Princeton University. After graduating from Princeton in 1955, Nader enrolled in Harvard University's law school and practiced law for several years following his graduation. Nader's book *Unsafe at Any Speed* (1965; revised in 1972) uncovered some of the more questionable manufacturing and design practices of the automobile industry and was influential in encouraging lawmakers to pass the National Traffic and Motor Vehicle Safety Act of 1966. Bringing together lawyers, students, and experts on consumer rights into teams known as Nader's Raiders, Nader has sought to expose the unethical or illegal practices of large corporations. Nader is acknowledged as a key figure in the establishment of a consumers' rights movement, and over the years uncovered information that would lead to the creation of several important agencies, including the Environmental Protection Agency (EPA), the Occupational Safety and Health Administration (OSHA), and the Consumer Product Safety Commission (CPSC). (See chapter 7 for more information on these organizations.) Nader also founded a number of consumers' rights organizations such as Public Citizen, Essential Information, and the Center for Auto Safety (see chapter 7 for more information on the Center for Auto Safety and Public Citizen, and chapter 8 for more information on Essential Information). In recent years, Nader has served as the Green Party's presidential candidate in 1996 and 2000.

References

Bollier, David. 1991. *Citizen Action and Other Big Ideas: A History of Ralph Nader and the Modern Consumer Movement.* Washington, DC: Center for Study of Responsive Law.

———. 2002. "The Nader Page." 7 February. http://www.nader.org/history_bollier.html [30 April 2003].

Mayer, Robert M. 1989. *The Consumer Movement: Guardians of the Marketplace.* Boston: Twayne.

Nader, Ralph. 1991. *Unsafe at Any Speed: The Designed-In Dangers of the American Automobile.* New York: Knightsbridge.

Vance Packard (1914–1996)

Sociologist Vance Packard earned a national reputation in 1957 with the publication of *The Hidden Persuaders,* an investigation into the U.S. advertising industry. In his book, Packard exposed the psychological tactics used by advertisers to manipulate consumers into desiring unnecessary goods. Packard argued that hidden symbols were being employed by advertisers to tap into the consciousness of potential consumers, and he identified several techniques used by advertisers then, and used extensively today, including especially the use of subliminal messages in text and voice and the appeal to the anxieties, fears, aspirations, and fantasies of consumers. It was hoped that exposure of these techniques, which Packard considered antihumanistic and regressive, would lead to a public outcry and a greater discussion and scrutiny of the manipulative practices of the advertising industry. *The Hidden Persuaders* sold over a million copies, topping the nonfiction best-seller list in the United States for six weeks. Packard went on to publish several more books, including *The Status Seekers* (1959), *The Waste Makers* (1960), *The Naked Society* (1964), *A Nation of Strangers* (1972), and *The People Shapers* (1977).

References

Horowitz, Daniel. 1994. *Vance Packard and American Social Criticism.* Chapel Hill: University of North Carolina Press.

Rothenberg, Randall. 1997. "How Powerful Is Advertising?" *The Atlantic.* http://www.theatlantic.com/issues/97jun/advert.htm [30 April 2003].

Queen Elizabeth I (1533–1603)

With her ostentatious style and love of embroidery and decoration, Queen Elizabeth I made a lasting contribution to the world of fashion. Some believe that her craving for flamboyant dresses stemmed not only from a certain amount of vanity, but also from a desire to use dress as a means of conveying political strength, nobility, and prestige. During this time, fancy clothing took time to make and was very expensive because items were often altered according to changing fashions and tastes. For example, parts of garments were often replaced or altered, older items had to be torn apart to provide fabric for other wardrobe pieces, and accessories were recycled from one item to the next. The queen also relied on items from the royal wardrobe to pay members of her royal entourage, including valets and ladies-in-waiting. However, despite the ostentatious and glamorous nature of the queen's wardrobe, she spent only one-fifth of the amount spent by her successor, King James, on clothing.

References

Erickson, Carolly. 1997. *The First Elizabeth.* London: St. Martin's Press.

Lasky, Kathryn. 1999. *Elizabeth I: Red Rose of the House of Tudor, England, 1544 (The Royal Diaries).* London: Scholastic Trade.

Leed, Drea. 2002. "Queen Elizabeth's Influence on Elizabethan Fashion." 10 June. http://costume.dm.net/influence.html [30 April 2003].

Tierney, Tom. 2002. *Queen Elizabeth I: Paper Doll.* Dover, UK: Dover Publications.

Thorstein Veblen (1857–1929)

Thorstein Veblen was the sixth of twelve children born to Norwegian parents in rural Wisconsin. He studied at Johns Hopkins University and then at Yale where he obtained his Ph.D. in 1884. In

1892, he became a fellow of Cornell University and was also hired to teach at the University of Chicago. An economist and sociologist, Veblen became famous for popularizing the term "conspicuous consumption" to signal the squandering of resources by the wealthy. In his most famous work, *The Theory of the Leisure Class* (1899), Veblen divided society into a "predator" or "leisure" class, which owns business enterprises, and an "industrious" class, which produces goods. In the book, Veblen criticized business owners for what he considered their "pecuniary" values, and he labeled the leisure class parasitic and harmful to the economy.

Despite the fame that came with the publication of *The Theory of the Leisure Class,* Veblen's tenure at Chicago from 1892 to 1906, and subsequently at Stanford University from 1906 to 1909, was limited due to his womanizing, making it difficult for Veblen to find another academic position. However, a colleague and friend who was the head of the Department of Economics at the University of Missouri helped Veblen to obtain a position there in 1911. In Missouri, Veblen published another of his best-known books, *The Instinct of Workmanship and the State of the Industrial Arts* (1914). Veblen left academia in 1917 and moved to Washington, D.C., where he worked for the U.S. Food Administration for a short time before working as the editor of a magazine. However, he soon made connections at the New School for Social Research, where he took an academic position in 1919. Though he was quite generously remunerated there, his lack of financial acumen and a series of economic mishaps meant a very modest life for Veblen from the time he retired from the New School in 1926 until his death in August 1929.

References

Riesman, David. 1995. *Thorstein Veblen*. Chicago: Transaction Press.

Ritzer, George, and Douglas Goodman. 2003. *Classical Sociological Theory,* 4th ed. New York: McGraw-Hill.

Tilman, Rick. 2003. *The Legacy of Thorstein Veblen*. Chicago: Edward Elgar Publishers.

Aaron Montgomery Ward (1843–1913)

Born on 17 February 1843 in Chatham, New Jersey, Aaron Montgomery Ward was apprenticed to a trade when he was fourteen, marking the beginning of a long career in retailing. Based on the comments of country proprietors and rural residents who complained that the comforts of the city were often overpriced, of poor quality, and difficult to purchase, Ward began to buy goods at low prices and then allowed individuals to send orders by mail and receive their purchases at their nearest railroad station. In 1872, Ward rented a small shipping room and began to publish a general merchandise mail-order catalog that listed just over 160 products. Retailers in rural parts of the country did not appreciate their business being cut, or their unfairness of their practices being exposed, and Ward's catalog was therefore burned in public. Nevertheless, the Wish Book, as Ward's catalog became known, was popular with consumers around the country. Due to this popularity, Ward's catalog was mimicked by, among others, Richard W. Sears and Alvah C. Roebuck, leading in turn to more imitation and eventually to the current importance of the mass-distribution mail-order industry in the U.S. retail economy. Along with the catalog, in 1975 Ward introduced the now ubiquitous phrase "satisfaction guaranteed."

In addition to heralding the catalog innovation, which greatly facilitated consumption within the home, Ward was also an early environmental advocate. After moving to Chicago in 1890, Ward filed four lawsuits in order to protect, restore, and clean up the lakefront of Chicago. As Ward commented, "Here is a park frontage on the lake, comparing favorably with the Bay of Naples, which the city officials would crowd with buildings, transforming the breathing spot for the poor into a show ground for the educated rich" (Baker 1956, 82). Ward fought city and park officials for two decades, using his own wealth to improve the waterfront area of Chicago. When Ward died in December 1913, his wife bequeathed a significant portion of his estate to Northwestern University.

References

Baker, Nina Brown. 1956. *Big Catalogue: The Life of Aaron Montgomery Ward*. New York: Harcourt, Brace.

Herndon, Booton. 1972. *Satisfaction Guaranteed: An Unconventional Report to Today's Consumers*. New York: McGraw-Hill.

Kim, Ann. 2000. *Montgomery Ward: The World's First Mail-Order Business*. April. http://www.lib.niu.edu/ipo/ihy000441.html [30 April 2003].

Latham, Frank B. 1972. *1872–1972: A Century of Serving Consumers—The Story of Montgomery Ward*. New York: McGraw-Hill.

Josiah Wedgwood (1730–1795)

Josiah Wedgwood was born in Burslem, Staffordshire, England, as the thirteenth and youngest son of the potter Thomas Wedgwood. In 1737, upon the death of his father, Josiah joined Churchyard Pottery Work, the family business. After suffering from smallpox two years later, Wedgwood's right leg became infected and had to be amputated. Due to his injuries, Wedgwood was unable to make his own pottery for some time, so instead he conducted research into the craft of pottery. In 1759, Wedgwood established a pottery works in Burslem, and in 1762, Queen Charlotte appointed Wedgwood as the royal supplier of dinnerware. "Queen's Ware," as it came to be known, was successful, enabling Wedgwood to build a village, which he named Etruria, near Stoke-on-Trent, as well as a second factory and housing for his employees.

At his pottery factory at Etruria, Wedgwood introduced the concept of "division of labor," whereby greater output was achieved by assigning the various tasks of the potter, such as mixing, shaping, firing, and glazing, to individual workers who specialized in each particular skill. The economic importance of transportation was also foreseen by Wedgwood, who assisted in the building of the Trent and Mersey Canal in northwest England, which when completed in 1877 allowed Wedgwood to transport supplies such as Cornish clay to his factory in Etruria. Wedgwood marketed his decorated and glazed earthenware not only to members of the European bourgeoisie, but also the working classes, for whom he created creamware. Aside from his reputation as the father of English pottery, Wedgwood was active in political and social reform movements, helping to form the Society for the Abolition of the Slave Trade in 1787.

References

McKendrick, N. 1959. "Josiah Wedgwood: An Eighteenth-Century Entrepreneur in Salesmanship and Marketing Techniques." *Economic History Review* 12, no. 3: 408–433.

Tames, Richard. 2002. *Wedgwood.* Lancashire, UK: Shire.

Wedgwood, C. W. 1978. *Last of the Radicals: The Life of Josiah Clement Wedgwood.* New York: Jonathan Cape.

Helen Rosen Woodward (1882–1960)

Helen Rosen Woodward was born in New York City. Considered the most intelligent of the three children in her family, Woodward was enrolled as a thirteen-year-old in the prestigious Girls' Latin School in Boston. After graduation, Woodward's family returned to New York, where Woodward began working for Merrill and Baker, a book company. At Merrill and Baker, Woodward wrote circular letters advertising the books, and in 1903 Woodward moved to the Ben Hampton advertising agency. While working at Ben Hampton, Woodward decided on a career as a copywriter, but was apprehensive about the way that copywriters were paid by the volume rather than the quality of advertisements. Woodward met her husband, W. E. Woodward, while working for the mail-order publisher J. A. Hill Company. Concerned about unequal pay rates between men and women, Woodward joined the Women's Trade Union League and assisted the organization by writing circulars and providing English lessons to immigrants.

After Woodward became a writer and account executive for the Frank Presbrey Company, a large advertising firm, she utilized the technique of "emotional advertising," which relies on evocative visual images and dramatic text to entice readers into wanting a product. Frustrated about the salary structure of the advertising industry and ambivalent about conveying advertising messages that she herself doubted, Woodward left advertising for good in 1942. Although having worked for much of her life in the field of advertising, Woodward nonetheless remained uncomfortable about the manipulative tactics employed by advertisers. For example, in her book *It's an Art* (1938), Woodward divulged information on the various tricks of the advertising trade, and she eventually wrote a number of consumer-oriented columns for *The Nation* magazine.

References

Brock, Sharon S. 1994. "Helen Rosen Woodward." In E. Applegate, ed., *The Ad Men and Women*, 344–353. Westport, CT: Greenwood Press.

Fox, Stephen. 1984. *The Mirror Makers: A History of American Advertising and Its Creators.* New York: William Morrow.

Hotchkiss, George Burton. 1949. *Advertising Copy.* New York: Harper & Brothers.

Rowsome, Frank, Jr. 1959. *They Laughed When I Sat Down*. New York: McGraw-Hill.

Woodward, Helen Rosen. 1938. *It's an Art*. New York: Harcourt, Brace.

———. 1938. "Pocket Guide: About Coffee." *The Nation* 147, no. 22 (25 December): 565–566.

———. 1938. "Pocket Guide: How to Swing an Election." *The Nation* 147, no. 18 (11 December): 450–451.

———. 1960. *The Lady Persuaders*. New York: Ivan Obolensky.

———. 1985. *Through Many Windows*. New York: Garland.

Events, Trends, and Organizations

Bourgeois Culture

In medieval France, inhabitants of walled towns were known as bourgeois, and the technical definition of bourgeois, according to the Oxford English Dictionary, is "of or pertaining to the French middle classes." During the transition from feudalism to capitalism, merchants and small shop owners formed an emergent bourgeoisie class, and as capitalism grew to become the dominant system of social, economic, and political organization in Western Europe, bourgeois culture became associated with middle-class values and lifestyles. The term bourgeoisie was popularized in the lexicon of social theory when Karl Marx (1818–1883) used the term to denote the class that grew out of the feudal system and eventually enjoyed power in capitalism through its ownership of the means of production. Bourgeois culture includes not only social class, but also a set of words, objects, gestures, and even worldviews. Bourgeois culture is associated with several characteristics, some of which conflict with one another: the exercise of self-control, materialism, the importance of appearance and status, the ritualization of daily routines, and a desire for respectability.

The "fetishism" of commodities—which according to Marx occurs when commodities are treated as fetishistic objects divorced from the relationships and forces that went into creating them—shapes bourgeois culture by making monetary value and the accumulation of commodities the source of meaning and value. Contemporary critics of bourgeois, middle-class culture indicate that, unlike in past eras when spiritual systems of belief were said to guide ethics and morality, ethical questions in bourgeois culture are influenced more by monetary concerns. However, though consumer culture grew out of bourgeois culture, the emphasis in early bourgeois culture on self-restraint, sacrifice, and community complicate the relationship between the birth of bourgeois culture centuries ago and the emergence of a consumer society.

References

"Bourgeois." 2002. In "Glossary of Terms," MIA Encyclopedia of Marxism. 8 June. http://www.marxists.org/glossary/terms/b/o.htm [30 April 2003].

Kocka, Jurgen. 1994. *Bourgeois Society in Nineteenth-Century Europe.* New York: Berg.

Le Wita, Beatrix. 1994. *French Bourgeois Culture.* Cambridge, UK: Cambridge University Press.

Civil Rights Boycotts (1950s and 1960s)

Though calls for racial equality have been voiced by a minority of individuals throughout the history of the United States, the modern U.S. Civil Rights Movement took off only after the 1954 Supreme Court decision in *Brown v. Board of Education.* Since the Civil Rights Movement demanded sweeping legal and cultural changes, mass boycotts organized by civil rights workers—such as the 1955 Montgomery bus boycotts organized in response to the arrest of Rosa Parks for refusing to give up her bus seat to a white passenger—and nonviolent acts of civil disobedience were met head on by a violent counteroffensive mounted by white supremacists in the South. Although the white supremacists' campaign targeted the homes, businesses, and churches of African Americans, and several civil rights leaders were assassinated, the Civil Rights Movement grew in strength and slowly broadened its base of support.

The Reverend Martin Luther King Jr., who emerged as the chief spokesperson of the Civil Rights Movement, led many visible protests, including the 1963 attack on civil rights protesters in Birmingham, Alabama, in which police and their dogs, along with the fire department and their fire hoses, dispersed the crowd of mostly young black demonstrators. Protests such as these produced dramatic images that were beamed across the United States on television, building sympathy and support for the movement. King's historic "I Have a Dream" speech, delivered on 28 August 1963 in Washington, D.C., was especially effective in conveying the purpose and tactics of the movement. Five years later, in April 1968, King was assassinated in Memphis, Tennessee. Despite the violence that accompanied efforts to promote equality and integration, the Civil Rights Movement achieved a great deal in a short amount of time and resulted in several legislative victories, including the Civil Rights Act in 1964, the Voting Rights Act in 1965, and the first implementation of affirmative action policies in the mid-1960s.

References

Hampton, Henry. 1990. *Voices of Freedom: An Oral History of the Civil Rights Movement from the 1950s through the 1980s.* New York: Bantam.

Leventhal, Willy S., ed. 1998. *The Children Coming On: A Retrospective of the Montgomery Bus Boycott.* Montgomery, AL: Black Belt Press.

Diners Club Card (1950)

Though currently a ubiquitous symbol of consumerism and convenience, it was not until 1914 when the very concept of the credit card began. In that year, the most reliable customers of Western Union were given the option of deferring their payments. Even so, the use of an actual plastic card did not begin until 1950, when Frank McNamara of Diners Club issued the first multiuse charge card that could be used in a number of different locations. The idea for the card came after an embarrassing incident where McNamara forgot his wallet and was unable to pay his restaurant bill because he did not have any cash. In 1951, Franklin National Bank in New York was the first bank to give its customers a credit card. By 1952, the Diners Club Card was accepted at thousands of merchants, and the use of charge cards continued to grow rapidly in the following decades, expanding to Canada, Cuba, and France. In 1962, the film *The Man from the Diners Club* starring Danny Kaye was released and soon after, the Ideal Toy Corporation created the Diners Club board game. Currently, 6.5 million merchants in 201 countries accept the Diners Club Card. Since the creation of the Diners Club Card, credit card use in the United States and the rest of the world has skyrocketed, leading to both convenience for retailers and consumers, but also to criticisms of the predatory practices of credit card companies (see annotation for Robert Manning's book in chapter 8 and Credit Card Nation in the "Selected Websites" section of chapter 8).

References

"Credit Card History." 2002. 8 June. http://bankcard.net/hist.htm [30 April 2003].

Diners Club International. 2000. "History of Diners Club, the First Charge Card." http://www.dinersclubnewsroom.com/anniversary.cfm?frame_src=anniversary.cfm [30 April 2003].

Ritzer, George. 1995. *Expressing America.* Thousand Oaks, CA: Pine Forge.

Great Depression (1929–1939)

The Great Depression was, and remains to this day, the worst economic depression ever suffered by the industrialized countries of the world. The depression began in 1929 and lasted until the outbreak of World War II in 1939. The U.S. economy began a downward slide in the early months of 1929, but this slide was precipitated greatly by the stock market collapse that commenced on 24 October 1929. Five days later, on what became known as Black Tuesday (29 October 1929), the New York Stock Exchange lost more value in one day than it had lost ever before, or since, and within hours of opening, the stock market's entire gains from the previous year vanished. This collapse was surprising because certain influential figures, including Yale University economist Irving Fisher and President Herbert Hoover, had assured the public just months and weeks earlier that the national economy was strong and that prosperity would continue unabated.

However, considering the disjuncture between stock values and actual profits that characterized the U.S. stock market for the five years prior to 1929, the crash should not have been completely unexpected. Rising stock market values prior to the crash proceeded despite a drop in merchandise sales and construction, key signals of economic health. After the crash, however, public confidence diminished and stock prices plummeted, reaching their lowest point on 13 November 1929. In the two weeks between Black Tuesday and 13 November, the U.S. economy lost a total of $30 billion. The social impact of the depression was immediate and widespread. One-third of Americans fell below the poverty line, homelessness and unemployment became endemic, high school dropout rates soared, and farmers suffered from the twin hits of drought and collapsing consumer demand. Although images of the Great Depression focus on examples of extreme poverty and desperation, sales of certain commodities such as cigarettes, gasoline, and movie tickets actually rose, indicating a desire to escape the dismal circumstances of everyday life at the time. Other than demonstrating the fickle and vulnerable nature of the stock market, the Great Depression, and the social deprivations that it caused, contributed to the idea that governments should intervene, through social spending, to ensure the welfare of those people most vulnerable to economic swings.

References

Beaud, Michel. 1983. *A History of Capitalism.* New York: Monthly Review Press.

Galbraith, John Kenneth. 1997. *The Great Crash 1929.* San Francisco: Mariner Books.

"Great Depression." 2003. *Encyclopædia Britannica.* http://www.britannica.com/eb/article?eu=38610> [30 April 2003].

Rothbard, Murray N. 2000. *America's Great Depression.* 5th ed. Auburn, AL: Ludwig von Mises Institute.

Schultz, Stanley K. 2003. "The Crash and the Great Depression." 26 February. http://us.history.wisc.edu/hist102/lectures/lecture18.html [30 April 2003].

The Peacock Revolution (1968)

Just as the peacock displays an ostentatious fan of plumage, the "peacock revolution" describes a dramatic change in what was considered acceptable clothing for men. During the 1960s, the mortality rate was in decline, and for the first time in the century, there were more boys than girls in the population. One of the results of such a demographic shift was an increase in pressure on boys and men to woo, attract, and court females. The peacock revolution, a term coined by a former *Esquire* and *Boston Globe* columnist George Frazier, was not only a result of demographic changes, but also, more importantly, reflected changing attitudes toward fashion, sexuality, and masculinity. On London's Carnaby Street, Frazier noticed that the clothing of boys was often more ostentatious than that of girls, with styles featuring suits, shirts, and ties with patterns and bold colors, as well as pointy-toed boots with Chelsea heels. The feminized clothing worn by boys was matched by long, styled hair and tall, lean physiques.

The peacock revolution soon influenced the world of popular music, which in turn solidified even further the emerging fashion tastes of youths. For example, members of bands such as the Rolling Stones and the Who wore hip-hugger pants, bold psychedelic prints, and open silk shirts or vests. Even the Beatles, associated in their early years with a clean-cut image, began sporting paisley scarves, flowered shirts, and striped bell-bottom pants. Carnaby Street tailors and designers, such as John Stephen, made the clothes that would define the peacock revolution and created a unisex dandy look that allowed males to express their own sexuality through flamboyant and spectacular fashion items.

References

Frank, Thomas. 1998. *The Conquest of Cool: Business Culture, Counterculture, and the Rise of Hip Consumerism.* Chicago: University of Chicago Press.

Tortora, Phyllis G., and Keith Eubank. 1998. *Survey of Historic Costume: A History of Western Dress.* 3d ed. New York: Fairchild.

Starbucks

Starbucks, the world's most famous and successful coffee retailer, opened its first store in Seattle's Pike Place Market in 1971. Named after mate Starbuck in *Moby Dick,* the company initially roasted and sold whole coffee beans to individual customers in its retail locations as well as to restaurants and espresso stands through its wholesale division. In 1982, Howard Schultz joined the company as director of retail operations and marketing. Five years later, Schultz bought the company for $3.8 million. From that time, Starbucks began to open "coffee bars" and offer coffee by the cup. Although expensive, high-quality coffee had been slowly growing in popularity for decades, the Starbucks brand name became synonymous with specialty coffees in the 1980s and 1990s. The current success of Starbucks is both a reflection and cause of the growing coffee culture found in the United States and other countries of the world.

With nearly 6,000 stores in twenty-eight countries, Starbucks remains a highly visible symbol of globalization, not to mention an influential "cathedral of consumption" that promotes the efficiency, predictability, and calculability associated with the "rationalization" of consumption (see annotation for George Ritzer's book in chapter 8). As a well-known symbol of corporate power, Western globalization, and consumerism, Starbucks has in recent years become the target of anticorporate protestors, most notably during the 1999 WTO meeting in Seattle, which saw the looting and destruction of the stores of famous multinationals such as Starbucks.

References

Schultz, Howard, and Dori Jones Yang. 1999. *Pour Your Heart into It: How Starbucks Built a Company One Cup at a Time.* Seattle, WA: Hyperion.

Starbucks. 2003. Starbucks' Timeline and History. http://www.starbucks.com/aboutus/timeline.asp [30 April 2003].

Volkswagen Beetle

In 1924, while in prison for treason, Adolf Hitler came up with the idea of state-built special highways (autobahns) and automobiles as a way of solving the high unemployment that plagued Germany between World War I and World War II. The mass-produced car would be called the Volkswagen, or "people's car," and would, as the name suggested, be available to the average German citizen. The issue of autobahns and Volkswagens came up at the very first cabinet meeting of the Nazi regime following their ascension to power in February 1933. In September of the same year, construction began on the autobahns, and in 1935, Dr. Ferdinand Porsche, the grandfather of Volkswagen AG's current chairman, designed the first Beetle prototype. Although Porsche's design for the car was chosen, Hitler specified that the car must have a top speed of sixty-two miles per hour, have an air-cooled engine, achieve forty-two miles per gallon, and have room for exactly two adults and three children. Most importantly, the price of the Volkswagen was fixed at the modern-day equivalent of $115, forcing Porsche to design a rear-engine automobile.

The first Beetle was produced in 1938, and by 1939, the factory was the largest motor factory in Europe, featuring an annual production capacity of 150,000 cars. By the end of World War II, the Volkswagen factory was almost completely destroyed by Allied bombing. Immediately following the war, the Allies rebuilt the factory and began placing orders for the car; the British army, for example, ordered 20,000 Volkswagens. In 1973, the production of Beetles surpassed 16.5 million, making it the best-selling car in the entire world. The next year, however, Volkswagen announced that it had recorded its first loss in history, a total that amounted to $200 million. In 1980, German production of the Volkswagens ceased, but production elsewhere continued. In the spring of 1998, Volkswagen released the much-anticipated New Beetle amidst great fanfare and publicity. Largely the result of a clever marketing campaign, initial demand for the New Beetle outstripped supply, and to this day demand remains high in the North American market.

References

"A Brief History of the Beetle." 2002. http://www.vwbeetle.org/briefhistory.php [30 April 2003].

Delorenzo, Matt. 1999. *The New Beetle (Enthusiast Color Series)*. Osceola, WI: Motorbooks International.

Frank, Thomas. 1998. *The Conquest of Cool: Business Culture, Counterculture, and the Rise of Hip Consumerism*. Chicago: University of Chicago Press.

Motavalli, Jim. 2002. "Hitler's 'People's Car': Did Adolf Really 'Design' the Beetle?" *Eugene Weekly* (21 November): C2.

Nelson, Walter Henry. 1998. *Small Wonder: The Amazing Story of the Volkswagen*. Cambridge, MA: Bentley.

Parkinson, Simon. 1996. *Volkswagen Beetle: The Rise from the Ashes of War*. Osceola, WI: Motorbooks International.

Shuler, Terry. 1997. *Volkswagen, Then, Now and Forever*. Munich: Beeman Jorgensen.

World Trade Organization (WTO)

Established on 1 January 1995 following the conclusion of the Uruguay Round negotiations (1986–1994), the World Trade Organization (WTO) defines itself as an international agency that encourages trade between member nations, administers global trade agreements, and resolves disputes when they arise. The WTO agreements, which are negotiated and then ratified in the parliaments or congresses of member nations, aim to remove barriers to free trade. Prior to the creation of the WTO, the General Agreement of Tariffs and Trade (GATT) served, since 1947, as the forum in which states discussed trade and negotiated to reduce customs, tariffs, and other barriers to trade. After 1995, the GATT became the key set of rules governing the WTO and its member states. The WTO resolves trade disputes between member states by adjudicating in closed tribunals and deciding on appropriate punitive measures against countries that violate the WTO agreements. Aside from establishing rules related to traditional manufactured goods, the WTO also enforces rules related to services such as insurance, financial services, and intellectual property. The WTO's intellectual property agreement regulates trade and investment related to copyrights, patents, trademarks, and geographical names used to identify products, integrated circuit layout designs, industrial designs, and undisclosed information such as trade secrets. By 2003, 145 countries had joined the WTO, with 30 more in the process of negotiating entry.

Critics of the WTO worry about the power of the WTO, an unelected and unaccountable organization that, in pursuit of free trade at any cost, nullifies laws passed by democratically elected governments. For instance, governments that pass laws aimed at ensuring ethical labor standards or environmentally friendly manufacturing practices can be found guilty, according to WTO rules, of imposing nontariff barriers to trade. Critics accuse the WTO of serving the interests of large multinational corporations and wealthy, industrialized countries. In 1999, large and violent demonstrations erupted in Seattle during the annual WTO meeting, sparking an ongoing global movement against what is termed "corporate globalization."

References

Krueger, Anne O., and Aturapane Chonira, eds. 1998. *The WTO as an International Organization*. Chicago: University of Chicago Press.

Schott, Jeffrey J., C. Fred Bergsten, and Renato Ruggiero. 2000. *The WTO after Seattle*. Chicago: Institute for International Economics.

Wallach, Lori, and Michelle Sforza. 1999. *Whose Trade Organization? Corporate Globalization and the Erosion of Democracy*. Washington, DC: Public Citizen.

World Trade Organization website. http://www.wto.org/index.htm.

7

Organizations, Associations, and Government and International Agencies

Selected Organizations Based in the United States

ACNielsen
770 Broadway
New York, NY 10003
Telephone: (646) 654-5000
Fax: (646) 654-5002
Website: http://www.acnielsen.com/site/about/

ACNielsen is a marketing information company. With 21,000 employees in more than 100 countries, ACNielsen provides market research, information, analysis, and insights on the consumer-product and service industries.

American Council on Consumer Interests (ACCI)
415 South Duff, Suite C
Ames, IA 50010-6600
Telephone: (515) 956-4666
Fax: (515) 233-3101

E-mail: info@consumerinterests.org
Website: http://www.consumerinterests.org/

Since 1953, the ACCI has been a membership organization for academics and other professionals involved in consumer and family economics. The ACCI headquarters office is in Ames, Iowa. The mission of ACCI is to provide a forum for the exchange of information about consumer issues and family economics to improve the well-being of individuals, households, and families.

Association for Consumer Research (ACR)
James Muncy, executive director
P.O. Box 2310
Valdosta, GA 31604
Telephone: (229) 244-2380
Fax: (229) 244-7881
E-mail: acr@acrweb.org
Website: http://www.acrweb.org/

The ACR is an organization comprised primarily of academic researchers in the field of consumer behavior.

Aveda
4000 Pheasant Ridge Drive
Blaine, MN 55449
Telephone: (866) 823-1425 (North America only)
Website: http://www.aveda.com/

Founded by Austrian Horst Rechelbacher in 1978, Aveda is a company specializing in an herbal-based product range as well as a nationwide network of salons offering massage therapy and other beauty treatments. The Aveda website provides company history, guiding principles, and press releases.

Better Business Bureau (BBB)
The Council of Better Business Bureaus
4200 Wilson Boulevard, Suite 800
Arlington, VA 22203-1838
Telephone: (703) 276-0100
Fax: (703) 525-8277
Website: http://www.bbb.org/

The BBB system in the United States extends to over 98 percent of the nation, including Hawaii, Alaska, and Puerto Rico. It also has a partner BBB system that serves much of Canada. In total, 145 BBBs serve nearly 24 million consumers and businesses each year. Founded in 1912, the BBB claims that many marketplace problems can be solved fairly through the use of voluntary self-regulation and consumer education. The BBB's core services include business reliability reports; dispute resolution; truth-in-advertising, consumer and business education; and charity review.

Bureau of Consumer Protection—Federal Trade Commission (FTC)
Consumer Response Center
Federal Trade Commission
600 Pennsylvania Avenue NW
Washington, DC 20580
Telephone: (202) 326-2222
Website: http://www.ftc.gov/ftc/consumer.htm

The Bureau of Consumer Protection's mandate is to protect consumers against unfair, deceptive, or fraudulent practices. The bureau enforces a variety of consumer-protection laws enacted by Congress, as well as trade-regulation rules issued by the FTC. Its actions include individual company and industry-wide investigations, administrative and federal court litigation, rule-making proceedings, and consumer and business education. In addition, the bureau contributes to the FTC's ongoing efforts to inform Congress and other government entities of the impact that proposed actions could have on consumers.

Center for Auto Safety (CAS)
1825 Connecticut Avenue NW, Suite 330
Washington, DC 20009-5708
Telephone: (202) 328-7700
Website: http://www.autosafety.org/

The CAS provides information on common problems and advice on how to resolve them for most models of vehicles on the road. It also produces reports on fuel efficiency and issues pertaining to vehicle safety.

Center for Science in the Public Interest (CSPI)
1875 Connecticut Avenue NW, Suite 300
Washington, DC 20009
Telephone: (202) 332-9110

Fax: (202) 265-4954
E-mail: cspi@cspinet.org
Website: http://www.cspinet.org/

The CSPI is a nonprofit education and advocacy organization that focuses on improving the safety and nutritional quality of the food supply and on reducing the damage caused by alcoholic beverages. The CSPI seeks to promote health through educating the public about nutrition and alcohol. It also represents citizens' interests before legislative, regulatory, and judicial bodies, while working to ensure that advances in science are used for the public good. The CSPI is supported by more than 800,000 member-subscribers to its *Nutrition Action Healthletter*, as well as by foundation grants and sales of educational materials.

The Center for Study of Responsive Law (CSRL)
P.O. Box 19367
Washington, DC 20036
Fax: (202) 234-5176
E-mail: csrl@CSRL.org
Website: http://www.csrl.org/index.html

The CSRL is a nonprofit organization founded by Ralph Nader that supports and conducts a wide variety of research and educational projects that encourage greater awareness of the needs of the citizen-consumer among political, economic, and social institutions of the United States. The center publishes reports on a number of public-interest issues.

Consumer Action
717 Market Street, Suite 310
San Francisco, CA 94103-2109
Telephone: (415) 777-9635
E-mail: editor@consumer-action.org
Website: http://www.consumer-action.org/

Consumer Action is a nonprofit, membership-based organization that was founded in San Francisco in 1971. Since then, Consumer Action has referred consumers to complaint-handling agencies through a free hot line; published educational materials in Chinese, English, Korean, Spanish, Vietnamese, and other languages; advocated for consumers in the media and before lawmakers; and compared prices on credit cards, bank accounts, and long-distance services.

Consumer Federation of America (CFA)
1424 16th Street NW, Suite 604
Washington, DC 20036
Telephone: (202) 387-6121
E-mail: ajaeger@consumerfed.org
Website: http://www.consumerfed.org/backpage/about.html

The CFA is an advocacy organization that works to advance pro-consumer policy on a variety of issues before Congress, the White House, federal and state regulatory agencies, and the courts. Its staff works with public officials to promote beneficial policies, to oppose harmful policies, and to ensure a balanced debate on important issues in which consumers have a stake.

Consumer Product Safety Commission (CPSC)
4330 East-West Highway
Bethesda, MD 20814-4408
Telephone: (301) 504-7908
E-mail: info@cpsc.gov
Website: http://www.cpsc.gov/

The CPSC is an independent federal regulatory agency, created in 1972 by Congress under the Consumer Product Safety Act, which works to save lives and keep families safe by reducing the risk of injuries and deaths associated with consumer products.

Consumer Union (CU)
101 Truman Avenue
Yonkers, NY 10703
Telephone: (914) 378-2455
Fax: (914) 378-2928
Website: http://www.consumerreports.org/

Since 1936, the CU's mission has been to test products, inform the public, and protect consumers. It claims to provide unbiased advice about products and services, personal finance, health and nutrition, and other consumer concerns. Its income is derived solely from the sale of *Consumer Reports* (in print and on-line) and other services, as well as from nonrestrictive, noncommercial contributions, grants, and fees. The CU is governed by a board of eighteen directors, who are elected by CU members and meet three times a year. CU's president, James Guest, oversees a staff of more than 450. The CU operates three advocacy offices—in Washington, D.C.; Austin, Texas; and San Francisco, California—that work on consumers' behalf on such issues as health care, food safety, financial services, and product safety. The CU testifies before federal and state legislative and regulatory bodies, petitions government agencies, and files lawsuits on behalf of consumers. The Consumer Policy Institute, at the CU's Yonkers, New York, headquarters, conducts research and education projects on such issues as biotechnology, toxic air pollution, community right-to-know laws, and food safety.

The Cygnus Group
505 Pleasant Street, Suite 404
Saint Joseph, MI 49085
Telephone: (269) 982-7860
Fax: (269) 982-7861
Website: http://cygnus-group.com/

The Cygnus Group website is designed to provide individuals and organizations with information regarding the most efficient and effective ways to reduce waste and conserve resources. This site contains back copies of the bimonthly newsletter *Useless Stuff (ULS) Report* and information on packaging, including a new study on packaging efficiency and other documents pertaining to packaging and waste reduction. This site also provides numerous pathways and resources leading to databases on related subjects as well as Environmental Protection Agency (EPA) data on waste prevention.

Environmental Protection Agency (EPA)
Ariel Rios Building
1200 Pennsylvania Avenue NW
Mail Code 3213A
Washington, DC 20460
Telephone: (202) 260-2090
Website: http://www.epa.gov/

The EPA's mission is to protect human health and to safeguard the natural environment. Established in 1970, the EPA has 18,000 employees in headquarters program offices and in ten regional offices and seventeen labs across the country. The EPA employs engineers, scientists, and environmental protection specialists, as well as a large number of legal, public affairs, financial, and computer specialists. The EPA is led by an administrator who is appointed by the president of the United States.

Equality Project
185 East 85th Street, Suite 25A
New York, NY 10028-2147
Telephone: (212) 870-2296
Website: http://www.equalityproject.org/index.htm

The Equality Project was formed in 1992 to monitor the policies of major corporations that deal with sexual orientation in the workplace and to pressure companies to implement the policies expressed in the Equality Principles on Sexual Orientation. The Equality Principles are currently being updated to include transgender workplace concerns. Members include financial professionals, investors, writers, academics, lawyers, and artists.

Food and Drug Administration (FDA)
5600 Fishers Lane
Rockville, MD 20857
Telephone: 1-888-INFO-FDA (1-888-463-6332)
Website: http://www.fda.gov/

The FDA's mission is to promote and protect the public health by helping safe and effective products reach the market in a timely way and by monitoring products for continued safety after they are in use. Its work is a blending of law and science aimed at protecting consumers.

Friends of the Earth
1025 Vermont Avenue NW, Suite 300
Washington, DC 20005
Telephone: (877) 843-8687
Fax: (202) 783-0444
E-mail: foe@foe.org
Website: http://www.foe.org/

Founded in San Francisco in 1969 by David Brower, Friends of the Earth is the U.S. voice of an international network of grassroots groups in seventy countries. Its members were the founders of what is now the world's largest federation of environmental groups, Friends of the Earth International.

Make Trade Fair
Oxfam America
1112 16th Street NW, Suite 600
Washington, DC 20036

Telephone: (202) 496-1306
Fax: (202) 496-1190
E-mail: vrateau@oxfamamerica.org
Website: http://www.maketradefair.com/

The Fair Trade movement is a response to the problems facing commodity producers. It gives consumers an opportunity to use their purchasing power to assist the poor. The Make Trade Fair campaign aims to change the unfair rules of world trade so that they work for small-scale producers as well as rich multinationals. In the past decade, the Fair Trade movement has grown rapidly, as consumer awareness of the treatment of producers in poor countries has increased. More and more retailers are stocking Fair Trade goods, and the number of products offered continues to grow as demand increases.

National Association of Consumer Advocates (NACA)
1730 Rhode Island NW, Suite 805
Washington, DC 20036
Telephone: (202) 452-1989
Fax: (202) 452-0099
E-mail: info@naca.net
Website: http://www.naca.net/

The NACA is a nationwide association of more than 800 attorneys and consumer advocates with experience curbing abusive and predatory business practices and promoting justice for consumers.

National Consumer Law Center (NCLC)
1629 K Street NW, Suite 600
Washington, DC 20006
Telephone: (202) 986-6060
Fax: (202) 463-9462
E-mail: nclc@consumerlaw.org
Website: http://www.consumerlaw.org/

The NCLC is the nation's consumer-law expert resource, helping consumers, their advocates, and public-policy makers use consumer laws on behalf of low-income and elderly Americans seeking economic justice.

National Consumers League
1701 K Street NW, Suite 1200
Washington, DC 20006

Telephone: (202) 835-3323
Fax: (202) 835-0747
E-mail: info@nclnet.org
Website: http://www.natlconsumersleague.org/programs.htm

The National Consumers League participates in more than fifty coalitions, advisory committees, and boards. The league provides a consumer's perspective on concerns including child labor, privacy on the Internet, food safety, and medication information. The league operates the National Fraud Information Center, a toll-free hot line that offers help and support to victims of telemarketing and Internet fraud. It also monitors cyberspace through Internet Fraud Watch to help consumers distinguish between legitimate and fraudulent promotions in cyberspace and route reports of suspected fraud to the appropriate law enforcement agencies.

New Internationalist
P.O. Box 1143
Lewiston, NY 14092
Telephone: (905) 946-0407
Fax: (905) 946-0410
E-mail: magazines@indas.on.ca
Website: http://www.newint.org/

The New Internationalist is a communications cooperative based in Oxford, with editorial and sales offices in Toronto, Canada; Adelaide, Australia; Christchurch, New Zealand; and Lewiston, United States. It reports on issues of world poverty and inequality, focuses attention on the unjust relationship between the powerful and the powerless in both rich and poor nations, and debates and campaigns for radical changes.

North American Free Trade Agreement (NAFTA) Secretariat
NAFTA Secretariat, U.S. Section
14th Street and Constitution Avenue NW, Room 2061
Washington, DC 20230
Telephone: (202) 482-5438
Fax: (202) 482-0148
E-mail: Webmaster@nafta-sec-alena.org
Website: http://www.nafta-sec-alena.org/english/index.htm

The NAFTA Secretariat website contains all documents pertaining to this trade agreement between the United States, Canada, and Mexico.

Occupational Safety and Health Administration (OHSA), U.S. Department of Labor

U.S. Department of Labor Occupational Safety and Health Administration
200 Constitution Avenue
Washington, DC 20210
Telephone: 1-800-321-OSHA (6742)
Website: http://www.osha-slc.gov/as/opa/oshafacts.html

The OSHA's mission is to ensure safe and healthful workplaces in America. Since the agency was created in 1971, workplace fatalities have been cut in half and occupational injury and illness rates have declined 40 percent.

Public Citizen

1600 20th Street NW
Washington, DC 20009
Telephone: (202) 588-1000
E-mail: slittle@citizen.org
Website: http://www.citizen.org/

Public Citizen is a national, nonprofit consumer advocacy organization founded by Ralph Nader in 1971 to represent consumer interests in Congress, the executive branch, and the courts. It fights for openness and democratic accountability in government, as well as for the following rights: the ability of consumers to seek redress in the courts; clean, safe, and sustainable energy sources; social and economic justice in trade policies; strong health, safety, and environmental protections; and safe, effective, and affordable prescription drugs and health care.

Purdue University, Consumer Sciences and Retailing

812 West State Street
West Lafayette, IN 47907-2060
Telephone: (765) 494-8292
Fax: (765) 494-0869
E-mail: csr@cfs.purdue.edu
Website: http://www.cfs.purdue.edu/conscirt/

This is an academic institution with programs in apparel retailing and planning, retail management, consumer behavior, textile science, and consumer economics.

Slow Food
434 Broadway, 7th floor
New York, NY 10013
Telephone: (212) 965-5640
Fax: (212) 226-0672
E-mail: info@slowfoodusa.org
Website: http://www.slowfood.com

Slow Food is an international movement that was founded in Paris in 1989. Its head offices are in Bra, in the Piedmont in northern Italy. Other offices have been opened in Switzerland (1995), Germany (1998), and New York (2000). Slow Food boasts 65,000 members in 45 countries, organized into 560 local groups. Slow Food's manifesto lays out the principles of a movement for the protection of the "right to taste." By this the movement means to convince people that in order to fully appreciate food, it should be produced, prepared, and eaten in an unhurried, relaxed manner.

Starbucks
Starbucks Customer Relations
P.O. Box 3717
Seattle, WA 98124-3717
Telephone: (206) 447-1575
Website: http://www.starbucks.com/aboutus/timeline.asp

This is the official website of Starbucks, the world's most famous coffee company. The website includes the company's mission statement, time line, and history of the company's development, as well as press releases.

University of Utah, Family and Consumer Studies (FCS)
225 South 1400 East
Alfred Emery Building 228
University of Utah
Salt Lake City, UT 84112
Telephone: (801) 581-6521
Fax: (801) 581-5156
Website: http://www.fcs.utah.edu/

FCS is an interdisciplinary department where faculty and students examine how the social, economic, political, and physical environments affect families, individuals, and consumers. The teaching, research, and service performed in the department focuses on how the welfare of individuals, and the families in which they live, are affected by external forces and internal forces. As such, the department emphasizes applied social science research and teaching with a strong public-policy orientation. The department offers two undergraduate majors: Consumer and Community Studies and Human Development and Family Studies.

University of Wisconsin-Madison, Consumer Science Program
1300 Linden Drive
Madison WI 53706
Telephone: (608) 263-5675
Fax: (608) 265-6048
E-mail: akskram@facstaff.wisc.edu
Website: http://www.sohe.wisc.edu/depts/cs/csmaj.html

The Consumer Science Program at the University of Wisconsin-Madison offers undergraduate, masters, and doctoral level education in consumer science and retailing. The program is interdisciplinary and integrative, focusing on consumers as individuals and household members, and on their interactions with the marketplace and the public sector. The Consumer Science Department offers an interdisciplinary approach to consumer economics, consumer behavior, family resource management, retailing, public-policy issues, and historical consumer issues. The Consumer Science major meets the needs of students interested in qualifying for employment or graduate study in business, economics, finance, consumer law, specialized areas of family and consumer finance, or family economics.

U.S. Bureau of Labor Statistics (BLS)
Postal Square Building
2 Massachusetts Avenue NE
Washington, DC 20212-0001
Telephone: (202) 691-5200
Fax: (202) 691-6325
E-mail: blsdata_staff@bls.gov
Website: http://stats.bls.gov/

The BLS is the principal fact-finding agency for the federal government in the broad field of labor economics and statistics. The BLS is an independent national statistical agency that collects, processes, analyzes, and disseminates statistical data to the American public, the U.S. Congress, other federal agencies, state and local governments, business, and labor. The BLS also serves as a statistical resource to the Department of Labor.

U.S. Energy Information Administration (EIA)
U.S. Department of Energy
1000 Independence Avenue SW
Washington, DC 20585
Telephone: (202) 586-8800
E-mail: infoctr@eia.doe.gov
Website: http://www.eia.doe.gov/

The EIA provides monthly energy statistics from 1992 to the present, a summary of greenhouse gas statistics for the United States, energy models, articles, U.S. and international energy statistics, and "World Energy," a database containing statistics on energy consumption and production for all countries of the world.

U.S. International Trade Commission
500 E Street SW
Washington, DC 20436
Telephone: (202) 205-2000
E-mail: webmaster@usitc.gov
Website: http://www.usitc.gov/default.htm

The U.S. International Trade Commission is an independent, nonpartisan, quasi-judicial federal agency that provides trade expertise to both the legislative and executive branches of government, determines the impact of imports on U.S. industries, and directs actions against certain unfair trade practices, such as patent, trademark, and copyright infringements.

Selected Organizations Based Abroad

Association of European Consumers (AEC)
Rue du Commerce, 70-72
B-1040 Brussels, Belgium
Telephone: 32 2 545 9074
Fax: 32 2 545 9076
E-mail: aec@belgacom.net
Website: http://www.consumer-aec.org

The AEC is a European organization that brings together thirty-three consumer organizations from seventeen different countries from the European Union (EU) and Central and Eastern Europe. The AEC and its members aim to work together in the interest of strengthening consumer influence in society, particularly on issues related to social and environmental awareness.

Benetton
Villa Minelli
31050 Ponzano
Treviso, Italy
Telephone: 0039 0422 519036
Fax: 0039 0422 519930
Website: http://www.benetton.com/colors/

The Benetton Group, an Italian clothing company, has stores in 120 countries. It produces 100 million garments per year and generates an annual turnover of 2 billion Euros of retail sales. Featuring an extensive archive of articles, the Benetton website features many links that serve to spark debates about consumption.

Center for Science in the Public Interest, Canada
1 Nicholas Street, Suite 412
Ottawa, Ontario K1N 7B7
Telephone: (613) 565-2140
Fax: (613) 565-6520
E-mail (for policy issues): jefferyb@istar.ca
Website: http://www.cspinet.org/canada/

The Canadian branch of Center for Science in the Public Interest (see entry above in "Selected Organizations Based in the United States" section) supports over 135,000 members in Canada.

Consumer Rights Commission of Pakistan (CRCP)
House Number 270, Street Number 37, G-9/1
P.O. Box 1379
Islamabad, Pakistan
Telephone: 92 51 285 5402
Fax: 92 51 285 5403
E-mail: crcp@comsats.net.pk
Website: http://www.crcp.sdnpk.org/pr_21_september_2002.htm

The CRCP is a rights-based civil initiative registered under the Trust Act of 1882. Established in 1998, the CRCP is an independent, nonprofit, and nongovernmental organization. It largely works through local fund-raising and by attracting volunteers. It is the first national consumer organization in Pakistan and claims to approach the issue of consumer protection in comprehensive and holistic terms. Its vision and strategies are meant to share significant cross-linkages with both market practices and issues of governance.

Consumers' Association (CA)
2 Marylebone Road
London NW1 4DF, United Kingdom
Telephone: 44 207 770 7262
Fax: 44 207 770 7666
E-mail: helen.west@which.co.uk
Website: http://www.which.co.uk

The CA produces *Which?* magazine, Britain's version of *Consumer Reports. Which?* contains product guides, forums, and reports.

Consumers International (CI)
Consumers International Head Office
Julian Edwards, director general
24 Highbury Crescent
London N5 1RX, United Kingdom
Telephone: 44 207 226 6663
Fax: 44 207 354 0607
E-mail: consint@consint.org
Website: http://www.consumersinternational.org/

CI supports, links, and represents consumer groups and agencies all over the world. It has a membership of over 250 organizations in 115 countries. It strives to promote a fairer society by defending the rights of all consumers, especially the poor, marginalized, and disadvantaged.

Consumers Protection Center (KEPKA), Greece
54 Tsimiski Street
GR-546 23 Thessaloniki, Greece
Telephone: 30 31 233 333
Fax: 30 31 242 211
E-mail: consumers@kepka.org
Website: http://www.kepka.org/

KEPKA is an independent, nonprofit, and nongovernmental consumer organization. KEPKA is the first recognized consumers' association formed in Greece in response to the law 2251/94, which aims to protect consumers.

Environment Agency (EA), United Kingdom
Rio House Almonsbury
Bristol BS32 4UD, United Kingdom
Telephone: 08 45 9333111
Website: http://www.environment-agency.gov.uk/

The EA tackles flooding and pollution incidents and makes sure that industry keeps its impacts on air, land, and water quality to a minimum. The EA cleans up rivers, coastal waters, and contaminated land and also looks after fish and wildlife habitats.

Environment Canada
Inquiry Centre
351 Saint Joseph Boulevard
Hull, Quebec, Canada K1A 0H3
Telephone: (819) 997-2800 or 1-800-668-6767
Fax: (819) 953-2225
E-mail: enviroinfo@ec.gc.ca
Website: http://www.ec.gc.ca

Environment Canada's website serves as a resource for weather and environmental information. The website offers advice for what one can do around the home to help the environment, as well as providing tips on how to protect wildlife.

Environmental Protection Agency (EPA), Denmark
Danish EPA
29 Strandgade
DK-1401 København K, Denmark
Telephone: 45 32 66 0100
Fax: 45 32 66 0479
E-mail: mst@mst.dk
Website: http://www.mst.dk/homepage/

The Danish EPA's spheres of activity center on preventing and combating water, soil, and air pollution. The agency reports to the Danish Ministry of the Environment and has approximately 360 employees.

Environmental Protection Agency, Scotland (SEPA)
SEPA Corporate Office

Erskine Court Castle Business Park
Stirling FK9 4TR, Scotland
Telephone: 01 786 457 700
Fax: 01 786 446 885
E-mail: scc@sepa.org.uk
Website: http://www.sepa.org.uk/

SEPA is the public body responsible for environmental protection
in Scotland. Its main aim is to provide an efficient and integrated
environmental protection system for Scotland that will improve
the environment and contribute to the government's goal of sustainable development. SEPA was established by the Environment
Act of 1995 and became operational on 1 April 1996. The Environment Act of 1995 also sets out SEPA's powers and responsibilities.

Environmental Protection Agency, Sweden
Naturvårdsverket
Blekholmsterrassen 36
SE-106 48 Stockholm, Sweden
Telephone: 46 8 698 1000
Fax: 46 8 20 29 25
E-mail: natur@naturvardsverket.se
Website: http://www.internat.naturvardsverket.se/

The Swedish Environmental Protection Agency is the central environmental authority under the Swedish government. Its main
tasks are to coordinate and promote environmental work on both
a national and international level.

**European Association for the Co-ordination of Consumer
Representation in Standardization (ANEC)**
36, avenue de Tervueren
B-1040 Brussels, Belgium
Telephone: 32 2 743 2470
Fax: 32 2 706 5430
E-mail: anec@anec.org
Website: http://www.anec.org

ANEC is the European consumer voice in standardization. ANEC
was established in 1995 as an international nonprofit association
under Belgian law. Its mission is to represent consumers on any
matter concerning the standardization of consumer-product regulations.

European Bureau of Consumers Union (BEUC)
36/4, avenue de Tervueren
B-1040 Brussels, Belgium
Telephone: 32 2 743 1590
Fax: 32 2 740 2802
E-mail: consumers@beuc.org

The BEUC coordinates consumer policy among the member countries of the European Union (EU). Thirty-three independent consumer organizations from twenty-three countries are represented.

European Union (EU) Director-General of Consumer Affairs
European Commission Directorate, General Health and
Consumer Protection
200, rue de la Loi / Wetstraat 200
B-1049 Brussels, Belgium
Telephone: 32 2 299 1111
E-mail: sanco-mailbox@cec.eu.int
Website: http://europa.eu.int/comm/consumers/index_en.html

The mission of the EU Director-General of Consumer Affairs is to ensure the proper integration of consumer concerns in all EU policies and to complement the consumer policy conducted by member states. Within this general context, the commission supports consumer organizations and seeks to enhance the role of consumer representatives in decision making. At the international level, the commission aims to ensure the proper application by candidate countries of the same standards of consumer protection and consumer safety as exist in the European Community (EC). The commission also promotes consumer policy and high consumer safety standards in international forums and in relation to Third-World countries.

Fairtrade Foundation
16 Baldwin's Gardens, Suite 204
London EC1N 7RJ, United Kingdom
Telephone: 44 207 405 5942
Fax: 44 207 405 5943
E-mail: mail@fairtrade.org.uk
Website: http://www.fairtrade.org.uk/

The Fairtrade Foundation exists to advocate for a better deal for marginalized and disadvantaged Third-World producers. The foundation awards a consumer label, the FAIRTRADE Mark, to products that meet internationally recognized standards of fair trade.

Foodaware: The Consumer's Food Group
36 Leyland Avenue
Saint Albans, Herfordshire, AL1 2BE, United Kingdom
Website: http://www.nfcg.org.uk/intro.htm

Foodaware coordinates the UK consumer movement's work on food safety, nutrition, and standards. Its mission is to give UK consumers a strong voice on food policy by bringing together the organizations that represent consumers. Foodaware also consults and supports the UK consumer representatives on food-related committees, while furthering the public understanding of science.

Friends of the Earth International, The Netherlands
P.O. Box 19199
1000 GD, Amsterdam, The Netherlands
Telephone: 31 20 622 1369
Fax: 31 20 639 2181
Website: http://www.foei.org/

The Dutch branch of Friends International initiated the Sustainable Societies Program, which assumes that the earth cannot support the wasteful production and consumption patterns established by the industrialized countries.

Health Action International (HAI), The Netherlands
Health Action International, c/o HAI Europe
Jacob van Lennepkade 334-T
1053 NJ Amsterdam, The Netherlands
Telephone: 31 20 683 3684
Fax: 31 20 685 5002
E-mail: info@haiweb.org
Website: http://www.haiweb.org/

HAI is a nonprofit, global network of health, development, consumer, and other public-interest groups in more than seventy countries working for a more rational use of medicinal drugs. HAI represents the interests of consumers in drug policy and believes that all drugs marketed should be safe, effective, affordable, and necessary. HAI also campaigns for better controls on drug promotion and for the provision of balanced, independent information for prescribers and consumers.

Institute of Consumer Protection (ICP), Mauritius
Main Office Institute for Consumer Protection
Hansrod Building, Second Floor
Corner Jummah Mosque and Sir Virgil Naz Streets
Port Louis, Mauritius
Telephone: (230) 210-4433
Fax: (230) 211-4436
E-mail: icpmapbi@intnet.mu
Website: http://icp.intnet.mu/Contact1.htm

The ICP was set up in 1983. Originally, it started as a breast-feeding promotion group and later evolved into a national consumer-protection agency. ICP has three distinct departments: the consumer-protection department, the maternal and child health department also known as MAPBIN, and the information and education department.

International Labor Office (ILO)
4 route des Morillons
CH-1211 Geneva 22, Switzerland
Telephone: 41 22 799 6111
Fax: 41 22 798 8685
E-mail: ilo@ilo.org
Website: http://www.ilo.org/

The ILO is the UN agency that seeks the promotion of social justice and internationally recognized human and labor rights. It was founded in 1919 and is the only surviving creation of the Treaty of Versailles, which brought the League of Nations into existence. The ILO became the first specialized agency of the UN in 1946. The ILO formulates international labor standards in the form of Conventions and Recommendations, setting minimum standards for the following labor rights: freedom of association, the right to organize, collective bargaining, abolition of forced labor, equality of opportunity and treatment, and other standards regulating conditions across the entire spectrum of work-related issues.

McSpotlight
BM McSpotlight
London WC1N 3XX, United Kingdom
E-mail: info@mcspotlight.org
Website: http://www.mcspotlight.org

McDonald's spends over $2 billion a year broadcasting its image to the world. This organization aims to provide a small space for alternatives to be heard. McSpotlight was created by the McInformation Network, an independent group of volunteers working in twenty-two countries on four continents. The McInformation Network is dedicated to compiling and disseminating factual, accurate, and up-to-date information about the workings, policies, and practices of the McDonald's Corporation. The network also highlights opposition to McDonald's and other transnational companies.

Ministerial Council on Consumer Affairs (MCCA), Australia
Department of the Treasury
Langton Cres
CANBERRA ACT 2600, Australia
Telephone: 02 6263 3997
Fax: 02 6263 2830
Website: http://www.consumer.gov.au/html/protection.htm

The MCCA consists of all Australian and New Zealander government ministers responsible for fair trade, consumer-protection laws, and credit laws. The role of the MCCA is to consider consumer affairs and fair trade matters of national significance and, where possible, to develop a consistent approach to those issues.

National Consumer Council (NCC), United Kingdom
20 Grosvenor Gardens
London SW1W 0DH, United Kingdom
Telephone: 44 207 730 3469
Fax: 44 207 730 0191
E-mail: jj@ncc.org.uk
Website: http://www.ncc.org.uk

The NCC is an independent consumer organization that attempts to champion the consumer interest in order to bring about change for the benefit of consumers. It does this by working with governments, regulators, businesses, and people and organizations that speak on behalf of consumers.

National Federation of Consumer Groups (NFCG)
c/o Centre for Consumer and Commercial Law Research
Brunel University
Uxbridge, Middlesex UB8 3PH, United Kingdom

Telephone: 44 1895 203 069
Fax: 44 1895 203 085
E-mail: office@nfcg.org.uk
Website: http://www.nfcg.org.uk

The NFCG was established in 1963 to bring together local consumer groups that were first set up from 1961 with the encouragement of Consumers' Association (CA), publishers of *Which?* magazine. The NFCG individual membership scheme was introduced in 1977 for people who do not live near enough to a group to make membership feasible.

North American Commission for Environmental Cooperation (CEC)
Commission for Environmental Cooperation
393 rue St-Jacques Ouest
Bureau 200 Montréal, Québec H2Y 1N9, Canada
Telephone: (514) 350-4300
Fax: (514) 350-4314
E-mail: info@cecmtl.org
Website: http://www.cec.org/home/index.cfm?varlan=english

The CEC is an international organization created by Canada, Mexico, and the United States under the North American Agreement on Environmental Cooperation (NAAEC). The CEC was established to address regional environmental concerns, to help prevent potential trade and environmental conflicts, and to promote the effective enforcement of environmental law. The agreement complements the environmental provisions of the North American Free Trade Agreement (NAFTA).

United Nations Environmental Program (UNEP)
United Nations Avenue, Gigiri
P.O. Box 30552
Nairobi, Kenya
Telephone: 254 2 621 234
Fax: 254 2 624 489 (or 254 2 624 490)
E-mail: eisinfo@unep.org
Website: http://www.unep.org/

UNEP provides leadership and encourages environmental partnerships that inform and enable nations and peoples to improve their quality of life without compromising that of future generations.

World Trade Organization (WTO)
Centre William Rappard
Rue de Lausanne 154
CH-1211 Geneva 21, Switzerland
Telephone: 41 22 739 5111
Fax: 41 22 731 4206
E-mail: enquiries@wto.org
Website: http://www.wto.int/index.htm

The WTO, located in Geneva and established on 1 January 1995, is the only global international organization dealing with the rules of trade between nations. At its core are the WTO agreements negotiated, signed, and ratified by most of the world's trading nations (144 countries as of January 2002). The goal is to help producers of goods and services, exporters, and importers conduct their business. Aside from administering WTO trade agreements, the WTO handles trade disputes, monitors national trade policies, and provides technical assistance and training for developing countries.

8

Print and Nonprint Resources

The sheer volume of available material addressing the issue of consumption can be overwhelming at first glance. A search of the word *consumption* in many library catalogs will produce a list of over 2,300 items. In this chapter, we provide a sample of the available materials that we consider important for a variety of reasons. Some of the items are considered "classics" in the field and thus are included in the list. Others contain the most recent data available on a particular aspect of consumption. Also, when making the selections for this chapter, care was taken to include a diverse range of materials; therefore, the reader will find books and articles focusing on consumption in countries other than the United States and will also find material addressing the consumption patterns of different segments of American society. Finally, in this chapter references for publications that focus on many of the ideas discussed in chapters 1 through 5 are provided. To better facilitate your reading and research, the chapter is divided into four sections: books; print articles, book chapters, and journals; videos; and websites.

Books

Adorno, Theodor W. 1991. *The Culture Industry: Selected Essays on Mass Culture.* London: Routledge. 224 pages.

This book is a collection of essays by Theodor Adorno (1903–1969), a leading member of the group of theorists known as the Frankfurt school. The unifying theme of the essays found in this book is a critique of the "culture industry" and mass culture. Adorno argues that consumer culture serves the interests of capitalism by creating false needs, discouraging political participation, and limiting opportunities for critical thinking. Adorno's writings on consumer-driven capitalism are difficult, groundbreaking, and indispensable.

Alfino, Mark, John S. Caputo, and Robin Wynyard, eds. 1998. *McDonaldization Revisited: Critical Essays on Consumer Culture.* London: Praeger. 232 pages.

The essays in this book extend the concept of McDonaldization, first presented by George Ritzer in *The McDonaldization of Society* (first edition, 1994). McDonaldization refers to the process by which the principles associated with fast food restaurants, including efficiency, calculability, predictability, and control through technology, have begun to permeate more and more sectors of American society. In addition to pointing out the limitations of the McDonaldization thesis, the authors in this collection demonstrate the relevance and applicability of the concept to such areas as feminist theory, semiotics, the hospitality industry, and consumer choice.

Antonides, Gerrit, and W. Fred Van Raaij. 1998. *Consumer Behaviour: A European Perspective.* New York: John Wiley and Sons. 642 pages.

This book offers a European perspective on consumer behavior and situates the discussion within psychological, economic, sociological, and historical contexts. In addition to exploring the determinants and consequences of consumer decision making, the authors examine all aspects of the consumption cycle, from the initial orientation and purchase to product disposal and its consequences for the environment. Chapters of particular interest include "Consumption and the Environment" and "Shopping Behaviour."

Appadurai, Arjun, ed. 1988. *The Social Life of Things: Commodities in Cultural Perspective.* Cambridge, UK: Cambridge University Press. 352 pages.

This edited collection of essays by anthropologists and historians examines the process by which "things" come to be seen as commodities. The contributors point out that desire, taste, and fashion are not inherent or natural, but are instead culturally mediated and socially constructed. Locations such as Europe, the Solomon Islands, France, and India provide case studies for the examination of topics such as the process of commoditization, sacred consumption, the politics of value, and notions of authenticity in consumption.

Barber, Benjamin R. 1995. *Jihad vs. McWorld: How Globalism and Tribalism Are Reshaping the World.* New York: Random House. 432 pages.

Barber argues that there are two competing forces in the world today. First, "McWorld" is the cultural homogenization produced by economic globalization and a corporate-manufactured popular culture. Second, "Jihad" is the term used by Barber to connote racial, ethnic, and religious-based resistance to this McWorld. While McWorld is eroding cultural differences around the world, Jihad is at the same time tearing the world apart. Nevertheless, Barber's thesis is that McWorld and Jihad are linked and not really oppositional forces. McWorld needs the racial, ethnic, and religious difference produced by Jihad in order to produce niche products. Although Jihad is a reaction against the entertainment and consumption values promoted by McWorld, it nevertheless needs the tools produced by McWorld such as cell phones, the Internet, and satellite news stations. Together these represent threats to democracy, and thus should concern those interested in active citizenship and the survival of the inclusive nation-state.

Belasco, Warren, and Phillip Scranton, eds. 2002. *Food Nations: Selling Taste in Consumer Societies.* New York: Routledge. 320 pages.

Warren Belasco is professor of American studies at the University of Maryland and one of the leading scholars in food studies. Though food is often not associated with larger issues of power, consumption, and class, the chapters in this book illustrate the important role played by food in the United States today. The collection examines an eclectic range of topics, including wine in France, donuts in Canada, baby food in the United States, and hybrid cuisines in Mexico.

Brower, Michael, and Warren Leon. 1999. *The Consumer's Guide to Effective Environmental Choices: Practical Advice from the Union of Concerned Scientists.* Pittsburgh, PA: Three Rivers. 304 pages.

This book serves as a resource guide for those concerned about the environmental impacts of their consumption patterns. The book identifies consumer-related environmental problems and statistical data to highlight the environmental consequences of various commodities and consumer choices. Priority actions and rules for responsible consumption are also provided.

Campbell, Colin. 1987. *The Romantic Ethic and the Spirit of Modern Consumerism.* Oxford: Basil Blackwell. 301 pages.

Campbell shows how the consumer revolution in eighteenth- and nineteenth-century England is related to wider cultural developments. He argues that central features of modern consumer culture, such as fashion and an addiction to novelty, have their cultural origin in romantic values that evolved from Protestant religious movements. These religious movements are the source of our modern pleasure-seeking outlook. Drawing on and enriching Weber's argument in *The Protestant Ethic and the Spirit of Capitalism* (1904), Campbell provides an exemplary model for how important, venerable ideas can be transformed and enriched by a focus on consumption.

Clammer, John R. 1997. *Contemporary Urban Japan: A Sociology of Consumption.* Oxford: Basil Blackwell. 256 pages.

This volume examines contemporary Japanese urban lifestyles and assesses consumption behavior in the Japanese context. Clammer demonstrates the link between consumption and urbanization in Japan and highlights the role played by consumption patterns in the social stratification of Japanese society. He shows how the apparently individual concerns that drive consumption are related to global changes.

Corrigan, Peter. 1997. *The Sociology of Consumption.* Thousand Oaks, CA: Sage. 197 pages.

This is an introductory primer to the sociology of consumption. Corrigan traces the history of consumerism in Western capitalist societies, outlines the ideas of key theorists, and explains some of the more complex concepts. A comprehensive array of topics is covered including advertising, fashion, tourism, and food.

Cowen, Tyler. *In Praise of Commercial Culture.* Cambridge, MA: Harvard University Press. 278 pages.

Cowen's argument in this volume is that the commercialization of consumption in modern societies can and should be viewed in a positive light. In the main, capitalism permits and encourages a wide array of vibrant artistic visions and representations. In short, Cowen praises commercial culture in all its manifold manifestations including theater, art, and popular music.

Crocker, David A., and Toby Linden, eds. 1997. *Ethics of Consumption: The Good Life, Justice, and Global Stewardship.* Lanham, MD: Rowman & Littlefield. 564 pages.

This collection of over twenty-five chapters brings together scholars from many fields to discuss both the practical and philosophical implications of American consumption patterns. The essays examine the causes and impacts of contemporary consumption patterns, touching on issues such as carrying capacity, the consumption of grain-fed meat, alternatives to the consumer society, global inequality, and religious perspectives on consumption.

Cross, Gary. 1993. *Time and Money: The Making of Consumer Culture.* London: Routledge. 294 pages.

In this historical analysis, Cross explains why consumer culture is biased toward goods and against free time. Drawing on American, British, and French experiences in the 1920s and 1930s, Cross reveals why hopes that mass production would create a leisure society proved illusory and why a work-and-spend culture prevailed instead.

de Graaf, John, David Wann, and Thomas H. Naylor. 2002. *Affluenza: The All-Consuming Epidemic.* San Francisco: Berrett-Koehler. 268 pages.

This book is derived from the PBS program of the same name. According to de Graaf, Wann, and Naylor, affluenza is a socially transmitted condition of overload, anxiety, debt, and waste that results from people's pursuit of an ever-increasing number of commodities. The book outlines some political, historical, and socioeconomic reasons for affluenza's prominence in contemporary American society. The authors liken affluenza to a powerful, contagious virus that hurts people's financial well-being, health, and family life. The book draws on the real-life stories of people who have chosen to fight affluenza by living a simpler life, and uses such stories to offer practical solutions to the problems caused by affluenza. (See *Affluenza* and *Escape from Affluenza* below in the "Videos" section.)

De Grazia, Victoria, and Ellen Furlough, eds. 1996. *The Sex of Things: Gender and Consumption in Historical Perspective.* Berkeley: University of California Press. 433 pages.

This collection of essays examines the historical relationships between gender, politics, and consumerism. Featuring both historical case studies as well as essays on methodology and social theory, the book integrates material from two centuries and covers topics such as the gendering of consumer practices in nineteenth-century France, consumer credit and the debtor family in turn-of-the-century England, cosmetics and women's identity, the diffusion of appliances in interwar England, and consumer nationalism in West Germany.

Deaton, Angus. 1992. *Understanding Consumption.* Oxford: Oxford University Press. 242 pages.

In this book, Deaton presents research from microeconomics, macroeconomics, and econometrics on the topic of saving and consumption. As an overview of empirical and theoretical work on saving and consumption patterns, this book includes a large amount and wide variety of data.

Douglas, Mary, and Baron Isherwood. 1996. *The World of Goods: Towards an Anthropology of Consumption.* Rev. ed. New York: Routledge. 169 pages.

Written by anthropologist Mary Douglas and economist Baron Isherwood, this book examines the relationship between material goods and interpersonal communication. The authors discuss food, clothing, cars, and homes as some examples of the commodities through which people communicate information about themselves, information that advances their particular interests, and shared meanings with others. This book is meant as a counterweight to economic approaches to consumption that neglect the cultural dimensions of consumer activity. Few anthropologists who study consumption have been unaffected by this book.

Edwards, Tim. 1997. *Men in the Mirror: Men's Fashions and Consumer Society.* London: Cassell. 150 pages.

The myth that women are interested in fashion while men are not has been challenged in both the popular press (visible in the proliferation of men's style magazines such as *GQ* and *Arena*) and academic writings in recent years. In this book, Edwards provides a sociological analysis of men's fashion, linking it to notions of masculinity, effeminacy, and homosexuality. Edwards explores how masculinity and men's fashions are constructed in an increasingly commodified society.

Ewen, Stuart. 1976. *Captains of Consciousness: Advertising and the Social Roots of the Consumer Culture.* New York: McGraw-Hill. 261 pages.

Ewen traces the roots of consumer culture in American society to the 1920s when advertising first began to infiltrate the popular consciousness of American workers by offering the "good life" to those who invested in an ever-expanding array of consumer goods. According to Ewen, the newly developed media became a tool by which capitalists kept workers passive through both the creation of an enticing and fantastic visual spectacle and, where necessary, the co-optation of voices of resistance.

Ewen, Stuart. 1988. *All Consuming Images: The Politics of Style in Contemporary Culture.* New York: Basic Books. 306 pages.

Ewen argues that our culture is increasingly dominated by style. The research reported in this book reveals the diverse and often contradictory ways that people view and understand style. Although recognizing that interpretations of style are often specific to a particular person or historical epoch, Ewen notes that among all of the respondents who provided him with a definition of style, two overarching themes emerged: First, style is linked to consumption; and second, the mass media play a central role in shaping and determining popular notions of style.

Fine, Ben, and E. Leopold. 2002. *The World of Consumption: The Material and the Cultural Revisited.* 2d ed. London: Routledge. 313 pages.

This book challenges standard economic studies of consumption that ignore issues of power and inequality. Fine and Leopold provide an overview of the many studies on consumption and focus particularly on issues such as economic imperialism, globalization, public consumption, systems of provision, and the world of commodities.

Finkelstein, Joanne. 1996. *After a Fashion.* Melbourne: Melbourne University Press. 127 pages.

In this broad and rigorous introduction to the study of fashion, Finkelstein argues that any analysis of fashion needs to recognize the complex and paradoxical influences that affect fashion, including economic activity, social context, sexual mores, aesthetic trends, and psychological formations. Fashion is looked at as simultaneously a globalizing and culturally homogenizing phenomena, as an ever-pervasive arm of big business, as a gimmick that sustains vast economic structures such as shopping malls and trade expositions, and as a principal impetus behind international advertising.

Finnegan, Margaret. 1999. *Selling Suffrage: Consumer Culture and Votes for Women.* New York: Columbia University Press. 222 pages.

Finnegan examines women's suffrage from the perspective of consumer history and details the various ways in which commodities and consumer activities were used to win the support of the public. In particular, Finnegan points out that commodities such as sunflower badges and Kewpie dolls, and activities such as pantomimes, pageants, and advertising campaigns, allowed suffragists to associate themselves with consumer culture, and thereby claim legitimacy in a capitalist society. Finnegan claims that prevailing historical assessments of the suffrage movement overemphasize the more radical suffragists and neglect the active role played by ordinary women in the commercialization of politics.

Fox, Richard W., and T. Jackson Lears, eds. 1983. *The Culture of Consumption: Critical Essays in American History, 1880–1980.* New York: Pantheon. 236 pages.

The thread that unites the essays in this collection is an interest in the ways in which an emerging consumer culture of the late-nineteenth-century United States emphasized the ownership of material goods rather than morality, self-control, and individual accomplishment. It contains a seminal essay by Lears, "From Salvation to Self-Realization: Advertising and the Therapeutic Roots of the Consumer Culture, 1880–1930," as well as articles about the rhetoric of advertising, consumption and Henry James, and early sociological studies of consumer culture, politics, and commodity scientism.

Frank, Robert H. 2000. *Luxury Fever: Why Money Fails to Satisfy in an Era of Excess.* Princeton, NJ: Princeton University Press. 326 pages.

This book takes a look at the consequences of the growth of conspicuous consumption and makes the point that the behavior of people's peers determines one's spending habits. Frank traces the history of the "consumption tax" and argues that despite its failure in the past, it would encourage a much-needed shift in economic priorities. Frank also discusses luxury spending and its relationship to economic inequality.

Frank, Thomas. 1998. *The Conquest of Cool: Business Culture, Counterculture, and the Rise of Hip Consumerism.* Chicago: University of Chicago Press. 278 pages.

Frank explores how the youth culture that emerged in the 1960s, along with its symbols and language, were intertwined from the start with the advertising industry. The cultural impact of this is continued in the move toward "hip consumerism." The book looks at the relation between advertising leaders and the ideas of the counterculture and discusses examples such as the 1960s "peacock revolution" in men's clothing, car advertising, and the cola wars. Frank provides an overview of how advertising changed from hard sell to ironic critic and demonstrates how the counterculture has become interchangeable with the business culture that it supposedly opposed.

Frank, Thomas. 2001. *One Market under God: Extreme Capitalism, Market Populism, and the End of Economic Democracy.* New York: Anchor Books. 436 pages.

This book argues that the free market economy, especially in the way that it operated in the 1990s, proved destructive for some people, contrary to the claim that unfettered capitalism benefits everyone. "Market populism," the belief that free markets allow more democracy than elected governments, is challenged through evidence suggesting that corporate America is more interested in its own growth and profits rather than the well-being of all members of society.

Frith, Katherine, ed. 1996. *Advertising in Asia: Communication, Culture, and Consumption.* Ames: Iowa State University Press. 313 pages.

Advertising and capitalism are closely intertwined in the newly emerging economies of Asia. The essays in this book examine the political, cultural, economic, and social aspects of advertising in countries such as Japan, Taiwan, Korea, China, India, the Philippines, Indonesia, Malaysia, and Singapore.

Gabriel, Yiannis, and Tim Lang. 1995. *The Unmanageable Consumer.* London: Sage. 213 pages.

This book discusses the various representations of the consumer: chooser, communicator, identity seeker, explorer, hedonist, victim, and rebel. The authors argue that contemporary patterns of consumption in the West are too complex and dynamic to be neatly represented by any one image of the consumer. Consumers are unmanageable because rather than consuming in predictable, consistent, or one-dimensional ways, they often contradict established theoretical models and maintain multifaceted identities.

Galbraith, John Kenneth. 1969. *The Affluent Society.* 2d ed. London: Hamish Hamilton. 333 pages.

In this important and influential book, Galbraith examines the social and political consequences of growing inequality between rich and poor. Galbraith claims that aside from threatening social cohesion, the "economics of affluence" also undermine economic stability and security. This book argues for extensive government spending on public goods such as education and transportation in order to combat the inflation and economic downturns that eventually accompany social inequality.

Goldman, Robert, and Stephen Papson. 1998. *Nike Culture: The Sign of the Swoosh.* London: Sage. 194 pages.

This book examines the social importance of signs and symbols in contemporary capitalist societies and uses the Nike "swoosh" symbol as the prime example of how successful marketing campaigns lead to economic success for image-savvy corporations. Goldman and Papson take a close look at the advertising efforts of Nike and demonstrate how certain issues, such as race, community, and the "spirituality" of sports, are represented and obscured by the images and messages found in Nike advertising.

Goodwin, Neva R., Frank Akerman, and David Kiron. 1997. *The Consumer Society.* Washington, DC: Island Press. 385 pages.

This collection includes summaries of close to 100 papers from economics and sociology on the topic of consumption. The book is divided into ten sections, including some based on the following themes: consumption in the affluent society; family, gender, and socialization; the history of the consumer society; foundations of economic theories of consumption; media, advertising, and wants creation; and consumption and the environment.

Goody, Jack. 1982. *Cooking, Cuisine and Class: A Study in Comparative Sociology.* Cambridge, UK: Cambridge University Press. 253 pages.

In this book on culinary practices around the world, Goody extends and challenges work already done by anthropologists on the cultural significance of food. In addition to providing an overview of culinary practices in various historical eras, including ancient Egypt, imperial Rome, and early modern Europe, Goody explores the reasons why haute cuisine is absent in Africa but not in other parts of the world. This book links the preparation and consumption of food in different societies to historical and socioeconomic circumstances.

Gronow, Jukka. 1997. *The Sociology of Taste.* London: Routledge. 199 pages.

In this book, Gronow discusses the relationship between fashion, taste, and consumer culture, using historical case studies from Europe. Gronow integrates the work of social theorists such as Thorstein Veblen and Georg Simmel in order to discuss the role of fashion in fostering social cohesion in modern societies.

Hebdige, Dick. 1979. *Subculture: The Meaning of Style.* London: Methuen. 195 pages.

This book examines the origins and social and cultural importance of subcultures in the United Kingdom. Hebdige takes a historical and sociological perspective on youth culture, fashion, and music. He links the motivations and actions of working-class members of subcultures—including mods, skinheads, and punks—to various social movements and trends. Hebdige provides some hope that consumer culture may provide for the emergence of progressive social movements based on subcultural styles.

Hochschild, Arlie Russell. 1985. *The Managed Heart: Commercialization of Human Feeling.* Berkeley: University of California Press. 307 pages.

Hochschild examines the changing nature of labor in an economy that focuses less on production and more on consumption. *The Managed Heart* examines the personal price paid by flight attendants and others who must exert "emotional labor," defined as labor that requires the constant expression, or suppression, of feelings and emotions. Hochschild argues that rationalization and inequality based on gender and class exacerbate the dehumanizing and alienating effects of emotional labor and cause burnout among workers who are required to utilize their feelings and emotions as labor skills.

Horowitz, Daniel. *The Morality of Spending: Attitudes toward the Consumer Society in America, 1875–1940.* Chicago: Ivan R. Del. 254 pages.

Horowitz demonstrates that consumption has long been considered a social problem, although concerns about that nature of its impact on the moral fiber of society have changed over time. Focusing on the period between 1875 and 1940, Horowitz shows that household budget studies from the era contain implicit and explicit concerns about how the pursuit of affluence affects the moral "health" of any nation that has an insatiable appetite for commercial goods and novel experiences.

Howes, David, ed. 1996. *Cross-Cultural Consumption: Global Markets, Local Realities.* London: Routledge. 214 pages.

The notion of firm cultural borders is challenged in this collection. The chapters in this book illustrate the increasingly global nature of consumer culture and demonstrate how the flow of goods and services around the world has eroded cultural barriers and differences. The topics covered in this book include perishable goods in the Pacific islands, contemporary British food cultures, the role of coffee breaks in Tanzania and Europe, Mayan export products in American catalogs, and cultural performances by women in the Ecuadorean tourist market.

Humphrey, Kim. 1998. *Shelf Life: Supermarkets and the Changing Cultures of Consumption.* London: Cambridge University Press. 270 pages.

This book provides an analysis of the contemporary Australian supermarket in its historical and cultural contexts. Humphrey contrasts the emergence of large supermarkets with the declining popularity of small counter-service grocery stores. Integrating oral histories with social theory, Humphrey uses the shoppers' views of supermarkets to offer insights into the everyday experience of living in a consumer society.

James, Jeffrey. 2000. *Consumption, Globalization, and Development.* New York: St. Martin's Press. 142 pages.

James addresses the relationship between globalization and consumption in the developing world and tackles issues such as conspicuous consumption, the "demonstration effect," preference changes, and consumer welfare. Approaching the issue of globalization as a set of trade-offs, James argues that globalization produces winners and losers simultaneously and creates new opportunities for developing countries to address key problems through social marketing campaigns.

Kaplan, E. Ann. 1987. *Rocking around the Clock: Music Television, Postmodernism, and Consumer Culture.* London: Methuen. 196 pages.

This is a study of Music Television (MTV), the first nonstop, rock-video channel. In the first part of the book, Kaplan looks at the similarity between music videos and advertisements. In the second part of the book, she analyzes a number of rock videos, focusing particularly on gender issues in videos by both male and female artists. Kaplan concludes that MTV represents a particular stage in the development of consumer culture, whereby distinguishing between reality and fiction becomes extremely difficult.

Klein, Naomi. 2002. *No Logo: Taking Aim at the Brand Bullies.* New York: Picador. 490 pages.

No Logo critiques the omnipresence of brands, the images of which are increasingly permeating such settings as schools and other locations that were once free of commercial messages. Klein also takes exception with the version of democracy and diversity promoted by multinational corporations in which consumer choice is likened to free choice and democracy. Klein points out that such corporations undermine the institutions of democracy while offering less and less choice due to the merger and acquisition frenzy that began during the 1990s and continues today unabated. In addition to discussing the plight of workers in well-known multinational retailers, Klein discusses recent efforts—such as culture jamming, human rights "hacktivism," and ethical shareholding—aimed at countering the harmful consequences of corporate branding.

Kowinski, William Severini. 2002. *The Malling of America.* Reissued ed. New York: Morrow. 415 pages.

In this book, Kowinski studies the way in which shopping malls both reflect and perpetuate consumerism in the United States. Kowinski discusses topics such as the land-appropriation efforts of malls, the mandatory hours of operation for tenants, the environmental impacts of mall construction, the privatization of public market spaces, and the move toward consumerism and away from citizenship and public involvement.

Larson, Erik. 1992. *The Naked Consumer: How Our Private Lives Become Public Commodities.* New York: Holt. 275 pages.

The Naked Consumer outlines the ways in which the desires, habits, and preferences of American consumers have been tracked and documented through the use of company spies, computers, hidden cameras, and sonar technology. Larson argues that the privacy rights of individuals around the world are undermined by technologies that are purportedly meant only to survey consumer preferences and behaviors but that, in practice, serve the interests of those in power who wish to monitor and control large groups of people.

Lasn, Kalle. 2002. *Culture Jam: How to Reverse America's Suicidal Consumer Binge—And Why We Must.* New York: Quill. 247 pages.

Lasn, the founder of *Adbusters* magazine, argues in this book that the United States has become a multimillion-dollar brand and that it is up to "culture jammers" to disrupt the commercialization promoted by the marketing campaigns of multinational food, fashion, sports, and music corporations, among others. Lasn claims that by "uncooling" consumer items, challenging the dominance of television marketing, and "demarketing" heavily stylized goods and even celebrities, people can deconstruct and resist the meanings and symbols created by the advertising industry.

Leidner, Robin. 1993. *Fast Food, Fast Talk: Service Work and the Routinization of Everyday Life.* Berkeley: University of California Press. 278 pages.

In this book, Leidner studies the lives of the employees of McDonald's and Combined Insurance. Leidner looks at the way in which the standardization and routinization of service work undermines individual autonomy, social responsibility, and spontaneous expression. The effects of this are felt by everyone who participates in these scripted, inauthentic performances of service work whether they are employees or customers.

Mackay, Hugh, ed. 1997. *Consumption and Everyday Life.* London: Routledge. 320 pages.

This book is a collection of closely related chapters that evaluate contemporary debates about consumption and its role in shaping everyday life. Countering simplistic accounts of the passive consumer, the chapters in this collection depict the consumer as active and critical, capable of making informed and deliberate choices. Case studies from around the world illustrate the rich variety of local consumption practices throughout the world and provide empirical context for the theoretical ideas examined by contributors to the book.

Mamiya, Christin J. 1992. *Pop Art and Consumer Culture: American Super Market.* Austin: University of Texas Press. 215 pages.

This study traces the rise and decline of the pop art era (1958–1968), exploring the linkages between pop art and the growth of consumer culture. When pop art first emerged in the United States in the late 1950s, many art critics predicted that it would rapidly disappear. In this book, Mamiya shows that pop art became the principal art movement in the 1960s. The financial success of American pop art could not have occurred without its close reliance on images from American consumer culture.

Manning, Robert D. 2001. *Credit Card Nation: The Consequences of America's Addiction to Credit.* New York: Basic Books. 406 pages.

Manning addresses the issue of national and individual credit card debt. Using data on debt from the past two decades, Manning identifies an alarming trend toward less savings and a greater amount of debt for both families and corporations. Manning discusses various aspects of the "credit card nation," including the historical emergence of the current debt problems in U.S. society, credit card debt among the young, and the predatory practices and advertising strategies employed by credit card companies.

Marchand, Roland. 1986. *Advertising the American Dream: Making Way for Modernity, 1920–1940.* Berkeley: University of California Press. 445 pages.

This book discusses the modernization of print advertising from the 1920s to the 1940s and traces the linkages between consumer culture and the print advertisements of this period. Marchand argues that advertising is a fairly reliable reflection of the needs and desires of a culture, even if it is a very poor expression of what may be needed to fill those needs and desires.

McCracken, Grant. 1990. *Culture and Consumption: New Approaches to the Symbolic Character of Consumer Goods and Activities.* Bloomington: Indiana University Press. 174 pages.

McCracken challenges conventional theories of consumption that pay little attention to the structural and personal functions played by consumption in modern capitalist societies. McCracken emphasizes the symbolism behind people's purchasing patterns, preferences, and tastes, pointing out that the consumerism often reviled by critics actually serves to create and maintain social cohesion and order. The book introduces two ideas that are now standard in studies of consumption. First is the disappearing importance of "patina," the signs of a commodity's age. Second is the idea that buying one new object will lead to the purchase of a number of related products, which McCracken calls a Diderot effect, after the French philosopher who described the room he had to furnish to match his new dressing gown.

McKendrick, Neil, John Brewer, and J. H. Plumb. 1982. *The Birth of a Consumer Society: The Commercialization of Eighteenth-Century England.* Bloomington: Indiana University Press. 345 pages.

This is a collection of essays by three historians, which argues that our consumer culture had its birth in eighteenth-century England. The thesis of the book is that there was a consumer revolution that predated the advent of industrialization as well as the advent of mass production. The book focuses on the impact of altered and increased consumption on the emergence of the Industrial Revolution.

Miller, Daniel. 1987. *Material Culture and Mass Consumption.* Oxford: Basil Blackwell. 240 pages.

This book uses the idea of objectification as developed by G. W. F. Hegel, Karl Marx, and Georg Simmel in order to develop a theory of the relationship between society and material culture. In objectification, we take an idea in our mind and create it as a material object. In consumer society, these objectifications are usually produced by large, abstract institutions such as companies and government agencies. Miller agrees with many that such objectifications are alienating and isolating, but he argues that these very consumer objects can be used as the basis of pluralistic, small-scale communities. Miller thus tries to avoid treating the consumer as a passive, alienated recipient of the intended messages of those in control of production.

Miller, Daniel. 1995. *Acknowledging Consumption: A Review of New Studies.* London: Routledge. 341 pages.

This book is meant to serve as an interdisciplinary text on consumption for undergraduate students. Scholars from fields such as anthropology, consumer behavior, economics, geography, history, media studies, psychology, and sociology contribute chapters to this collection, bringing together a large variety and quantity of material on consumption produced in the ten years prior to 1995.

Miller, Daniel. 1998. *A Theory of Shopping.* Ithaca, NY: Cornell University Press. 180 pages.

In this book, Miller presents the results of a year long ethnographic study of shopping on a North London street. Shopping is treated as more than just a trivial and meaningless activity, and this book frames the act of shopping in terms of familial relationships and "sacrificial ritual." Miller argues that shopping reveals significant information about how we think of our social relationships.

Miller, Daniel. 2001. *Consumption: Critical Concepts in the Social Sciences.* Vols. 1–4. London: Routledge. 2,200 pages.

These expansive volumes range from classic theoretical discussions of consumption to recent work detailing the diversity of consumption as it is actually practiced. These volumes provide an exhaustive and extensive guide to past and current research on the topic of consumption.

Miller, Michael B. 1994. *The Bon Marché: Bourgeoisie Culture and the Department Store, 1869–1920.* Princeton, NJ: Princeton University Press. 266 pages.

This book is a social history of Le Bon Marché, the famous Parisian department store that, prior to 1914, was the world's largest store of its kind. The rise of Le Bon Marché reflected the ambitions and anxieties of Parisian culture at the time, and Miller illustrates the success of Le Bon Marché's owners and directors in accommodating the conflicting forces of modern mass consumption on the one hand and traditional social and cultural values on the other. The book includes material on not only the business and organizational aspects of running a store like Le Bon Marché, but also the techniques used to manipulate consumer desire and promote mass consumption.

Mintz, Sidney W. 1986. *Sweetness and Power: The Place of Sugar in Modern History.* Harmondsworth, UK: Penguin. 274 pages.

Mintz traces the history of sugar production and consumption and shows how Europeans and Americans transformed sugar from a rare foreign luxury consumed by the aristocracy to a staple in the diet of the new industrial workers. Mintz claims that this transformation from luxury to mass-consumed commodity changed the trajectory of capitalism. Sugar not only reflected patterns of race, class, and gender, but also permanently influenced eating habits, work patterns, and health.

Nava, Mica, Iain MacRury, Andrew Blake, and Barry Richards, eds. 1997. *Buy This Book: Studies in Advertising and Consumption.* London: Routledge. 355 pages.

Buy This Book is an examination of advertising and consumption since the 1950s. The editors bring together work from many disciplines, including cultural studies, psychoanalysis, social history, sociology, politics, art and design history, and business studies. The twenty chapters cover a large range of topical areas and are placed into sections based on the following themes: theories and histories, the advertising industry, case studies, textual strategies, readers as producers of meaning, and consumption and identity.

Nixon, Sean. 1996. *Hard Looks: Masculinities, Spectatorship and Contemporary Consumption.* London: Palgrave Macmillan. 241 pages.

Nixon examines how feminism's effect on popular consciousness has influenced new representations of masculinity. The book addresses assorted aspects of representations of masculinity in consumer culture, including the following issues: the "New Man" as represented by the retail, advertising, and publishing industries; the distinctive visual codes of these representations and their impact; and the relationship between this imagery and the institutional practices that underlie a wider representation.

Olney, Martha L. 1991. *Buy Now, Pay Later: Advertising, Credit and Consumer Durables in the 1920s.* Chapel Hill: University of North Carolina Press. 424 pages.

Olney examines how advertising and the increasing availability of credit during and after the 1920s encouraged more and more people to purchase durable goods that only a century ago were rare possessions in the average American home. Clever marketing, credit, and the possibility of purchasing durable goods on installment plans facilitated a revolution in consumer spending.

Packard, Vance. 1985. *The Hidden Persuaders.* New York: Pocket Books. 288 pages.

Packard argues that by the mid-1950s, efficiency and technology had overcome traditional problems related to the production and distribution of goods. However, the efficiency of the industrial production system necessitated the need for consumption to increase in order to absorb excess production of goods. Packard illustrates how advertising at this time switched from a focus on the attributes and reliability of goods to a focus on psychological techniques aimed at persuading individuals in both obvious and subtle ways to purchase commodities. Although he may have overestimated the power of advertising, this book was very influential in the public debate around advertising, especially the idea of subliminal advertising, which it popularized.

Pendergrast, Mark. 2000. *For God, Country and Coca-Cola: The Definitive History of the Great American Soft Drink and the Company That Makes It.* 2d ed. London: Basic Books. 621 pages.

This is an unauthorized history of the product that began as a patent medicine after the Civil War and eventually became a dominant consumer beverage in the United States and the rest of the world. Rather than merely trace the history of the Coca-Cola Company, Pendergrast links the rise of the soft drink to the development of capitalism and the rising global power and influence of American corporations.

Radin, Margaret Jane. 2001. *Contested Commodities.* Cambridge, MA: Harvard University Press. 279 pages.

This book is a philosophical and legal examination of the commodification of the human body. Radin looks at what happens when the values of consumer culture invade such areas as sex, the sale of human organs, and commercial surrogate motherhood. Radin argues that controversies surrounding commodification are better addressed by careful regulation than by unfettered markets or complete prohibitions.

Ritzer, George. 1995. *Expressing America.* Thousand Oaks, CA: Pine Forge. 240 pages.

Ritzer illustrates the ways in which consumers and credit card companies contribute to an expanding cycle of credit card debt in the United States and the rest of the world. Ritzer also examines how credit cards serve as expressions and symbols of American-style wealth and prosperity. Using sociological concepts to illustrate the theoretical significance of credit card use, Ritzer argues that the credit card is transforming social and economic relations throughout the world.

Ritzer, George. 1999. *Enchanting a Disenchanted World.* Thousand Oaks, CA: Pine Forge. 258 pages.

Ritzer claims that consumption is increasingly rationalized, that is, it is more predictable, efficient, calculable, and involves attempts to control and manipulate people. This rationalization also leads to disenchantment, which alienates consumers. To draw consumers back in, producers have been forced to develop new means of consumption that employ strategies aimed at reenchanting consumers. According to Ritzer, the new means of consumptions—such as theme stores, chain stores, shopping malls, electronic shopping centers, casinos, discounters, superstores, cruise ships, and entertainment facilities—urge and manipulate people into "hyperconsumption."

Ritzer, George. 2000. *The McDonaldization of Society.* 3d ed. Thousand Oaks, CA: Pine Forge. 278 pages.

This book outlines the ways in which the principles of the fast food industry, particularly of its most powerful player, McDonald's, have come to permeate many sectors of society. Though the process of rationalization—which involves efficiency, predictability, calculability, and control though technology—assists and is logical for businesses, it also ironically carries irrational social, health, cultural, and environmental consequences for consumers and communities. Rationalization brings with it some benefits, and on the surface seems logical and inevitable, but Ritzer argues that people should rethink the long-term consequences of uncritically accepting the McDonaldization of society.

Robbins, Richard. 2002. *Global Problems and the Culture of Capitalism.* 2d ed. Boston: Allyn and Bacon. 421 pages.

Robbins traces the roots of problems such as inequality, hunger, environmental destruction, disease, and global inequality to the culture of capitalism. Robbins incorporates anthropological, economic, and historical perspectives in order to counter the view that problems in the developing world stem from internal, local deficiencies rather than from conditions imposed or encouraged by external forces linked to the global search for profit and the idea that trade and economic growth represent the source of human well-being.

Robison, Richard, and David S. G. Goodman, eds. 1996. *The New Rich in Asia: Mobile Phones, McDonald's and Middle-Class Revolution.* London: Routledge. 253 pages.

This book examines the ways in which the emergence of new business and professional classes in East and Southeast Asia are altering the global economic balance of power, consumption, and opposition. This book examines whether the rising consumerism of Asia's burgeoning middle classes will give rise to political upheaval and demands for Western-style, liberal-democratic forms of governance.

Ryan, John C., and Alan Thein Durning. 1997. *Stuff: The Secret Lives of Everyday Things (New Report, No 4).* Seattle: Northwest Environment Watch. 86 pages.

This book reveals the hidden costs associated with the goods owned by the average North American consumer. The authors start with individual acts of consumption and trace the linkages associated with the production, consumption, distribution, and disposal of commodities such as sugar, coffee, clothing, automobiles, food, and computers. In addition to providing readers with detailed information on commodity chains, the authors attempt to encourage people to reflect on the unintended consequences of their everyday consumption decisions.

Schlosser, Eric. 2001. *Fast Food Nation: The Dark Side of the All-American Meal.* Boston: Houghton Mifflin. 356 pages.

Fast Food Nation documents the damaging effects of America's obsession with fast food. Using firsthand observations from Colorado Springs, Schlosser discusses the following problems associated with the rising consumption of fast food: the targeting of youth by advertisers, obesity and other health concerns such as food-borne illnesses, urban sprawl, water pollution, the financial and physical exploitation of immigrant workers, and the lack of government oversight and regulation over the meatpacking industry.

Schor, Juliet B. 1999. *The Overspent American: Why We Want What We Don't Need.* New York: HarperCollins. 253 pages.

In this book, Schor argues that despite rising prosperity, Americans report feeling no better off than in the past. The reason that Americans want what they do not need is related to what Schor calls "new consumerism," a form of "upscale spending" in which people seek status within a reference group that includes not neighbors or the stereotypical "Joneses" but rather the wealthiest part of the population. Through media images and advertising messages, people are led to believe that the lifestyles and preferences of the wealthy represent middle-class lifestyles and preferences. The final chapters feature testimonies from "downshifters," individuals who reject "upscale spending" and instead live more simply and without concern for achieving status through conspicuous consumption.

Schor, Juliet B., and Douglas B. Holt, eds. 2000. *The Consumer Society Reader.* New York: The New Press. 502 pages.

This collection gathers together key works in the field of consumption and addresses the underlying nature, evolution, and features of consumerism. The book includes chapters from renowned scholars (many of which are featured in this chapter), including Theodor Adorno, Max Horkheimer, John Kenneth Galbraith, Betty Friedan, Stuart Ewen, Jean Baudrillard, Dick Hebdige, Thornstein Veblen, Pierre Bourdieu, and James Twitchell.

Slater, Don. 1997. *Consumer Culture and Modernity.* Oxford, UK: Polity Press. 230 pages.

Slater provides an overview of theories on consumption and examines the primary issues through which people organize their approach to consumption and its effects on personal identity and status in contemporary Western societies. Slater critiques what he sees as a productivist bias in studies of modernity and argues instead that demand from the sixteenth century onward linked consumer culture firmly to modernity. Although useful as an introduction to the study of consumption, Slater also provides a sustained argument regarding the meaning of consumer objects and the production and use of that meaning in social practices.

Snow, Nancy. 2002. *Propaganda, Inc.: Selling America's Culture to the World.* 2d ed. New York: Seven Stories Press. 124 pages.

Using insights gained during two years of employment as a cultural affairs specialist in the U.S. Information Agency, Nancy

Snow argues that the agency, which is responsible for the dissemination of information about the United States overseas, serves more as a propaganda machine selling consumer culture for the benefit of corporate interests than as a facilitator of global intercultural communication.

Strasser, Susan, Charles McGovern, Matthias Judt, and Daniel S. Mattern, eds. 1998. *Getting and Spending: European and American Consumer Societies in the Twentieth Century.* Cambridge, UK: Cambridge University Press. 477 pages.

This collection features essays that tackle the history of consumption by examining various aspects of political, social, and economic life in locations throughout the world. Some of the topics covered include consumption and citizenship in the United States between 1900 and 1940; the New Deal state and the making of citizen-consumers; consumer behavior and economic reform in East Germany in the 1960s; gender, generation, and consumption in the United States; housewives and the politics of consumption in interwar Germany; and modern subjectivity and consumer culture.

Twitchell, James. 2000. *Lead Us into Temptation.* New York: Columbia University Press. 310 pages.

Twitchell argues that instead of being led around by the nose and manipulated into cultivating false desires, individuals reinforce their status and derive meaning from consuming material goods. Thus, even while decrying the negative costs of materialism and consumerism, individuals living in modern societies also pursue a consumer lifestyle in order to find the security and comfort that once came from organized religion. Twitchell refuses to blame greed or ignorance for the high levels of consumption in the United States.

Twitchell, James. 2002. *Living It Up—Our Love Affair with Luxury.* New York: Columbia University Press. 309 pages.

Twitchell defines luxury as a tool with which to judge the taste of others. In this book on the American interest in all things luxurious, Twitchell points out that the availability of credit has created the impression that luxury is available to all members of society. Twitchell uses the term "opuluxe" to denote universally craved name-brand objects, the image of which often proves more important than its quality. Regardless of the status seeking inherent in people's pursuit of luxury, Twitchell defends luxury in that its mass consumption could ultimately prove to be an economic equalizer for the masses, a positive influence on taste levels, and a factor in improving standards of living around the world.

Underhill, Paco. 2002. *Why We Buy: The Science of Shopping.* New York: Simon and Schuster. 255 pages.

This book is based on field research in shopping malls, department stores, and supermarkets across America and illustrates that marketing, retailing, and purchasing all entail precise complex processes whereby all three parties—marketers, retailers, and shoppers—are in a perpetual competition to come out the "winner."

Veblen, Thorstein. [1899] 2001. *The Theory of the Leisure Class.* New York: Penguin Books. 400 pages.

Though this book is over a century old, it still provides a scathing dissection of consumer culture. Veblen chronicles the ethical and economic impact of the rise of a new elite whose status stems primarily from monetary wealth. He calls them the leisure class and describes their tendency toward conspicuous consumption and idleness. Veblen critiques those individuals who acquire status through consumption and who link feelings of accomplishment to the ostentatious display of wealth.

Weber, Max. [1904] 1958. *The Protestant Ethic and the Spirit of Capitalism.* New York: Charles Scribner's Sons. 292 pages.

This book, Max Weber's best-known work that was first published in 1904, traces the roots of capitalism in the West to changes in religious practice. In particular, the savings, thrift, and sacrifice encouraged by the emergence of Protestantism facilitated the discipline of labor, accumulation of capital through savings, and reinvestment of profits that proved helpful in hastening the transition from a feudal to a capitalist more of production.

Williams, Rosalind H. 1991. *Dream Worlds: Mass Consumption in Late Nineteenth-Century France.* Berkeley: University of California Press. 451 pages.

Using the consumer revolution that occurred in France between 1850 and the start of World War I, Williams examines the events and ideas that were influential in the development of a "prototype of consumption" that includes "civilized" manners, fashion, furniture, and leisure activities, all of which were emulated by European aristocrats and, subsequently, among the elites in the American colonies. Having traced the development of consumer lifestyles in the first half of the book, Williams analyzes, in the latter half, a number of key theoretical responses to consumption and offers suggestions for reconciling feelings of guilt and fear that have been experienced by, and directed toward, consumers in Western societies.

Articles, Book Chapters, and Journals

Agnew, Jean-Christophe. 1993. **"Coming Up for Air."** In J. Brewer and R. Porter, eds., *Consumption and the World of Goods*, 19–39. New York: Routledge.

Agnew provides an overview of the sea change in historian's thinking about consumer culture from utterly critical to more celebratory. In the conclusion of this article, Agnew suggests that scholars of consumer culture would benefit from taking some "breathing space" in order to appreciate important recent developments in the field. Agnew argues that recent studies that have integrated historical and political events, as well as reexamining assumptions of causality, offer more nuanced, complex, and thus more useful explanatory tools for analyzing patterns of consumption and consumer motivations and behavior.

Allen, Jeanne T. 1980. *"The Film Viewer as Consumer."* *Quarterly Review of Film Studies* 5, no. 4: 481–499.

Allen outlines the ways in which the goals of the market economy are present in the practices of those who make and watch films. In particular, she illustrates how film viewing has become integrated into the sphere of mass consumption, evident in the physical proximity of movie theaters to shopping malls, and the increasing prevalence of advertisements prior to the start of a film.

Anderson, Fiona. 2000. **"Museums as Fashion Media."** In S. Bruzzi and P. Church Gibson, eds., *Fashion Cultures: Theories, Explorations and Analysis,* 371–389. London: Routledge.

Using three British museums as case studies, Anderson argues that fashion has become ever present and popular as museum curators recognize fashion's potential to draw young audiences into new arenas of cultural consumption.

Arnould, Eric J., and Richard Wilk. 1984. **"Why Do the Natives Wear Adidas?"** *Advances in Consumer Research* 11: 748–752.

Arnould and Wilk attempt to answer why and how Western consumer goods penetrate non-Western material cultures. They explore the roots of consumption of Western objects within primitive ritual behaviors. The authors argue that the concepts of socially distant reference groups and emerging elites help to explain this type of consumption.

Belk, Russell. 1988. **"Possessions and the Extended Self."** *Journal of Consumer Research* 15: 139–168.

The central premise of this article is that possessions function as an extension of the self. Belk argues that if we examine why certain items and artifacts are routinely considered critically important to the development of personal identity, then we can better understand consumer behavior and how consumer behavior is indicative of human motivations, needs, and desires.

Bently, Amy. 2002. **"Inventing Baby Food: Gerber and the Discourse of Infancy in the United States."** In W. Belasco and P. Scranton, eds., *Food Nations: Selling Taste in Consumer Societies,* 92–112. London: Routledge.

Bently argues that Gerber and other baby food manufacturers advocated the early introduction of solid foods for infants less than four months old with the express goal of expanding the market share of this new product. Advertising copy and photographs suggest that manufactured baby food was a mark of technological advancement and modernity.

Blumer, Herbert. 1969. **"Fashion: From Class Differentiation to Collective Selection."** *Sociological Quarterly* 10: 275–291.

Blumer examines the development, selection, and "success" of styles and fashions in modern societies. He argues against the idea that fashions are simply a creation of the elite dutifully copied by the lower class. In line with his "symbolic interactionist" approach, Blumer analyzes how fashions emerge through social interaction with like-minded individuals of similar social standing.

Carter, Erica. 1984. **"Alice in the Consumer Wonderland: West German Case Studies in Gender and Consumer Culture."** In A. McRobbie and M. Nova, eds., *Gender and Generation*, 185–215. London: Macmillan.

Although many studies of female consumers and their patterns of consumption have suggested that women blindly accept fashion trends, this case study of West German women indicate that consumption is often used as a means to oppose dominant codes of social taste. For example, in postwar West Germany, donning the accoutrements of an American feminine ideal—high heels, red lipstick, and nylon stockings—was, in part, an effort to register a public disavowal of fascist images of femininity: sturdy childbearing hips, sensible shoes, and a scrubbed-clean, rosy complexion.

Chaney, David. 1983. **"Department Stores as Cultural Form."** *Theory, Culture and Society* 1, no. 3: 22–31.

The department store transformed retailing and urban life by facilitating impersonal shopping, an ideology of consumerism, and spectacular developments in urban architecture. Chaney addresses three main concerns: the economic significance of new forms of retailing, their physical or ecological significance for the late nineteenth century, and the cultural significance of opportunities to create a personal lifestyle through impersonal consumption.

Clarke, Alison. 1997. **"Tupperware in the 1950s: Gender and Consumption."** In R. Silverstone, ed., *Visions of Suburbia*, 132–160. London: Routledge.

Analyzing Tupperware as an icon of suburbia, Clarke considers the role of mass consumption and material culture as a potentially active rather than passive aspect of the formation of postwar feminine identity.

Cohen, Lizabeth. 2001. **"Citizens and Consumers in the United States in the Century of Mass Consumption."** In M. Daunton and M. Hilton, eds., *The Politics of Consumption: Material Culture and Citizenship in Europe and America,* 203–221. New York: Berg.

This article examines the impact of mass consumption on the political culture of the United States. Although the roles of "citizen" and "consumer" are, in many ways, antithetical, Cohen's examination of three eras of U.S. history—the Progressive Era of the late nineteenth and early twentieth centuries, the New Deal from the early 1930s through World War II, and the post–World War II era—indicate that these two roles have merged into a vision of citizenship that is primarily concerned with consumption, which Cohen calls a "citizen-consumer."

Consumption, Markets & Culture

This is a journal devoted to the analysis of consumption for those particularly interested in marketing. Its focus is visual interpretations and representations of material culture and consumption patterns. Drawing from a range of theoretical traditions including literary criticism, feminism, media studies, sociology, and anthropology, the journal features submissions by scholars from around the world.

Creighton, Millie. 1998. **"Something More: Japanese Department Stores' Marketing of 'A Meaningful Life.'"** In K. L MacPherson, ed., *Asian Department Stores,* 206–230. Richmond, VA: Curzon Press.

Creighton illuminates the intersections between department stores and personal identity in contemporary Japan. In particular, she assesses the belief of many department store employees that they offer "something more" than simply displaying merchandise or selling goods.

Douglas, Mary. 1992. "Why Do People Want Goods?" In S. Hargeaves Heap and A. Ross, eds., *Understanding the Enterprise Culture: Themes in the Work of Mary Douglas,* 19–31. Edinburgh, UK: Edinburgh University Press.

Criticizing much of the economic analysis of consumption, central to which is the concept of "rational choice," and basing the analysis of consumption on rational choice means, according to Douglas, that society is making moral judgments about consumers who are thus perceived to be either irrational or greedy. Douglas argues that a much more complex analysis of rationality is needed if we are to fully understand why people consume. In particular, she suggests that rather than moralizing about greed and envy, society should consider the role of exclusion and rejection, which are central in the advertising and marketing of consumer goods.

Douglas, Mary. 1997. **"In Defense of Shopping."** In P. Falk and C. Campbell, eds., *The Shopping Experience*, 15–30. Thousand Oaks, CA: Sage.

As the title indicates, Douglas presents a defense of shopping. In particular, Douglas defends women's shopping and the demeaning and oversimplistic ideas that men have about female shoppers. Douglas challenges popular depictions of shopping as trivial and shoppers as vacuous dupes who respond like Pavlovian dogs to fashion items and consumer durables. Instead, Douglas presents the female shopper as rational and strategic, making important political and moral statements as much by what is not purchased—through the rejection of commodities—as by those that are procured.

Ehrlich, Paul R., et al. 1997. **"No Middle Way on the Environment."** *Atlantic Monthly* (December): 98–104.

This article is a response to a 1997 article by Mark Sagoff (see "Sagoff, Mark" entry later in this section). The authors warn against assuming that there is a viable middle ground in the debate between those who believe society is consuming too much and those who think it is not. They argue that the preponderance of scientific evidence points to the need for restraint both in the growth of population and in the overconsumption of developed countries.

Etzioni, Amitai. 1998. **"Voluntary Simplicity: Characterization, Select Psychological Implications, and Societal Consequences."** *Journal of Economic Psychology* 19, no. 5: 619–643.

Etzioni describes the concept of voluntary simplicity, exploring its manifestations and its relationship to competitiveness. Since increased consumption has been shown not to result in increased contentment, Etzioni argues that voluntary simplicity offers an opportunity to enhance personal satisfaction, socioeconomic equality, and environmental responsibility.

Fantasia, Rick. 1995. **"Fast Food in France."** *Theory and Society* 24, no. 2: 201–243.

Fantasia considers the cultural production of consumer goods, in this instance how the fast food phenomenon is perceived and received in France, a country that features a deep cultural pride in its national gastronomy.

Featherstone, Mike. 1987. **"Lifestyle and Consumer Culture."** *Theory, Culture and Society* 4, no. 1: 55–70.

Using theoretical perspectives developed by Pierre Bourdieu, Featherstone argues that postmodern consumer culture features the aestheticization of everyday life and encourages social groups to pursue status through the cultivation of superior taste and lifestyle. As a system of free-floating signifiers, postmodern culture emphasizes form over function, attaching symbolic value to goods through culturally mediated signs and images. The "new petite bourgeoisie," a group with poor economic but high cultural capital, is especially concerned with using lifestyle as a means of establishing class and status superiority.

Featherstone, Mike. 1991. **"The Body in Consumer Culture."** In M. Featherstone, M. Hepworth, and B. S. Turner, eds., *The Body: Social Processes and Cultural History*, 170–196. London: Sage.

In this article, Featherstone argues that consumer culture in capitalist society encapsulates two prevailing ideas about the body: that it should be preserved at any cost and that it is a vehicle of self-expression and beauty. As a result, taking care of one's body is divorced from notions of spiritual salvation that characterized earlier decades, and, instead, cosmetic benefits of body maintenance are emphasized. The advertising industry is critiqued for breeding insecurities in people who are constantly fearful of exhibiting bodily imperfections.

Fine, Ben, and Ellen Leopold. 1990. **"Consumerism and the Industrial Revolution."** *Social History* 15: 151–179.

Fine and Leopold discuss the history of the Industrial Revolution and argue that contemporary events shape people's interpretation of the Industrial Revolution. For this reason, studies of the events associated with the Industrial Revolution have changed over the years as contemporary circumstances have changed. In this article, Fine and Leopold critique, and claim as narrow, the "consumerist approach" to the Industrial Revolution taken by McKendrick (see entry on McKendrick, Brewer, and Plumb's *Birth of a Consumer Society* in the "Books" section in this chapter).

Firat, A. Fuat. 1991. **"The Consumer in Postmodernity."** *Advances in Consumer Research* 18: 70–76.

Firat argues that postmodern culture, a phenomenon rapidly expanding in advanced capitalist countries, is a "new perspective on life," largely influenced by the marketing industry and is characterized by five basic traits: hyperreality, fragmentation, reversal of production and consumption, juxtaposition of opposites, and decentering of the subject. Firat concludes that as a result of the changes evident in postmodern culture, the postmodern consumer is radically different from consumers in former epochs.

Fiske, John. 1989. **"Shopping for Pleasure."** In J. Fiske, *Reading the Popular,* 13–42. Boston: Unwin Hyman.

Fiske argues that the religious metaphors, such as the now popular description of shopping malls as "cathedrals of consumption," that have been used to describe consumerism and commodities ignore the potential of the shopping mall to be a site of resistance or "terrain of guerilla warfare" for marginalized elements in society. In particular, women and unemployed youth often frequent shopping malls not to purchase items but, in the case of women, to socialize or exercise (e.g., mall walking) in a safe and unthreatening environment and, in the case of the unemployed, to prevent boredom by engaging in various tactics aimed at evoking the ire of security guards.

Foster, Robert J. 1995 **"Print Advertisements and Nation Making in Metropolitan Papua New Guinea."** In R. J. Foster, ed., *Nation Making: Emergent Identities in Postcolonial Melanesia,* 151–181. Ann Arbor: University of Michigan Press.

Foster demonstrates the usefulness of seeing a nation as an imagined community of consumption. He examines the way that particular advertisements have contributed to the conception of Papua New Guinea as a nation as well as helping its inhabitants to view themselves as Papua New Guineans. He shows that our conception of a nation functions very much like a commodity.

Fox-Genovese, Elizabeth. 1987. **"The Empress's New Clothes: The Politics of Fashion."** *Socialist Review* 19, no. 1: 7–32.

Fox-Genovese argues against those theorists who treat fashion as either a form of political resistance or a system of representation. Fox-Genovese claims instead that fashion is a market-driven, multibillion-dollar enterprise that exacerbates social class and gender inequality.

Frith, James. 1994. **"Radical Shopping in Los Angeles: Race, Media and the Sphere of Consumption."** *Media, Culture and Society* 16, no. 3: 469–487.

Frith discusses the cultural dimensions of looting as a kind of radical shopping and the mass media coverage devoted to its incidence in South Central Los Angeles following the initial Rodney King verdict.

Gabaccia, Donna R. 2002. **"As American as Budweiser and Pickles? Nation Building in American Food Industries."** In W. Belasco and P. Scranton, eds., *Food Nations: Selling Taste in Consumer Societies*, 175–193. London: Routledge.

Using biographies of seventy business leaders in the nineteenth and twentieth centuries that pioneered the mass production of food and drink in the United States, Gabaccia explores the link between industrial production and the notion of "American" food. She takes into consideration whether these pioneers were native- or foreign-born and whether or not certain foods became labeled "American" or "ethnic."

Galilee, John. 2002. **"Class Consumption: Understanding Middle-Class Young Men and Their Fashion Choices."** *Men and Masculinities* 5, no. 1: 32–52.

Consumption, especially fashion and shopping, has traditionally been seen as a feminine practice. Some have argued that since the

1980s consumption has been "masculinized." In this article, Galilee presents the results of interviews with thirty-five middle-class young men about their clothing choices. Assumptions about young men's consumer independence and the "masculinization of consumption" thesis are both challenged by this research.

Gell, Alfred. 1986. **"Newcomers to the World of Goods: Consumption among the Muria Gonds."** In A. Appadurai, ed., *The Social Life of Things,* 110–140. Cambridge, UK: Cambridge University Press.

This article argues that consumption is a form of symbolic action, and the desirability of consumer goods is often dependent on the role that they play in a particular symbolic system. Gell discusses observations of consumption behavior among the Muria of Madhya Pradesh, India. The Muria consider conspicuous consumption as especially threatening and disruptive.

Glennie, Paul, and Nigel Thrift. 1996. **"Consumption, Shopping and Gender."** In E. Wrigley and M. Lowe, eds., *Retailing, Consumption and Capital: Towards the New Retail Geography,* 221–237. London: Longman.

The authors take an optimistic look at consumption, claiming that it offers liberating experiences and provides the opportunity for individuals to escape the class-centered social constellations of the past. This chapter examines the behavior of consumers in urban retail environments and analyzes the interactions of specific consumers within a group, or "throng." The gendered practices of shopping in urban retail centers are also examined in detail.

Goldman, R. 1987. **"Marketing Fragrances: Advertising and the Production of Commodity Signs."** *Theory, Culture and Society* 4, no. 4: 691–725.

Goldman examines fragrances as an example of both the power of advertising in a consumer society and the symbolism, desire, and emotional connections associated with commodities. Goldman focuses on three advertisements in particular in order to demonstrate the symbolic cultural content, lifestyle associations, and reification attached to the packaging and marketing of fragrances.

Gottdiener, Mark. 2000. **"Approaches to Consumption: Classical and Contemporary Perspectives."** In M. Gottdiener, ed., *New Forms of Consumption: Consumers, Culture and Commodification*, 3–31. Lanham, MD: Rowman & Littlefield.

Gottdiener traces shifting approaches to the study of consumption, covering both classical and contemporary theorists. The first half of the chapter outlines the ideas of classical theorists including Karl Marx, Max Weber, Émile Durkheim, and Thorstein Veblen. The second half addresses key concepts developed by contemporary scholars such as George Ritzer, Grant McCracken, Chandra Mukerji, and Jean Baudrillard. At the end of the chapter, the author synthesizes this diverse range of scholarly literature by offering an integrated approach to the symbolic, economic, and personal aspects of the consumer experience.

Hannerz, Ulf. 1990. **"Cosmopolitans and Locals in World Culture."** *Theory, Culture and Society* 7, no. 2: 237–251.

Hannerz argues that in a unified global culture, cosmopolitans and locals are structurally linked, with the former seeking identity and definition through conceptual difference with the latter. Among the components of cosmopolitanism identified by Hannerz are competence, orientation, types of mobility, and the meaning of home.

Hendrickson, Carol. 1996. **"Selling Guatemala: Maya Export Products in US Mail-Order Catalogues."** In D. Howes, ed., *Cross-Cultural Consumption: Global Markets, Local Realities*, 106–124. London: Routledge.

Hendrickson analyzes the ways in which Guatemalan products are marketed to American consumers in mail-order catalogs. Depictions often discuss "traditional," "simple," "remote," or "authentic" aspects of the artisans and the production process. Although in many cases this does serve as an important opportunity to educate Americans about Guatemala, and while Mayan artisans do earn money from such transactions, for the most part product control (design, color, size, etc.) and financial arrangements are not in the hands of local producers. Further, the reality of the hardships and challenges experienced by the artisans is inevitably absent since the primary purpose of the informational exchange is to sell products.

Humphrey, Caroline. 1995. **"Creating Culture of Disillusionment: Consumption in Moscow: A Chronicle of Changing Times."** In D. Miller, ed., *Worlds Apart: Modernity through the Prism of the Local*, 43–68. London: Routledge.

Humphrey connects the creation of the consumer under the Soviet regime to present patterns of consumption in Russia. Humphrey claims that the consumption practices of Russians are determined largely by values and perceptions shaped by recent historical events.

Janus, Norene Z. 1981. **"Advertising and the Mass Media: Transnational Link between Production and Consumption."** *Media, Culture and Society* 3: 13–23.

Janus argues that transnational advertising is an important component of global media flows. The output and organization of mass media has been greatly influenced by its dependence on advertising, and Janus demonstrates the vital link between mass media and advertising, whereby an increase in multinational manufacturing has encouraged the "transnationalization" of advertising agencies. This article documents the ways in which global patterns of commerce and consumption determine the nature and consequences of transnational advertising in developing countries.

Journal of Consumer Culture

The *Journal of Consumer Culture* is devoted to issues of consumption from a social scientific perspective, with a focus on sociological themes such as social change, social stratification, and social disorganization. Its principal goal is to illuminate the central role of consumer culture in contemporary social interactions both locally and globally.

Kline, Stephen. 1988. **"The Theatre of Consumption: On Comparing American and Japanese Advertising."** *Canadian Journal of Political and Social Theory* 12, no. 3: 101–120.

This article explores the impacts of the internationalization of Japan's economy and pays particular attention to the issue of cultural homogenization in Japanese society. Kline conducts a content analysis of sixty television commercials from Japan and compares these to an equivalent number of advertisements from the United States. Television advertising is chosen over other kinds of advertising because it plays an important role in Japan, as elsewhere, in depicting and shaping cultural meanings. Kline discovers that rather than representing an external cultural force, consumerism is accommodated and naturalized into Japanese society.

Laermans, Rudi. 1993. **"Learning to Consume: Early Department Stores and the Shaping of the Modern Consumer Culture (1860–1914)."** *Theory, Culture and Society* 10, no. 4: 79–102.

Laermans examines the rise of consumer culture in France and the United States from 1860 to 1914 and highlights the central role played by the department store in encouraging mass consumption. As female leisure centers, department stores at this time encouraged passive shopping and strove to attach symbolic meaning and importance to merchandise; these trends, and the growth of the department store in general, feminized consumption, facilitated the expansion of the urban middle class, and permanently altered the nature of consumer behavior and preferences.

Lamont, Michele, and Virag Molnar. 2001. **"How Blacks Use Consumption to Shape Their Collective Identity: Evidence from Marketing Specialists."** *Journal of Consumer Culture* 1, no. 1: 31–45.

Drawing on interviews conducted with black marketing experts working in black advertising agencies in New York and Chicago, the authors explore the linkages between notions of collective identity and patterns of consumption. The interview data indicate that black Americans consume in order to express solidarity and acquire membership in various social niches, to illustrate a unique cultural identity, and to demonstrate distinctiveness from mainstream American society. However, the role of marketing professionals, who frequently link group membership and solidarity with conspicuous consumption and thus influence and shape the consumption patterns of black consumers, cannot be overlooked.

McGovern, Charles. 1998. **"Consumption and Citizenship."** In S. Strasser, C. McGovern, and M. Judt, eds., *Getting and Spending: European and American Consumer Societies in the Twentieth Century*, 37–58. Cambridge, UK: Cambridge University Press.

McGovern examines how notions of consumption and citizenship became intertwined in U.S. political discourse. It is argued that the

Great Depression increased government involvement in the economy, and thus recognizing an important opportunity to profit from the government's commitment to increase consumer spending, advertising executives promoted the idea that consumption was the medium by which individuals could achieve independence and agency. As a result, consumption was commonly evoked as a mark of patriotism—the badge of a true American.

McRobbie, Angela. 2000. **"Fashion as a Culture Industry."** In S. Bruzzi and P. Church Gibson, eds., *Fashion Cultures: Theories, Explorations and Analysis*, 253–263. London: Routledge.

McRobbie discusses the ways in which governments become involved in industries that are perceived to be important to the "national" culture. In this instance, McRobbie focuses on the British fashion industry and how Tony Blair's commitment to making over Britain into a "young country" led to photo opportunities between politicians and representatives from the fashion industry.

Miller, Peter, and Nikolas Rose. 1997. **"Mobilizing the Consumer: Assembling the Object of Consumption."** *Theory, Culture and Society* 14, no. 1: 1–36.

Miller and Rose analyze the consulting work undertaken by the Tavistock Institute of Human Relations in England on behalf of advertising agencies and manufacturers, looking particularly at the ways in which the agency and creativity of consumers is acknowledged in advertisements. This article demonstrates that in addition to creating artificial desires and exploiting the emotions of consumers, advertising also opens up space for consumers to exert their intelligence, enhance their knowledge, and mobilize their desires in a deliberate and active manner.

Porter, Roy. 1993. **"Consumption: Disease of the Consumer Society?"** In J. Brewer and R. Porter, eds., *Consumption and the World of Goods*, 58–81. New York: Routledge.

In this chapter, Porter examines the various ways that food, the rhetoric of "excessive consumption," and "waste" have been used to justify overeating or the withholding of food. For example, the British gentry justified gluttony as an effective mechanism for warding off the ever-present threat of "consumption" or tuberculosis, whereas in Victorian England, food was withheld from girls to promote thinness and delicacy. In sum, although we are presently in an era where the overconsumption of food and drink are condemned as detrimental to one's health, there are numerous recent examples where the opposite was believed to be true.

Prus, Robert, and Lorne Dawson. 1991. **"'Shop 'Til You Drop': Shopping as Recreational and Laborious Activity."** *Canadian Journal of Sociology* 16, no. 2: 145–164.

Based on interviews with ninety-five consumers in Kitchener-Waterloo, Ontario, Prus and Dawson explore people's definitions of shopping and discover that purchasing behaviors stem from social needs and perceptions. In particular, the degree to which a person sees shopping as laborious or recreational determines that person's enjoyment and interpretation of interpersonal interactions in shopping settings. The authors argue that shopping is not a static, one-dimensional action, bur rather a dynamic process imbued with personal meaning for individual consumers.

Ritzer, George, Douglas Goodman, and Wendy Weidenhoft. 2001. **"Theories of Consumption."** In G. Ritzer and B. Smart, eds., *Handbook of Social Theory*, 410–427. Thousand Oaks, CA: Sage.

Compared to an excessive amount of attention devoted to the process of production as a key human activity, it is argued that the significance of consumption was, until recently, ignored. Yet, a recent and growing interest in the study of consumption has become sufficiently established to merit an overview. To this end, the authors outline the development of contemporary theories of consumption and mine classical theories for concepts that prove useful in understanding patterns of consumption. In the conclusion, it is argued that theories of consumption need to be more balanced in their assessment of the positive and negative impacts of consumption as well as more broad in scope, for example, including analyses of the sites of consumption and the objects that are consumed.

Sagoff, Mark. 1997. **"Do We Consume Too Much?"** *Atlantic Monthly* (June): 80–96.

Sagoff argues that the expanding world economy will not irrevocably deplete natural resources. He believes that the case against overconsumption should be made on moral rather than economic grounds. Sagoff claims that a lost reverence for the natural world will undermine important cultural values.

Schudson, Michael. 1988. **"Delectable Materialism: Second Thoughts on Consumer Culture."** In D. A. Crocker and T. Linden, eds., *Ethics of Consumption: The Good Life, Justice, and Global Stewardship*, 249–268. Lanham, MD: Rowman & Littlefield.

Schudson attempts to present a more positive alternative to the negative "rational left" view of consumption by noting the complex ways in which people incorporate commodities into their everyday lives. In effect, such commodities are often used to serve particular needs, but even when used in standard fashion, they are used quite pragmatically and are rarely imbued with spiritual or romantic qualities. Although agreeing with the need to critique consumer culture, Schudson complains that the judgmental tone that often accompanies critiques hinders an accurate understanding of the reasons why people choose to consume.

Slater, Don. 1996. **"Consumer Culture and the Politics of Need."** In M. Nava, A. Blake, I. MacRury, and B. Richards, eds., *Buy This Book: Studies in Advertising and Consumption*, 51–63. New York: Routledge.

Slater argues that some important questions about consumer culture remain to be answered and have been marginalized or ignored altogether in current scholarly debates. The questions include: What constitutes the good life? How can we evaluate "needs" in the context of achieving the good life? How does consumer culture measure up as a system that produces and mediates these needs? Slater concludes that until these questions are addressed and answered, theories of consumer culture cannot adequately identify the structural constraints that hinder or facilitate participation in consumer culture and the political sphere.

Stevenson, Nick. 2002. **"Consumer Culture, Ecology and the Possibility of Cosmopolitan Citizenship."** *Consumption, Markets, Culture* 5, no. 4: 305–319.

In this article, Stevenson argues that current theorizing on citizenship often overlooks the importance of culture, the environment, and the impact of consumerism in contemporary societies. Challenging two popular arguments—first, that democracies in the West are compromised by a "culture of contentment," and second, that consumerism offers "ordinary people" the opportunity to participate in a populist democratic revolution—Stevenson argues that the benefits and drawbacks of consumerism could be channeled into a new mode of thinking about citizenship—"cosmopolitan democracy"—in which questions of pleasure are connected to questions of ethics. By situating environmental questions centrally in discussions of consumption, and encouraging members of every nation to imagine themselves as global citizens, a civic solidarity distinct from the nation-state might be possible.

Wallendorf, Melanie, and Eric J. Arnould. 1988. **"My Favorite Things: A Cross-Cultural Inquiry into Object Attachment."** *Journal of Consumer Research* 14: 521–547.

Using cross-cultural data collected from adults in America and the Niger Republic, the authors examine the attachments people form to objects they deem "favorite" or "special." Strong attachments to these kinds of objects are not usually based on monetary value, and thus these attachments are distinct from the possessiveness intrinsic to materialism. It is argued that more attention needs to be paid to the meanings attributed to favorite objects such as photos and to the differences in object attachment by gender, age, and culture.

Warde, Alan. 1990. **"Introduction to the Sociology of Consumption."** *Sociology* 24: 104.

Although sociologists have tended to overlook consumption in their analyses, Warde suggests that there are important social, political, and cultural reasons for the recent sociological interest in consumption. Although recent research has focused on two distinct, and rarely overlapping, areas—the study of consumerism and consumption patterns, and consumption as a collective endeavor—Warde believes that consumer activities are more effectively analyzed as "episodes" and that comprehensive accounts of single episodes of consumption must examine "not just production and access, but also the nature of delivery and the enjoyment of a service."

Wilk, Richard. 1994. **"Consumer Goods as Dialogue about Development."** *Culture and History* 7: 79–100.

Wilk argues that the role of consumer goods in Belize is more complex than has been claimed by those who focus exclusively on their use in status competition. In fact, consumer goods create and maintain all kinds of social relationships, and although they do play a role in the creation of personal identity, they are also commonly used in the expression of egalitarian ideals rather than as a means of maintaining hierarchy or exclusion of socially inferior elements of Belizean society.

Willis, Susan. 1994. **"I Want the Black One: Is There a Place for Afro-American Culture in Commodity Culture?"** In S. Willis, ed., *A Primer for Daily Life*, 108–132. London: Routledge.

Willis looks at the way in which the dominant white culture industry has produced consumable images of blacks. Her analysis ranges from the essential "blackness" produced by Toni Morrison, to the racial homogeneity produced by fashion marketing, to the physical transformations of Michael Jackson. She concludes that in a world that is unified by the commodity, we can only practice partial resistances.

Yan, Yunxiang. 1997. **"McDonald's in Beijing: The Localization of Americana."** In J. L. Watson, ed., *Golden Arches: McDonald's in East Asia*, 39–66. Stanford, CA: Stanford University Press.

Yan discusses the relationship between McDonald's and the local Chinese communities in which it operates. In particular, Yan indicates that while many ordinary Chinese view a meal at McDonald's as an opportunity to sample American culture, and thereby attain social status, others perceive the limited and standardized menu as a rare opportunity to partake in a moment of equality.

Videos

The Ad and the Ego
Date: 1997
Length: 57 min.
Source: Parallax Pictures
http://www.parallaxpictures.org/

The Ad and the Ego reedits and restructures thousands of contemporary and classic television commercials in order to illustrate the destructive power of the mass media. The video traces the history of advertising from its descriptive nineteenth-century roots to the high-tech manipulation of powerful symbols and imagery common in advertising today.

Advertising and the End of the World
Date: 1998
Length: 47 min.
Source: Media Education Foundation
http://www.mediaed.org/

This video exposes the ways in which advertisers tap into human needs, desires, and fantasies to sell products. By linking the world of commodities to the world of social relationships, family, love, emotions, and fears, advertisers attempt to connect with potential consumers.

Affluenza
Date: 1997
Length: 56 min.
Source: Bullfrog Films
http://www.bullfrogfilms.com/

Affluenza outlines of the features of the "disease" of materialism and discusses how the concept of simple living offers one way around the social and environmental problems caused by affluenza. (See also listing below for sequel film *Escape from Affluenza* and summary of the book *Affluenza* under "de Graaf, John" in the "Books" section of this chapter.)

Beyond Killing Us Softly: The Strength to Resist
Date: 2001
Length: 34 min.
Source: Cambridge Documentary Films
http://www.cambridgedocumentaryfilms.org/beyond.html

Beyond Killing Us Softly is the most recent of four films by Jean Kilbourne on the image of women in advertising. The views of girls and young women are complemented by the comments of women's studies scholars and advocates of women's rights. In addition to giving firsthand accounts of the ways in which individuals deal with pressures to conform to stereotypical gender images, the video emphasizes practical solutions for resisting the dominant gender ideologies that are reproduced through advertising and popular culture.

Escape from Affluenza
Date: 1998
Length: 56 min.

Source: Bullfrog Films
http://www.bullfrogfilms.com/

This sequel to the film *Affluenza*, which premiered on PBS in September 1997, documents how some Americans have left the proverbial rat race, choosing instead to resist consumer pressure and live a more simple life. (See summary of the book *Affluenza* under "de Graaf, John" in the "Books" section of this chapter.)

The Gleaners and I
Date: 2001
Length: 82 min.
Source: Zeitgeist Films
http://www.zeitgeistfilms.com/current/gleaners/gleaners.html

This film focuses on "gleaners," people who pick at already harvested fields for vegetables that are left behind. More generally, gleaners seek to find uses for those items deemed useless by the rest of society. Director Agnes Varda interviews a diverse range of subjects in settings such as the French countryside and green markets in Paris.

The Merchants of Cool
Date: 2001
Length: 60 min.
Source: WGBH Educational Foundation
http://www.pbs.org/wgbh/pages/frontline/

This video, an episode from the PBS Frontline series, explores the impact of advertising, style, and fashion on the tastes, preferences, and relationships of contemporary American teenagers.

Sell and Spin: A History of Advertising
Date: 1999
Length: 91 min.
Source: A&E Store
http://www.aetv.com/

This film illustrates the ways in which advertisers promise happiness to consumers and claim that desire can be satisfied as long as one purchases *their* particular product or service. The video is divided into several subsections: advertisements in ancient times, the dawn of newspaper and magazine advertising, outdoor advertisements (barns, billboards, electric signs, blimps, and skywriting), radio and television commercials, political advertising, the development of the *"Yo quiero* Taco Bell" advertising campaign, and selling in cyberspace.

Sweating for a T-Shirt
Date: 1998
Length: 23 min.
Source: Global Exchange
http://store.globalexchange.org/sweating.html

Produced by Global Exchange in San Francisco, this film chronicles the difficult conditions under which clothing is manufactured in *maquiladora* plants in Honduras: excessive work hours, low wages, harsh labor discipline, illness and fatigue among workers, and management that is hostile to unionization.

Thirty Second President
Date: 1988
Length: 60 min.
Source: PBS Video
http://www.shop.pbs.org/

Thirty Second President discusses the impact of the media on presidential elections, in particular the role played by advertising in election campaigns and general perceptions of political candidates. The video includes advertisements used by Dwight Eisenhower, John F. Kennedy, Lyndon Johnson, Richard Nixon, and Ronald Reagan.

Selected Websites

Adbusters
http://www.adbusters.org

Adbusters is a global network of artists, writers, environmentalists, ecological economists, media-literacy teachers, ecofeminists, and green entrepreneurs. They describe themselves variously as: "idealists, anarchists, guerilla tacticians, pranksters, campus rabble-rousers, downshifters, neo-Luddites, poets, philosophers, and punks." Their aim is to topple existing power structures and forge a major rethinking of the way we live in the twentieth century. They want to change the way information flows; the way institutions wield power; the way television stations are run; and the ways in which the food, fashion, automobile, sports, music, and culture industries set their agendas. Above all, they want to change the way people interact with the mass media and the way in which meaning is produced in our society.

Business Ethics
http://www.business-ethics.com/100best.htm

Business Ethics has for fifteen years served as a publication of the movement for greater social responsibility in business.

The Center for a New American Dream
http://www.newdream.org

The Center for the New American Dream is an organization dedicated to reducing and shifting American consumption.

Consumer Culture and Modernity
http://homepages.gold.ac.uk/slater/consumer/about.html

This website offers resources and communication links for those interested in the study of consumer culture and topics such as leisure and critical investigations of everyday life.

Consumer Culture Bibliography
http://homepages.gold.ac.uk/slater/consumer/biblioa.htm

This bibliography was created by Don Slater (see "Slater, Don" entry in the "Books" section of this chapter) and contains approximately 1,500 references pertaining to consumption.

Consumer WebWatch
http://www.consumerwebwatch.com/project/index.html

The Consumer WebWatch mission is to investigate, inform, and improve the quality of information published on the World Wide Web.

Consumer World
http://www.consumerworld.org/

Consumer World is a public service noncommercial guide cataloging over 2,000 of the most useful consumer resources. It was founded in 1995 by Edgar Dworsky, a consumer advocate, educator, and attorney.

Consumers against War
http://www.consumers-against-war.de/caw.htm

This site is the brainchild of a group of young Europeans who protested the war in Iraq. Their principal goal is to boycott American products and thus the American economy, which they hold responsible for the war. The war is viewed as a breach of international law.

Corporate Predators
http://www.corporatepredators.org

The point of the list contained in this report, "The Top 100 Corporate Criminals of the Decade" (1990s), is to focus public attention on a wave of corporate criminality that has swamped prosecutors' offices around the country. The "Top 100 Corporate Criminals of the Decade" includes corporations that have pled guilty or no contest to crimes and have been criminally fined.

CorpWatch
http://www.corpwatch.org/

CorpWatch critiques corporate-led globalization through education and activism. It aims to foster democratic control over corporations by building grassroots globalization, a diverse movement for human rights, labor rights, and environmental justice.

Credit Card Nation
http://www.creditcardnation.com/

This is the inspiration of Dr. Robert D. Manning, a leading expert on the credit card industry. Manning is the author of *Credit Card Nation: The Consequences of America's Addiction to Credit* (2001), a study of credit card use and debt in the United States. (See "Manning, Robert D." entry in the "Books" section of this chapter.)

Essential Information
http://www.essential.org/EI.html

Founded in 1982 by Ralph Nader, Essential Information is a nonprofit, tax-exempt organization. It is involved in a variety of projects that encourage citizens to become active and engaged in their communities. It provides information to the public on topics neglected by the mass media and policymakers.

George Ritzer
http://www.bsos.umd.edu/socy/ritzer/

This is the website of George Ritzer (Department of Sociology, University of Maryland), author of some of the seminal works on consumer culture (see "Ritzer, George" entries in the "Books" section of this chapter).

Global Issues
http://www.globalissues.org/

This website, created and maintained by Anup Shah, examines the ways in which interrelated global issues affect people. The site features over 5,000 links to external articles, website reports, and analyses that are used to provide credence to the arguments made on this website.

Indymedia
http://www.indymedia.org/

Indymedia is a collective of independent media organizations and hundreds of journalists offering grassroots, noncorporate coverage. Indymedia is a democratic media outlet committed to the creation of radical, accurate, and passionate truth telling.

Multinational Monitor
http://www.multinationalmonitor.org

Published by Essential Information, the *Multinational Monitor* tracks corporate activity, especially in the Third World, and focuses on the export of hazardous substances, worker health and safety, labor union issues, and the environment.

No Logo
http://nologo.org/

No Logo is a website born out of an antibranding book entitled *No Logo: Taking Aim at the Brand Bullies*, written by Naomi Klein between 1995 and 1998 and published in English in January 2002 (see "Klein, Naomi" entry in the "Books" section of this chapter). The site is a portal to the evolving and expanding movements chronicled in the book. For the most part, it is a place where readers and researchers can connect with one another and learn about various campaigns, issues, and organizations.

PBS Kids
http://pbskids.org/dontbuyit/

This site aims to expose kids to the seduction and manipulation behind much of advertising.

Stop SUVs
http://www.stopsuvs.org

This organization feels that each time the choice to purchase a SUV is made, the quality of life in our society suffers. Claiming that the sum of consumer choices has great consequences on the environment, economy, politics, and safety, Stop SUVs aims to persuade people to consider alternate, more sustainable means of transportation.

U.S. Department of Energy
http://www.energy.gov/efficiency/index.html

The Department of Energy is a $21-billion-per-annum organization that employs more than 115,000 people in thirty-five states. The site provides information on such topics as gas mileage (MPG), greenhouse gas emissions, air pollution ratings, and safety information for new and used cars and trucks.

Worldwatch Institute
http://www.worldwatch.org/

Worldwatch is a nonprofit, public-policy research organization dedicated to informing policymakers and the public about global problems and trends, as well as the links between the world economy and the environment.

Index

About the Authors

Douglas J. Goodman is an assistant professor of comparative sociology at the University of Puget Sound. He is the coauthor (with G. Ritzer) of three textbooks: *Sociological Theory* (6th ed.), *Modern Sociological Theory* (6th ed.), and *Classical Sociological Theory* (4th ed.). He has also published numerous articles on social theory, consumer culture, and social problems.

Mirelle Cohen is an assistant professor of comparative sociology at the University of Puget Sound. Her interests include the sociology of religion, race relations, gender and sexuality, and deviance. Her current work explores the challenges experienced by female juvenile offenders in Tacoma, Washington.